PETER YU KIEN-HONG

HU JINTAO
AND THE
ASCENDANCY
OF
CHINA

**A Dialectical
Study**

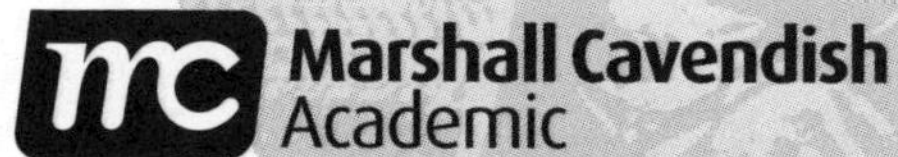

© 2005 Marshall Cavendish International
(Singapore) Private Limited

Published 2005 by Marshall Cavendish Academic
An imprint of Marshall Cavendish International
(Singapore) Private Limited
A member of Times Publishing Limited

Times Centre, 1 New Industrial Road,
Singapore 536196
Tel:(65) 6213 9288
Fax: (65) 6284 9772
E-mail: mca@sg.marshallcavendish.com
Website:
http://www.marshallcavendish.com/academic

ISBN: 981-210-423-2

A CIP catalogue record for this book is available from
the National Library Board (Singapore).

Printed by Times Graphics Pte Ltd, Singapore
on non-acidic paper

**London • New York • Beijing • Shanghai
• Bangkok • Kuala Lumpur • Singapore**

This book is dedicated to James C. Hsiung,
Richard W. Wilson, and those who are fond
of studying international/global governance
and international regimes.

Contents

Acknowledgement

I wish to thank H. T. Sam, a Singaporean lawyer, and Andrew Scobell for their critical commentaries on Part I. Of course, I alone am responsible for its content.

Preface

I finished my graduate study at the age of 30.[1] At that time, I only had a vague idea of what a model or theory was. Five years later, I finally understood what a non-dialectical model or theory was all about. In September 1994, I constructed my first dialectical model.[2] What I am going to say below may create some pressure on those who still do not fully understand what a model or theory in social sciences is.[3]

A Dutch sinologist, Hans Kuijper, once wrote a paper, arguing that if you do not apply a model or theory in your study of Chinese (Communist) affairs, you are a pseudo-scientist. The paper was published in the July-September 2000 issue of *China Report*. To him, sinology is not a science. This Dutch expert, in his letter dated April 24, 2001 to me, said he had not submitted his paper to *China Quarterly*, *Modern China*, *The China Journal*, *China Information*, *China: An International Journal*, etc. for possible publication. These journals do not usually encourage people to apply a model or theory in the study of (Bicoastal) China.

A theory can be a word, a symbol, a letter, a number,[4] a phrase, a sentence, etc. A theory can be elevated to the status of a school or even paradigm,[5] if it can describe, explain, and predict phenomena over a long period of time, say 100 or more years, implying acceptance by many, if not most, people. Zbigniew K. Brzezinski, a former National Security advisor in the Jimmy Carter administration, treated his totalitarian theory as a paradigm. That is a mistake. In the non-dialectical social sciences of the West, we can, at best, only apply a theory, not a paradigm.

Strictly speaking, the title or sub-title of your background brief, working paper, occasional paper, monograph, or book should be or mention the theory. The table of contents or sections and sub-sections should be the model or framework of thought and action.

A theory has several major functions: to rationalize phenomena, to solve and resolve contradictions, to predict (or infer) the future, etc.

Many people say reality and theory do not match. These people do not really understand what a theory is all about, and they have not chosen the right theory. * is a model or theory, because it reflects something. But, its descriptive and explanatory power is extremely limited and, therefore, only a few people would employ * as a model or theory.

In the non-dialectical social sciences of the West, academics have constructed many models and put forward many theories. Professor Lowell Dittmer has observed that the field of (Bicoastal) China Studies is littered with many abandoned models and theories. Why? This is because these non-dialectical theories do not fit into the world of what I would call Chinese (Communist) Dialectical Politics.

Why do we need a theory or a model? I would argue that it is because we as human beings cannot fully understand or remember everything that has been said or written. We can only have an impression of what has been said or written. Of course, only the author knows fully and probably remembers best the things he or she has written.

So, in order to attract other people's attention, we should rely on a model or theory. A model or theory is a simplification or compression of reality. We can test the model or theory over a period of time. If it can still describe and explain in depth new phenomena 20 or 30 years from the time it was first propagated, it is a valid and good one. So, a theorist must know the past, the present, and especially the future.

Why do we need to apply a model or a theory? This is because a model or a theory is supposed to be logically, systematically, and coherently developed or constructed. A good model or theory can help us protect ourselves from criticisms. For example, if we were to write a background brief, we ought to make use of a model or theory. This is to protect government officials and help them not to make contradictory remarks, decisions, or policies. In other words, the making and executing of a policy must be made within a theoretical framework. A government must rely on theorists. The same thing speaks for any political party. A theorist certainly stresses ideology. When there is an ideology, there is a framework of thought and action. So, we must find out what Beijing's is and, for that matter, what Taipei's framework is at a particular time/space sequence. If you carefully read *all* the publications related to mainland China, Taiwan, Hongkong, Macao, and the Overseas Chinese, you would have noticed that there are so many contradictory descriptions, explanations, etc. This is because we write and think differently. But, because most government officials who read publications are not trained in dialectical and non-dialectical social sciences and are hence unfamiliar with models or theories, we will face obstacles if we apply a theory or a model in our writings.

I think many, if not most, government officials do not understand the power of a model or a theory. If they did, they would certainly require think tank researchers to apply a model or a theory in their writings.

It takes time to come up with a new model or theory, which can describe and explain Chinese (Communist) affairs, be it political, economic, social, or legal. It took me some 15 years to construct my version of a dialectical model, and I have slightly modified it for the third time over the last ten years or so in this book.

Kuijper said sinologists must command a theory of their own. I urge research centers like East Asian Institute (EAI), National University of Singapore (NUS) [or, for that matter, Institute of Defence and Strategic Studies (IDSS), Nanyang Technological University (NTU)], to have its own theory. This is the only way to emerge on top of all others. If EAI succeeds, the theory can be called the EAI school of thought and action (東亞研究所學派). I am deeply convinced that a One-Dot-School of Thought and Action should be developed.[6] It must incorporate your model/theory, my model/theory, and a newcomer's model/theory. This means the School is still pluralistic. After 100 or more years of repeated testing, it could evolve into the EAI paradigm (東亞研究所典範), for instance.[7]

Both parts of this book apply my version of dialectics (see p. xii for the primary model). Before the death of Deng Xiaoping, many observers were debating whether the People's Republic of China (PRC) would collapse, just like the former Soviet Union. It did not come to pass. Then, two major issues remain. First, we wanted to know whether the Communist Party of China (CPC) could remain the ruling party and whether both sides of the Taiwan Strait could be politically reunited. For this reason, the first part deals with Hu Jintao and other former Central Military Commission (CMC) leaders. To be sure, in October 2004, Hu for the first time, revealed his military thinking on how to administer and manage the Chinese People's Liberation Army (PLA). If they can do a good job, they can certainly help to maintain the ruling status of their political party and, as a next step, continue to build China from china to China and to CHINA and even reaching *CHINA*. The theory, CHINA, China, and china, could also incorporate the theory of China's peaceful rise (*Zhongguodehepingjueqi*), which was first put forward in October/November 2003 at the Boao Forum for Asia (BFA) in Hainan Province.[8] For this major reason, I have combined the two parts into one

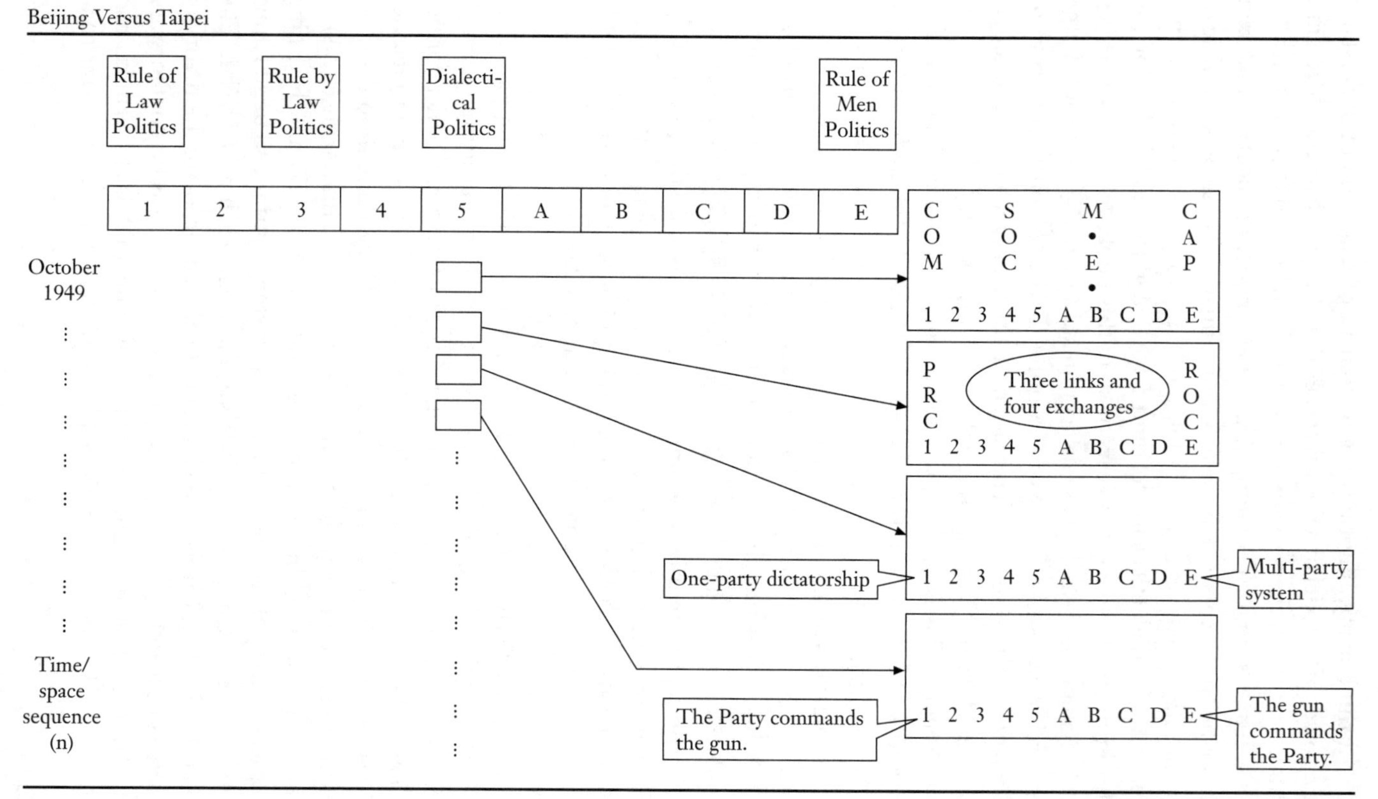
Beijing Versus Taipei
Rule of Law Politics
Rule by Law Politics
Dialectical Politics
Rule of Men Politics
1 2 3 4 5 A B C D E
COM SOC M E CAP
1 2 3 4 5 A B C D E
PRC Three links and four exchanges ROC
1 2 3 4 5 A B C D E
October 1949
One-party dictatorship
1 2 3 4 5 A B C D E
Multi-party system
The Party commands the gun.
1 2 3 4 5 A B C D E
The gun commands the Party.
Time/space sequence (n)

volume, and I would like to thank Anthony E. C. Thomas, Roy See and Joe Ng of Marshall Cavendish Academic as well as Lily Loy, the freelance copyeditor, for their professional work. Tsai Chih-hsuan should also be credited for creating the diagram on page xii.

Finally, as one Australia-based political scientist, He Baogang, said patience is needed when reading things related to dialectics. I sincerely hope readers have such patience. It took about one semester for my undergraduate students like Ala'a Shnoudi and Stephanie Houng to fully understand my model. To promote my intellectual growth, I sincerely welcome your challenge. As a last reminder, a dialectical remark is just the opposite of a non-dialectical (usually linear) remark or, at best, they must meet half-way.[9]

Peter Kien-hong Yu
Graduate School of International Affairs
Ming Chuan University
Guishan, Taoyuan, Taiwan 333
Republic of China

ENDNOTES

1   This is a revised version of my talk, dated April 17, 2001, at the East Asian Institute (EAI), National University of Singapore (NUS). Later, Professor and director Wang Gungwu wrote me and others about what he thought of my talk. It has been slightly revised and updated in December 2004. I wish to thank Aw Beng Teck for editing this piece.

2   In the last several years, at least three academics have told me that dialectics is "out," and political economy and rational choice theory are "in." In my view, dialectics is not dead. In the December 2001 issue of *PS: Political Science & Politics*, two scholars are still partially applying the dialectical method. Robert H. Salisbury of Washington University wrote on p. 767: "… [I]n part, the problem lies in the supposed incompatibility of the ostensible polarities; teaching versus research, technique versus substance, real world politics versus theoretical driven research. Of course, these are not either/or choices but questions of degree, and the appropriate balance may vary considerably across both time and the spectra of subject matter and professional career paths." Peter J. Katzenstein of Cornell University in the same issue on p. 791 said: "… [t]hese networks facilitate the creation of cross-regional perspectives on a range of dialectical processes confronting the social sciences everywhere: global versus local, basic versus applied, area versus disciplinary." In a word, dialectics is not dead. In July 2004, for the first time, I came across a book by William (Bill) H. Gates, III, the computer tycoon. In his November 1996 revised book, *The Road*

Ahead, he tried to describe and explain the binary system in computer science by depicting a diagram of light bulbs. The bulb on the left extreme has the largest watts, and the one on the right extreme, only one watt. In other words, there is a striking similarity between the light bulb arrangement and my dialectical model. By giving an analogy, 1 has the largest watts and 5 having only one watt. Similarly, E has the largest watts and A, only one watt. On July 31, 2004, I asked a professor of computer science at Qinghua University (Beijing), Li Chuang, whether we can say that the binary system is another way of saying *Yin* and *Yang*, and he said yes! Of course, Gates' light bulbs arrangement does not have safe zone and danger zone.

3 V. O. Key, Jr. said in his presidential address to the American Political Science Association (APSA) 40 years ago: "Method without substance may be sterile, but substance without method is only fortuitously substantial."

4 One of my papers was entitled *Island China in the Contexts of 1, 2, and 3*.

5 The word paradigm is enshrined in the German terms *Denkstil* (thought style) and *Denkkollektiv* (thought collective).

6 In the Fall of 2003, a student at Ming Chuan University's Department of Economics asked me whether we should begin to acquire knowledge from one dot. My reply was: Yes!

7 Both EAI and IDSS have the money. So, seize the moment! Seize the day!

8 We should go back to the Deng Xiaoping theory of Peace and Development (*hepingyufazhan*). A dialectical model can be set up as follows: Peace and Development Versus Non-Peace-and-development or Peaceful Development Versus Non-Peaceful-development. China's peaceful rise is actually Number 3 or 4, because there are three major phases in the development: nascent (or primary), ascendant, and mature. Those academics, experts, and practitioners who do not apply the dialectical approach will see tension, struggles, and resistance at the macro-level. See, for example, http://www.worldjorunal.com/wj-ch-news.php?nt_seq_id=1037880&sc_seq_id=3 (accessed August 25, 2004). However, the opposite is true. Of course, at the micro-level, there could be tension, struggles, and resistance. In April 2004, Hu Jintao at the Boao Forum for Asia (BFA) mentioned peace and development (as opposed to China's peaceful rise) more than 10 times. See *ibid*.

9 Academics like Gerald Chan said dialectics are colored with ideology. This non-dialectical statement is meeting only half-way, because dialectics can be used in playing politics and other non-ideological things, such as the birth and death of human beings. In other words, if the two remarks somehow match, it only means that the dialectician has only, at best, accepted half-way.

PART I

A Micro-Level Perspective

Hu Jintao and His Central Military Commission Predecessors: Navigating within a Series of Dialectical Frameworks

CHAPTER 1

Introductory Remarks

In November 2002, the 16th National Congress of the Communist Party of China (CPC) (hereinafter CPC Congress) was held. It was supposed to endorse Jiang Zemin's *Sangedaibiao* (Three Represents) important thought, which nicely and properly fit into what this author called the safe zone in my Socialism with (Distinct) Chinese Characteristics Versus Capitalism framework of thought and action, as we shall see later,[1] and to announce the beginning of political reforms, which are also to be carried out within a series of *youji* (organic), *huanhuanxiangkou* (interlinked), dialectical frameworks, after having carried out economic reforms from the Third Plenum (or Planning Session) of the 11th CPC Congress in December 1978 to the end of the 15th CPC Congress. In March 2004, at the Second Session of the Tenth National People's Congress (NPC), *Sangedaibiao* became part of the People's Republic of China (PRC)'s fourth amended Constitution since September 1982. The main purpose of holding the 12th Party Congress in September 1982 was an attempt at officially pulling the mainstream economic line from Communism back to Socialism (which was officially modified as Socialism with Chinese Characteristics). The aim of the 13th Congress from October 15 to November 1, 1987 was to announce the line of the nascent (or primary) stage of Socialism with Chinese Characteristics and the separation of functions of the party and state apparatuses. The 14th CPC Congress in October 1992 was to leap from the Maoist Communism Versus Capitalism framework of thought and action or what the Chinese Communists called *gangling* (program) to a smaller, Dengist *gangling*, to wit, Socialism with Chinese Characteristics Versus Capitalism, which is a part of the Maoist dialectical model, as we shall see clearly later on in Figure 2. The 15th Congress, held in September 1997, was to announce the party's policy of moving to the *zhongyongzhidao* (middle way), to wit, the Market Economy line (*luxian*) in the Dengist dialectical model, which is something that even Karl Marx had not dwelled on, as well as to separate politics from economics. At this Congress, *zheng* (administration) and *qi* (business/enterprise) have been separated, meaning that the latter can legally do whatever it wants to. We have also witnessed for the first time that none of the military figures could be Members of the Central Committee of the Political Bureau, the highest policy-making council. The 16th CPC Congress was to legitimize the Three Represents. The same Congress has also witnessed the further decline in the number of uniformed members in the new Political Bureau from two out of 21 in the last Party Congress to two out of 24.

The process for political reform may take a long period of time to complete. This is because the CPC must make sure that it can continue or sustain its ruling party status, so that it can bring its mainstream Market Economy line *qua* object, which was officially publicized at the 15th CPC Congress back to the Socialism with Chinese Characteristics line *qua* subject hopefully decades from now. In his Political Report at the 15th Congress, Jiang Zemin, the very first civilian Central Military Commission (CMC) Chairman who, on the day after the closing of the 16th CPC Congress, reminded the four new heads of the Chinese People's Liberation Army (Chinese PLA) General Departments who were taking their public pledge before him to "resolutely heed the commands of the party central authorities and CMC Chairman Jiang," said that it would take a few generations, several generations, and even more than 10 generations to finish walking, so to speak, the Market Economy line.

In September 1999, Hu Jintao became the Vice-Chairman of the CMC of the CPC's Central Committee and of the PRC. He belongs to what is popularly known as the core of fourth-echelon (or generation) leaders. He was perceived as someone who has been deliberately ensconced in a central position since the 14th CPC Congress. Although he was only referred to as the core of the new Central Committee in the November 17, 2002 edition of *Jiefangjunbao* (Liberation Army Daily) on page 1, Hu, in March 2003, became the President of the PRC. On September 19, 2004, Hu became the CMC Chairman of both the CPC and the PRC and promoted two generals on the next day. In other words, Jiang Zemin stepped down as the CMC Chairman of both the party and the state, a post he acquired in November 1989, with the blessing of Deng Xiaoping two months before that.

The armed forces of the PRC include the Chinese PLA, the People's Armed Police Force (PAPF), militia, and reserves. The Chinese PLA is headquartered at the August First Building in the capital, which is ostensibly a CPC organ or a core pillar of the dialectical Chinese

Communist power structure. On the other hand, the PAPF, formerly under the Ministry of Public Security (MPS), has also been headquartered in Beijing since April 1983. And, since the 15th CPC Congress, its *diwei* (position or standing) is in parallel with seven Military Regions (or Military Area Commands in the mainland China parlance), which could become *zhanqu* (*ad hoc* operational area commands) as in the case of Nanjing Military Region since December 1995.

The Chinese PLA and its relationship with the party still deserves in-depth, closer study, because, as of August 1, 2004, it has been unsuccessful for both Chinese and foreign academics and experts to non-dialectically decode and to decipher its words and deeds over the last 77 years as well its not-so-intricate relationship with the CPC, once my version of the dialectical model is fully understood.

I will first point out the major problems in the studies of the party and the Chinese PLA. Such problems can be logically, systematically, and coherently solved or resolved in the context of my dialectical framework(s), which will be introduced in a later section. First, David L. Shambaugh in his July 1999 commentary and elsewhere equated symbiosis and professionalism as "two sides of the same dialectical coin" in the Chinese PLA.[2] Yet, mere mention of this is not enough, because, unlike Western conceptual thinking, Chinese thinking is correlative. This author also has some reservation with regard to the usage of the word professionalism, which is only a part of the overall dialectical picture, which is People's War. Besides, the usage of the word coin is also not appropriate. This is because, throughout the paper, he has to apply a version of dialectics and to slot in the relevant data in his dialectical model. Only by doing this, will he be consistent and not distort basic facts. Alexander C. Huang suffers from the same problem. However, it is commendable that he may well be the first seasoned Chinese PLA observer outside of mainland China to have decoded Jiang Zemin's *wujuhua* (five sentences) for the Chinese PLA, which were first unofficially put forward in either December 1990 or September 1991 but officially on August 1, 1996. They are *zhengzhihege* (politically qualified), *junshiguoying* (militarily competent), *zuofengyouliang* (good work style), *jiluyanming* (strict discipline), and *baozhangyouli* (adequate logistics), which are the general requirements for army-building in the new era (*xinshiqijunduijianshedezongyaoqiu*). To be sure, these words are but another way of saying Red and Expert (both socialist-minded or politically progressive and professionally proficient), which later became the Red

Versus Expert framework in the Maoist Era.[3] Inspired by Huang's decoding, we can confidently say that revolutionization (*geminhua*), modernization (*xiandaihua*), and regularization (or standarization [*zhengguihua*]) (as opposed to professionalism [*zhiye*], professionalization [*zhiyehua*] or specialization [*zhuanyehua*]) are but another version of People's War, as this author will discuss more fully later on. Third, because about 95 per cent of the Chinese PLA analysts think about or perceive reality non-dialectically, that is, they do not apply my version or other versions of dialectics, contradictory remarks at least at the micro-level[4] can be easily spotted in their writings.[5] This is because, in my model, empirically speaking, whenever a move is made, be it a word or a deed, one only thinks about a Number or a Letter at any point in time/space sequence. Thus, there is no such thing as, for example, a pyramid or a policy formulation structure which comes in terms of several concentric rings[6] or circles in dialectical thinking. Everything is arranged in terms of 1, 2, 3, 4, 5, A, B, C, D, and E, as we shall see later.

This is a study of all the CMC Chairmen and Vice-Chairmen since October 1949, including Zhao Ziyang who was CMC's First Vice Chairman from November 1, 1987 to June 24, 1989 as well as Guo Boxiong and Cao Gangchuan who replaced Zhang Wannian and Chi Haotian at the 16th Party Congress. We do not have to study Chen Yun, who was the only leader who dared to challenge Deng in economic affairs since late 1970s, simply because he was basically not involved in military affairs. Hu Yaobang also needs no discussion for the same reason, even though he was promoted by Deng at the 12th Party Congress as the CPC General Secretary and placed in front of Marshal Ye Jianying, who was labelled by Mao as *baohuguojiadajiangjun* (a great general who can protect the country). One should also notice that there was a gap for a short period of time between the demise of Mao Zedong on September 9, 1976 and the official announcement of Hua Guofeng as his successor on October 6. This should be regarded as a problem, because the question is whether Hua could have ruled at that time as it was not possible for Mao's influence and clout to be automatically passed on to Hua? This problem will also be discussed in chapter 4 entitled "Comments and Major Observations."

This author strongly argues that, first, out of all the major frameworks mentioned in this study, the principal dialectical models of the CPC Commands the Gun (Barrel) and the Gun (Barrel) Commands the CPC Versus the Non-CPC Commands the Gun (Barrel) and the

Gun (Barrel) Commands the CPC as well as the CPC Commands the Gun Versus the Gun Commands the CPC which have been keeping the party and, as a consquence, the PRC, afloat since October 1949, and not necessarily the existence of Mao, Hua, Deng Xiaoping, Jiang Zemin, and Hu Jintao as well as their Vice-Chairmen in the respective periods. To be sure, at the climax of the Great Proletariat Cultural Revolution (GPCR), which took place from late 1966 to early 1967, the Chinese PLA, for the most part was still functioning as usual, with the exception of those departments related to propaganda, cultural work, military schools and academies as well as scientific research.[7] Second, with Mao, Deng, and Ye around, who, however brief for Ye, had *junshishiquan*[(([actual military power] as opposed to *junshixuquan* [nominal military power]), they can reinforce the execution of those major dialectical frameworks in general and those two quite different but unique dialectical models as mentioned in this paragraph in particular. But, Hu Jintao (and other core members) can only first rely on law to reinforce the compliance of those dialectical models, until the day when he and his core members can apply the Party Commands the Gun and the Gun Commands the Party Versus the Non-Party Commands the Gun and the Gun Commands the Party model. If Hua, who never possessed *junshishiquan*, were still the CMC Chairman after March 1997, he (and his core members) would also have to first rely on law to accomplish the same thing. Jiang Zemin was different. He (and other core members) first needed Deng to help them to reinforce the frameworks. After the 4th Plenum of the 14th Party Congress in September 1994, he (and other core members) have had the laws to rely on to play dual roles, to wit, the Party Commands the Gun and the Gun Commands the Party, as he (and other core members) see fit. As for General Secretary Hu (and his core members) prior to September 19, 2004, as well as CMC Chairman Jiang (and his core members) after November 2002, they have all had to rely on law to allow Hu (and his core members) to play the Party Commands the Gun role and Jiang (and his core members) to apply the other one, namely, the Gun Commands Party, both of which are intertwined in the safe zone and, therefore, dialectically acceptable at the macro-level.

To refresh our memory, in August 1927, Mao for the first time said that *qiangganzichuzhengquan* (all political power grows out of the barrel of a gun).[8] These words are derived from his bitter struggle against Chiang Kai-shek. Mao also knew that, once he had seized the *guojia* (state in general and government in particular, the latter of which, as a whole, was in charge of economic affairs) power, he and his successors would have to guard against anyone inside or outside of the CPC using real gun(s) to force them to do something that they did not want to. In March 1997, when the National Defense Law (NDL) was adopted as law by the Fifth Session of the Eighth NPC, the CPC Commands the Gun tenet (or dictum or *junhun* [spirit for the Red Army and later the armed forces]) legally became part of it as well as the PRC Constitution, and it has subordinated everyone, to begin with the CMC Chairman at both the CPC and *guojia* apparatus levels and anyone serving the armed forces or having military duties. In other words, military figures, high ranking or at entry level, come and go, but there is a thread of consistency for most, if not all, of them to adapt to changing circumstances by staying in the safe zones of any one of my version of dialectical frameworks and to realize that personalistic *guanxi* (ties or connections), primordial (ethnic, religious, parochial, and class) sentiments, etc. come second, third, fourth, or later priorities.

Gangjumuzhang (once the key link is grasped, everything falls into place) is the right Mandarin Chinese idiom to understand *gangling*; *luxian* (line)(*zhanlue* [strategic]) or *zong* [general]) *fangzhen* (guiding principle); and *zhengce* (policy) in that order of *huanhuanxiangkou* importance. According to Guoguang Wu in a short piece written 10 days after the 16th CPC Congress, four to six months after the January 1935 conference (*huiyi*) at Zunyi City, Guizhou Province, this principle (as expressed in Chinese) was applicable during the Long March prior to Mao's success in seizing the military power from Zhou Enlai and in getting rid of a foreign Communist International military advisor and pro-Moscow representatives like Wang Ming (or Chen Shaoyu). Before that, Zhang Guotao and Zhou in that order headed the Central Miliary Department of (Chinese Workers and Peasants') Red Army. In other words, before mid-1935, Mao could not do much to reinforce the dialectical model, to wit, the CPC Commands the Gun and the Gun Commands the CPC Versus the Non-CPC Commands the Gun and the Gun Commands the CPC, that is as applied to himself or to reinforce the Party Commands the Gun Versus the Gun Commands the Party framework which all the military officers and soldiers had to comply with. For example, in the early 1930s, Mao was in command of some troops in Jiangxi Province's Jianggang Mountains, which became the first revolutionary base in February 1928. But, he still had to bow to Wang or be *paiji* (discriminated against) by the same, the latter of whose headquarters was in Shanghai City.[9]

Because the CPC Commands the Gun tenet and its opposite appeared before the Zunyi Conference, my argument can still be applied to the period from December 1929, if not dating back to September and October 1927 when Mao at Sanwan Village, Yongxin County, Jiangxi Province reorganized the troops of *Qiushou* (Autumn Harvest) uprising and institutionalized the Party Commands the Gun, up to September 1946, when the Eighth Route Army and the New Fourth Army were renamed the Chinese PLA at the same time in the following month.

ENDNOTES

1   The first Represent (or subject) refers to the workers, peasants, and the armed forces and includes the Chinese People's Liberation Army (Chinese PLA). This is mentioned in the party Constitution. The second pillar or Number 3 in this author's model is equivalent to the intellectuals. And the third component or object or 5 in this author's framework of thought and action is those (new) businessmen and entrepreneurs who have Communism at heart and who support the ruling status of the Communist Party of China (CPC).

2   David L. Shambaugh, "Commentary on Civil-military Relations in China: The Search for New Paradigms," commentary presented at the "State of the PLA on the Eve of the Millennium: A Retrospective of the Last Twenty Years," conference as sponsored by the Chinese Council for Advanced Studies (CAPS) and Rand Corporation, Radisson Barcelo Hotel, Washington, D. C., dated July 8–11, 1999. In the November 2002 paper presented at a conference on the Chinese PLA which was held in Taipei, he mentioned the same thing. He also said that the symbiosis thesis is not dead or even moribund. See also his book, *Modernizing China's Military* (Berkeley, CA.: University of California Press, 2003). Earlier, he wrote that "The Party's control has atrophied and eroded more than many realize. Only the military can save it." See his article, "Chinese Hegemony Over East Asia by 2015?" *Korean Journal of Defense Analysis* (hereinafter KJDA), Vol. IX, No. 1 (Summer 1997), p. 27.

3   Alexander Chieh-cheng Huang, "Transformation and Refinement of Chinese Military Doctrine: Reflection and Critique on the PLA's View," paper presented at the "State of the PLA on the Eve of the Millennium: A Retrospective of the Last Twenty Years" conference as sponsored by the Chinese Council for Advanced Studies (CAPS) and Rand Corporation, Radisson Barcelo Hotel, Washington, D. C., dated July 8–11, 1999, p. 13 and *Guangjiaojingyuekan* (Hongkong), October 1996, p. 79 (mentioning December 1990) and July 1997, p. 16 (mentioning September 1991). Huang only wrote Red Versus Expert. This is not complete because it should be Red and Expert from the outset. During the Great Proletarian Cultural Revolution (GPCR), only Red was stressed.

4   Micro-level refers to the moves made by the CPC and/or the Chinese PLA. Applying my dialectical model, one would notice that there is contradiction at the macro-level where two extremes have been mentioned. Each Number or Letter, for exmaple, 1 and E reflects a concept.

5   Huang (note 3), p. 1. The following academics and experts have mentioned *Yin and Yang*, Hegelian, or Marxist dialectics: June Teufel Dreyer, Lin Chong-pin, Michael Y. M. Kau, Arthur S. Ding, David L. Shambaugh, Monte R. Bullard, Yitzhak Shichor, Andrew Scobell, Robert Suettinger, as well as Jorn Brommelhorster and John Frankenstein.

6   For example, one of Shambaugh's publications was entitled "The Pinnacle of the Pyramid: The Central Military Commission" in *The PLA as Organization*, edited by James Mulvenon (Santa Monica, CA: The RAND Corporation). In his discussion paper prepared for the October 26–27, 2000 conference sponsored by the National Defense University, Washington, D.C., he said there appeared to be five separate levels of doctrinal thinking and planning for the Chinese PLA and he also gave the parallels in Western doctrine. Well, the levels should be depicted vertically for the Chinese armed forces. If they are correct, they should be positioned horizontally. Tai Ming Cheung maintains that the CMC lies at the heart of the structure and is the core of the first inner ring, the scond inner ring, and the third outer ring. See Tai Ming Cheung, "The Influence of the Gun" in David M. Lampton, ed., *The Making of Chinese Foreign Policy and Security Policy in the Era of Reform, 1978–2000* (Stanford, CA: Stanford University Press, 2001), pp. 79–80. Dennis J. Blasko in one of his papers entitled "A New PLA Force Structure" wrote "The relationship of the three schools to one another and Chinese force structure can be visualized as a triangle or pyramid composed of three tiers." See also June Teufel Dreyer, "State of the Field Report: Research on the Chinese Military," *Access Asia Rewiew*, Vol. 1, No. 1 (Summer 1997), p. 26. Harlan W. Jencks in his October 26–27, 2000 paper on page 4 presented at the National Defense University, Washington, D.C. also mentioned, for example, "at the bottom of the pyramid, there were vast numbers of militia...." The conceptualization of a crisis as shown in Alastair I. Johnston's Figure 1 is also non-dialectical. See his article, "China's Militarized Interstate Dispute Behaviour 1949–1992: A First Cut at the Data," *China Quarterly*, No. 153 (March 1998), p. 4.

7   *Jiefangjunbao* (Beijing), December 18, 1998, p. 1 and Ke Li and Shengzhang He, *The Chinese People's Liberation Army During the Cultural Revolution* (Beijin Zhonggongdangshiziliaochubanshe, December 1989), p. 31. The first military academy was launched in January 1951. In 1966, there were 126 of these academies. In 1969, they were reduced to 43. And, in 1975, they were increased to 84. To emphasize the importance of training , the CMC and General Political Department used *hongtouwenjian* (colloquially, they are referred to as "red-headed documents," because the Chinese characters are printed in red ink). See *Jiefangjunbao* (Beijing), December 18, 1998, p. 1.

8   *Zhongguoguofangbao* (Beijing), June 25, 2001, p. 3. This remark was made after some one million CPC members and revolutionary masses from 1927 to 1930 were killed by the then ruling party in mainland China. See

Jiefangjunbao (Beijing), July 2, 2001, p. 6. At the 6th CPC Congress, Zhou Enlai's Military Report said that the party did not use the military and political organizations of the ruling party to help the CPC's political work in the army. According to an observer, this is what Deng Xiaoping thought: A General Secretary who does not have *junquan* (miltiary power) is a *guanggansiling* (a commander without troops). Once possessing the *junquan*, one can use the gun to take over *zhengquan*. Once having *jundangdaquan* (big power of the army and the party), the *zhengfu* (government) is only just a *banshijigou* (office) under the CPC and the Chinese PLA's command or order.

9   Xinyang Wang, "The Party Commands the Gun Versus the Gun Commands the Party," *China Forum* (Taipei), Vol. 28, No. 11 (September 10, 1989), p. 56 and Jin Xin and Xue Qing, editors, *Gongheguodajunqusilingchuanqi* (Legend of The Republic's Military Region Commanders)(Sichuan: Sichuanrenminchubanshe, May 1995), p. 406. Wang Ming after the outbreak of Sino-Japanese War in July 1937 said *yichejingguotongyizhanxian* (everything has to go through the untied front) or *yichefuchongtongyizhanxian* (everything has to obey the united front). In August 1937, the then ruling party announced the reorganization of the Red Army. But, Mao insisted on the Party commanding the 8th Army numbering more than 45,000 troops and the New 4th Army numbering more than 10,000 troops. See *ibid.*, pp. 409–410 and *Jiefangjunbao* (Beijing), July 2, 2001, p. 6. From April 1931 to January 1935, the CPC under Wang Ming was relying on the *maoxianzhuyi* (adventurism) versus *jijifangyu* (active defense) framework. Wang was tilting in favor of the former. In Fall 1938 at the 6th Plenum of the 6th CPC Congress, Wang was dismissed from his Changjiang (Long River) Bureau position.

CHAPTER 2

A Normative and Empirical Model: Decoding and Deciphering the Chinese Communist Politico-military Maze

Human beings suffer from one serious problem, to wit, we simply cannot remember everything. Therefore, many of us have learned to simplify or compress a myriad of things into a model or, as a step further, come up with a theory (or, more universally, a paradigm) which is again a logical simplification or compression of the model itself. To be sure, both model and theory must be able to describe, explain, and infer, predict, or forecast future. They can be elevated to the status of paradigms if and when many, if not most, model-builders and theorists collectively accept them.

Attempts have been made to describe and explain the relationship between the party and the Chinese PLA since the creation of the latter. Many, if not most, publications about them have been logically written. However, there are several objections. Firstly, they lack models. Even where models have been mentioned or introduced, none of them have depicted their models in a graphic manner to facilitate and improve our understanding.[1] In this electronic age, studies which do not apply models very quickly become out-dated or irrelevant in the face of new developments which could contradict facts appearing in the previous one. Secondly, some of these studies, taking chances, have made the wrong inferences, predictions or forecasts which, on occasion have proven to be disastrous.[2] For this reason, some authors have tried to protect themselves by reminding readers, at the outset, that there is not enough hard information due to the fact that mainland China is still shrouded in secrecy or mention that their work is speculative at best.[3] There is a third reservation. That is to say, the models are non-dialectical, whereas we know for certain that Chinese Communists and those in the military forces do apply a version of dialectics, just as *guanxi* are pervasive in Chinese culture and society. Mao once said that there are 600 million Chinese people and he wanted to convert all of them into dialecticians. A column in the January 24, 2004 edition of *Jiefangjunbao* (Liberation Army Daily) on page 3 was entitled "The dialectics of 1.3 billion Chinese people." To be sure, Chinese Communists repeatedly say that *luxianjuedingyiqie* (line determines everything). In the early 1980s, many military academics in the PRC began teaching military dialectics, a term which embraces Chinese characteristics, as coined by Mao.[4] Nie Fengzhi and Fu Quanyou are relatively obscure military figures, as compared to Mao, Zhou, and Deng. But, they apply dialectics in politico-military affairs.[5] It should be noted that the Anglo-American analytic philosophy, in the words of an Italian-American dialectician, Chris M. Sciabarra, "has never been friendly" to dialectical analysis. Thus, almost every student or scholar[6] of the relationship between the CPC and the Chinese PLA has refrained from applying the dialectical approach, for fear of not being able to gain recognition from their peers or get their manuscripts published by better publishers. Thomas J. Bickford in his doctoral dissertation put forward his moderator (or arbiter armies) model and mentioned continuum as well as Leninist and non-Leninist. He argued that with some modifications the moderator concept is "the most suited for understanding the (Chinese) PLA from 1949 to the present."[7] However, that might not really be the case for Andrew Scobell, using the frameworks of Chinese strategic and civil-military culture, did not mention this model in his 2003 book, *China's Use of Military Force: Beyond the Great Wall and the Long March*?

This author applies his own version of dialectics in decoding and deciphering the Chinese Communist politico-military maze, to wit, the relationship between the party and the Chinese PLA. Carl G. Jung, a well-known non-Chinese psychologist, should be credited for correctly reading the Chinese mind, to quote him at length:

> Just as causality describes the sequence of events, so synchronicity to the Chinese mind deals with the coincidence

of events. The causal point of view tells us a dramatic story about how D came into existence, how it took its origin from C, which existed before D, and C in its turn had a father, B, etc. The synchronicity view on the other hand tries to produce an equally meaningful picture of coincidence. How does it happen that 'A', 'B', 'C', 'D', etc., appear all at the same moment at the same time and in the same place? It happens in the first place because the physical events 'A' and 'B' are of the same quality as the psychic events 'C' and 'D', and further because all are the exponents of one and the same momentary situation. The situation is assumed to represent a legible or understandable picture.[8]

A very good example is reflected in Mao's letter to Lin Biao on May 7, 1966 when the GPCR was gradually gathering momentum: Chinese PLA soldiers were "to combine the roles of the military scholar, the military farmer, the military worker, and the military civilian *all in one* (emphasis mine)."[9] However, before moving on to introducing our model, several caveats are in order. First, dialectics, as Chinese Communists say, should not be associated with metaphysics nor idealism (*weixinglun*). In other words, there is an adjective "materialist" preceding the word dialectics. My version of the dialectical framework of thought and action, which provides the organic, *huanhunaxiangkou* functions of rationalization and self-protection (from criticisms), control and guide, as well as struggle, is as follows.

One paradigmatic way of simplifying complex, ever-changing, and ever-dynamic reality for a long period of time is to perceive or to present reality in terms of two dots/points (*liangdianlun*) or, to be more precise, two extremes, at any time/space sequence before the last one. The two dots/points/extremes, in parallel, are depicted below:

●　　　　●

But, these two dots/points/extremes are originally derived from one dot/point,[10] which is another way of referring to as the Roof/Housetop or Eaves:

●

That is to say, the extreme at the left is part of the above original dot/point, just as the other extreme at the right is also part of the original dot/point. In other words, if the original dot/point equals to 100, the left extreme dot/point could be 75 or 51, while the right extreme dot/point, 25 or 49 respectively. Or, if the original dot/point is 1, the left extreme dot/point could be .75 or .51, while the right extreme dot/point, .25 or .49 respectively. In this connection, there is a distance between the two dots/points/extremes. There is a reason for having the distance, as we shall see later.

To facilitate later discussion, I shall label the left dot/point/extreme as Number 1 and the right dot/point/extreme as Letter E.[11] Another way of depicting the two dots/points/extremes is as follows:

1   E

Each dot/point/extreme refers to something, be it a concept, a phrase, a sentence, a label, a symbol (which does not necessarily have any meaning but could just reflect something or represent something else). Each point in the two-dot system is just the opposite of the other dot/point/extreme (or, as one other possibility, it could be the dot/point half-way between two other extremes). If there are many issues which need to be dealt with or (re)solved, many working frameworks or sets of two dots/points/ extremes can be created or employed, linking each other. Players can manipulate or play a lot of games at once, by moving sideways like crabs within the framework of each game (or set of two dots/points/extremes) and by making leaps like frogs from one framework to another one at any time/space sequence. By "moving sideways like crabs," I mean the movement of a politico-military figure (or a political entity, political party, country, etc.) within the framework in any of the following manner: Remaining at or sticking to the left dot/point/extreme (or 1) or the right dot/point/extreme (or E); moving to the edge of the safe zone or 5 (which comes in terms of a spectrum or which extends from the left extreme to the centre-point between the two dots/points/extremes) of a framework or a set of two dots/points/extremes; moving to the edge of the danger zone or A (which comes in terms of a spectrum or which extends from the right extreme to the centre-point between the two dots/points/ extremes) of a framework or a set of two dots/points/extremes; staying at a dot/point/extreme in between the left dot/point/extreme and the centre-point or staying in between the centre-point and the right dot/point/ extreme; etc. However, the politico-military figure ought to concentrate on one primary game (working framework or set of two dots/points/

extremes) at a time/space sequence to enhance the figure's ability to be logical, systematic, and coherent in what he or she does and says. There should be one primary dialectical framework of thought and action at any time/space sequence. Choosing the right framework is very important. Failing to do that even by dialectical players would be disastrous.[12] If one framework does not fit into a particular time/space sequence, another can. In between them, one may have to construct another framework, so as to link them up. So, a dialectician, like a frog, would constantly leap from one framework to another. An outsider who does not understand dialectics, would certainly be confused, he or she is apt to conclude that the politico-military figure is illogical, unsystematic, and incoherent in what he or she does or says.

A politico-military figure may also make use of the frameworks (games or sets of two dots/points/extremes) to perform any one of the following functions: rationalization and self-protection, control and guidance, as well as struggle. The term rationalization means that whatever one does and says is done within the safe zone, preferably positioned at 1. Because it is safe, one can protect himself or herself from unnecessary criticisms while control, means that the politico-military figure will ensure that his or her (potential) enemy falls within the framework. Guidance is necessary, because some politico-military figures may deviate and enter into the danger zone. Thus, efforts must be made to bring them back to the safe zone. And struggle is obvious. The subject wants to eliminate, co-opt, or absorb the object, and vice versa, hence the tension, friction, conflict, etc.

Even more important still, the politico-military figure should preferably attempt to stay at the left dot/point/extreme at all time/space sequences or at least within the safe zone (which always refers to the spectrum made up of Numbers ranging from the left dot/point/extreme to the centre-point of the framework or 5). In this context, the safe zone is the opposite of the danger zone (which refers to the spectrum made up of Letters ranging from the right dot/point/extreme up to the centre-point of the framework or A). It is always possible that, owing to circumstances beyond his or her control, the politico-military figure may voluntarily or involuntarily venture into the danger zone for a period of time. However, in order to justify what he or she is doing and saying, he or she will attempt to rearrange the two dots/points/extremes, so that his or her actions can be seen as still taking place within the safe zone. That is to say, the politico-military figure will attempt to make the original centre-point or 5 into the new left dot/point/extreme or 1 with the right dot/point/extreme or E remaining in the same place. All games end when they reach the time/space sequence (n), in which the final and conclusive crab-like/sideways move takes place.

In order to help readers to acquire a better visual understanding of what has been said in the preceding paragraphs, I shall depict the working framework or the set of Numbers and Letters plus the time and space elements in Figure 1.

FIGURE 1

---

1 2 3 4 5 A B C D E

time/space sequence (1)
time/space sequence (2)
....
time/space sequence (n)

Numbers 2, 3, 4, and 5 are each a variation/synonym[13] of Number 1 which is the left extreme. For example, we can have CHINA as 1, "CHINA" as 2, CHINa as 3, CHIna as 4, and China as 5. Similarly, Letters A, B, C, and D are, again, each a variation/synonym of Letter E, which is the right extreme. We can refer to china as E. But, for D, it could be written in a different font so as to differentiate it, for example, from china. One might envisage more than just 5 numbers and 5 letters, if one chooses to extend the list. But, this is not really necessary, because, the dialectician would not burden himself or herself with too many things. In a word, dialectics might first appear complicated but actually is not. Within each Number or Letter, there is room for manoeuvre (or change) from right or the nascent (or primary) stage to the ascendant stage, and to left, the mature stage. The Numbers can be conceived of as a dot/point/extreme or *zheng* (thesis), and the Letters, another dot/point/extreme or *fan* (anti-thesis).

In the face of constant change, a dynamic, operational concept (or what the Chinese Communists called *fangzhen*) is required to reconcile the two dots/points/extremes or to eventually bring about the disappearance of the right extreme by elimination, co-optation, absorption, etc. Another way of expressing this concept is action. Conducting anti-corruption campaigns is one example of possible actions. Having three links and four exchanges (*santongsiliu*), such as shipping link between mainland China and Taiwan after January 1, 1979 is another example. Such a concept/action must work in favour of the left extreme.

To summarize the description and explanation above, Number 1 represents the left dot/point/extreme. Numbers 1 to 5 constitutes the safe zone/spectrum. Number 5 refers to the edge of the safe zone (which touches the framework centre-point). Letter E is the right dot/point/ extreme. Letters A to E fall into the danger zone/spectrum. Letter A refers to the edge of the danger zone (which also touches the framework centre-point). In a nutshell, Number 1 and Letter E are simply the two dots/points/extremes (*liangdianlun*) I referred to earlier (see Figure 1).

ENDNOTES

1	Li Nan proposed a model for civilian control of the Chinese PLA. But, can he simplify it in the form of a diagram? See his article, "From Revolutionary Internationalism to Conservative Nationalism," *Peace Works*, (Washington, D.C.: United States Institute of Peace), No. 39 May 2001, pp. 36–37. Ying-mao Kau mentioned "dialectic model." See his book, *The People's Liberation Army and China's Nation-building* (White Plains, New York: International Arts and Sciences Press, Inc., 1973), p. iii. See also Ellis Joffe, "Party-Army Relations in China: Retrospect and Prospect," paper presented to the conference, The PLA Towards 2000, co-sponsored by *The China Quarterly* and the Chinese Council of Advanced Policy Studies, Island Shangri-la Hotel, Hongkong, dated July 13–15, 1995 and Thomas J. Bickford, *Marching Into the Abyss: The Changing Role of the People's Liberation Army in Chinese Politics*, doctoral dissertation submitted to the Graduate Division of the University of California at Berkeley, 1995. Suzanne Ogden discussed the issue of distorting understanding between the Western and Chinese Communist definitions. The word dialectics was not mentioned in her book. See her book, *Chinese Unresolved Issues* (Englewood Cliffs, NJ: Prentice Hall, 192), Chapter 1.

2	See a paper presented at a November 2002 conference on the Chinese PLA in Taipei. Chong-pin Lin also made an erroneous prediction on the emergence of Yang Baibing. Fourth Annual Conference on China's People's Liberation Army, August 1993, Staunton Hill, Virginia, as sponsored by the American Enterprise Institute, p. 38.

3	See Michael D. Swaine, *The Military and Political Succession in China* (Sana Monica, CA: The Rand Corporation, 1992). Both Swaine and Shambaugh said news media in Taiwan and Hongkong more often than not have proven to be faulty guides to empirical uncerstanding of Chinese PLA words and deeds. See Shambaugh (note 2, chapter 1), p. 2.

4	See, for example, Boye Lin, *Junshibianzhengfajiaocheng* (A Course in Military Dialectics) (Beijing: Jiefangjunchubanshe, October 1985), p. 21. In 1936, Mao at Yanan's Red Army University first mentioned military dialectics. Karl (Carl) von Clausewitz (1780–1831), a Prussian general, applied Frederick Engel's version of dialectics. See p. 73.

5   Jin and Xue (note 9, chapter 1), pp. 239–250 and Haijian Ling, *The Profile of New Prominent Military Chiefs in China*, (Hongkong: The Pacific Century Press, 1999), p. 32.

6   Both Swaine and Shambaugh refer to Ellis Joffe as a scholar of politico-military affairs of the PRC. There are exceptions. Monte R. Bullard, for example, does "try to present both sides of a problem in a dialectical manner. [He likes] to think of it as a Max Weber value-free approach rather than a Marxist dialectical reasoning approach" adding "there is not much difference" between the two. His email to me, dated January 11, 2004. Andrew Scobell mentioned the adjectives dualistic and (Hegelian) dialectics. See his book, *China's Use of Military Force: Beyond the Great Wall and the Long March* (U.K.: Cambridge University Press, 2003), p. 15 and p. 51. Arthur S. Ding knows that the party applies a version of dialectics. But, he does not, in writing, apply the dialectical approach.

7   Bickford (note 1). In his paper, "A Retrospective on the Study of Chinese Civil-military Relations Since 1979: What Have We Learned? Where Do We Go," presented at the the "State of the PLA on the Eve of the Millennium: A Retrospective of the Last Twenty Years" conference as sponsored by the Chinese Council for Advanced Studies (CAPS) and RAND Corporation, Radisson Barcelo Hotel, Washington, D.C., dated July 8–11, 1999, he, while making a critique of other approaches, models, paradigms, etc., did not mention his model but credited works by Ellis Joffe, Paul H. B. Godwin, and Harlan W. Jencks for correctly perceiving developments made in the Chinese PLA professionalism. See p. 17. June Teufel Dreyer and Richard J. Latham have reservation with regarding to seeing the Chinese PLA as fitting Western concept of professionalism.

8   Cited in the Preface of my book, *The Crab and Frog Motion Paradigm Shift: Decoding and Deciphering Taipei and Beijing's Dialectical Politics* (Lanham, MD.: University Press of America, 2002), p. ix. See also my article, "The Dialectical Relationship of the Chinese Communist Party and the PLA," *Defense Analysis*, Vol. 16, No. 2 (August 2000), pp. 203–217.

9   Quoted in Chong-pin Lin, "Limits to Professionalism: The Extramilitary Roles of the People's Liberation Army in Modernization," *Security Studies*, Vol. 1, No. 4 (Summer 1992), p. 685.

10   If we look at earth from outer space, it is possible to see what is going on since the beginning of human beings as one dot. This is quantum physics.

11   In September 1994, I constructed my version of dialectical model. In October 2003, I realized that Chinese Communists like to mention three things at a time. For this reason, it is easier to slot in data if I were to use only five numbers and five letters. After going over my model, Bertell Ollman, a Marxist teaching dialectics at New York University (NYU) commented that it clear and has Marxist trimmings. His latest book is *Dance of Dialectic* (Chicago University of Illinois Press, 2003)

12   See *Zhongguo mianxiang ershiyi shiji de ruokan zhanlue wenti* (China Facing the 21st Century:Some Strategic Problems)(Beijing: Zhonggong Zhognyang Dangxiao Chubanshe, May 2000), p. 9.

13   A la manière de William (Bill) H. Gates, III, 1 can be a light bulb of 100 watts; 3, 50 watts; and 5, 1 watt. Similarly, E has 100 watts; C, 50 watts,

and A, 1 watt. In religion, they could be called *fenshen* (spare time to attend to something else or disengage oneself from [inf]), and Number 1 would be *benzun* (the revered or esteemed). The same thing applies to A, B, C, D, and E which are *fenshen*, and F is *benzun*. One good example is as follows: Dr. Sun Yat-sen is 1, whereas Wang Bingzhang could be 2, 3, 4, or 5 because a reporter said many people adore Dr. Wang and referred to Wang as "Contemporary Sun Yat-sen." Wang in November 1982 published the inaugural issue of *China Spring*. See *China Times* (hereinafter CT), March 28, 1998, p. 9.

CHAPTER 3

First, Second, and Other Multi-faceted Frameworks

Like accessing the Internet,[1] we must first go into a browser window. Then, in that window, we can click to see or open other smaller browser windows. In the latter, there could be even smaller windows. In this book, the very first window—and the biggest—is the Rule of Law Politics Versus Rule of Men (or Rule of Personality) Politics. Another way of saying the same thing is 1 Versus E. The framework could also be expanded to Rule by Virtue Politics Versus Rule by Men Politics. In this context, the former is 1 and the latter, E. At a national conference whose participants included heads of propaganda departments, in January 2001, Jiang Zemin stressed Rule by Virtue, which is akin to the ancient Chinese aphorism of *xiushenqijiazhiguopingtianxia* (cultivate oneself and make oneself useful to the society, look after the family and maintain strong sense of family responsibilities, look after the country, as well as have peace and harmony under heaven). In between the Rule of Law Politics and the Rule of Men Politics, there is what this author called Rule of Dialectical Politics.[2] It is designated as 5, and it is a mixture of Rule of Law Politics or 1 and Rule of Men Politics or E. This is indeed the case, because, in mainland China, there has been personality politics as well as rule of law and rule by law politics since October 1949. To be sure, in between Rule of Law Politics and Rule of Dialectical Politics, there is what this author called Rule by Law Politics (*yifazhiguo* as opposed to Rule of Law which has the same pronunciation but with different tone, meaning administering the state according to law). At the 15th CPC Congress and on earlier occasions, Jiang Zemin said the armed forces of the PRC must adhere to the Rule by Law Politics. As to those members in the Political Bureau, they can still play the Rule of Dialectical Politics. This means that having made that remark, Jiang Zemin returned to 5 from 3 in the framework of the Rule of Law Politics Versus Rule of Men Politics.

In a word, our analysis of the relationship of the party and the Chinese PLA at each time/space sequence should first figure out what the mainstream in the biggest window is. Otherwise, one will be confused and bewildered by the illogical, unsystematic, and incoherent nature of the moves made by the CPC and/or the Chinese PLA.

As soon as we have figured out the mainstream for each time/space sequence, we are in a position to apply the second framework of thought and action, as depicted in Figure 2. The application of the rest of the dialectical models is done in the context of this second dominant framework. As can be seen, there are four mainstream economic lines from October 1949 up to now. With Mao at the helm, the Chinese PLA, on the whole, had not tried to challenge his command. Not many people dared to, given Mao's charisma, contribution to the founding of the PRC, and other leadership qualities, especially during the GPCR. For example, Lin Biao, who had replaced Peng Dehuai as the Minister of Defence in September 1959, complied with Mao's economic line by cutting down military exercises and by eliminating many military academies, because, at least at the nascent Communist stage of economic development, there was no need for so many troops owing to the perception that *guojia* should gradually disappear before time/space sequence (n),[3] which would mean that Capitalism would almost be absorbed or defeated by Communism, the latter of which should have quite abundant (material) wealth.[4] But, because the mainland was still at the nascent stage of Communism, Lin did not eliminate once and for all the Chinese PLA. To be sure, Peng was criticized by Mao at the 8th Plenum of the 8th Party Congress held at Lushan (Lu Mountain, Guling County, Jiangxi Province) in August 1959 not because he had deviated from the Party Commands the Gun Versus the Gun Commands the Party framework but because he had challenged Mao's economic decision to ask all the PRC people to go to Number 1 in Figure 2. Peng in his 10,000-word letter (dated July 1959) to Mao was correct in saying that the time was not yet ripe for the Chinese people to practise Communism, be it the nascent, ascendant, or mature stage. At that time, Deng, who was in charge of economic affairs at the State Council, sided with Peng and others. They had to confront the Chinese PLA led by Mao. Unable to change or to modify Mao's economic line, Deng lost his struggle against Mao, and was branded a Second Capitalist Roader, after Liu Shaoqi, during the GPCR.[5]

FIGURE 2

	COM				SOC			CAP	
	1	2	3	4	5	A	B	C	D	E
	Safe Zone					Danger Zone				
1937.09								X		
1939.05								X		
1940.01								X		
1945.10								X		
1949.10					X					
1949.12					X					
1956.08					X					
1957.06					X					
1957.07	X									
1976.09	X									
1978.11	X									
1978.12					X					
1992.01.17					X					
1992.01.18								X		
1992.09								X		
1997.09 to the present								X		

FIGURE 2 (cont'd)

NOTE: Prior to January 18, 1992, Beijing leaders basically relied on the Communism (COM) Versus Capitalism (CAP) framework of thought and action or the Maoist framework. After that, the leaders chose a new but a smaller Socialism (SOC) (with Chinese Characteristics) Versus Capitalism framework which is supposed to function since April 1956 or the Dengist framework, in which 5 became 1 and C (Market Economy Under Socialism [with Chinese Characteristics][6]) became 5, thereby bringing mainland China back to the position where it was in January 1940, October 1945, the Xibaipo Village, Pinshan County, Hebei Province period from May 1948 to March 1949, or the days of the Republic of China (ROC) on the mainland.[7] At the 7th CPC Congress which took place from April to June 1945, creating a *Xinminzhuzhuyi* (New Democracy) China was the political line.

It is very important to understand where the mainstream line or economic base is, at each stage of the PRC's development. Based on this, can we talk about the superstructure, namely, *guojia*, ideology, and politics, to be followed by things related to military affairs such as war which could be either righteous (*zhengyi*) or non-righteous. To give an example.[8] Yang Shangkun's half-brother, Yang Baibing, was labelled *qiangyingpai* (hardliner) in June 1989, because he, largely backed by the 27th Group Army (*jituanjun*) of Beijing Military Region, not only signed the document but was for the brutal, military crackdown of the mass-scale student demonstration in Beijing (and elsewhere). The elder Yang was appointed the First Vice-Chairman of the CMC, while the younger Yang became the CMC Secretary General. Qin Jiwei who formerly commanded the Beijing Military Region and who had helped Deng to make a third come-back, and who later became the Defense Minister in April 1988 was regarded as a *wenjianpai* (moderate). In other words, they could not politically get along well with each other on the issue. Yet, why was Deng able to accomodate them in the first place? The reason is simple. The three of them before the Tiananmen massacre were for the Dengist *gangling* or Deng's decision to eventually leap from the Communism Versus Capitalism framework to the Socialism with Chinese Characteristics Versus Capitalism dialectical model. They also knew that Deng would eventually adopt the middle road, that is, Market Economy, in the Socialism with Chinese Characteristics Versus Capitalism framework, which is closer to Capitalism. This was something that Deng wanted to continue doing from June 1957. However, the Gang of Four led by Mao's wife, Jiang Qing, who were followers of Mao and who had labelled Deng a Second Capitalist Roader were opposed to that especially during the GPCR.

Once we are surfing on the right mainstream economic line, we are ready to apply the following third framework: The Party Commands the Gun Versus the Gun Commands the Party. To repeat, for Mao, Deng, and even Ye briefly, it is the Party Commands the Gun and the Gun Commands the Party Versus the Non-the Party Commands the Gun and the Gun Commands the Party which worked.[9] This is because they possessed actual power when they were in center stage. For others, like Hua, Chen Xilian, Zhao, the Jiang Zemin core (up to August 1994), Liu Huaqing, Zhang Wannian, the Hu Jintao core (until Hu acquires *junshishiquan*), and Guo-they like the rest of the military officers and soldiers-have to comply with the CPC Commands the Gun Versus the Gun Commands the CPC model. In other words, to the former, Mao, Deng, and Ye can make crab-wise moves in between the Party Commands the Gun or 1 and The Gun Commands the Party or 5, both of which are placed in the safe zone, as they see fit at any time/space sequence. Jiang was also able to do it, as seen in the way he prohibited the Chinese PLA in late 1998 from doing business or having enterprises. As for the latter, the Gun Commands the CPC is clearly designated the danger zone. Zhao failed to comply with the CPC commands the Gun tenet; this resulted in his downfall in late June 1989. A brief narration of history may be necessary.

The 9th CPC Congress was held in December 1929 at Gutian Town, Shanghang County, Fuijian Province, which was popularly known as the Gutian conference. Over there, Mao made the first part of the tenet, which was intended , among other things, to eliminate warlordism.[10] From June to October 1935, Mao, during the Long March, criticized Zhang Guotao for splitting the Red Army and the CPC, and he emphatically reiterated that their principle is for the party to command the gun, not vice versa. After the collapse of Communism in East Europe and the Soviet Union in that sequence, the Party re-emphasized *dangdejueduilingdao* (absolute loyalty to the CPC or absolute leadership of the Party over the army). For the record, in September 1932, *jueduilingdao*, for the first time appeared in *xunling* (directive or instructions), as a military document, for the Red Army.[11] Again, the same logic applies as in the first and second working frameworks.

Of course, there is the fourth framework as set up by the CPC in May 1953, which is: Revolutionization, Modernization, and

Regularization Versus Non-Revolutionization, Modernization, and Regularization. We should spread the troops into the safe zone. 1 represents Revolutionization. 3 is Modernization. And 5 would be Regularization. To be sure, this spectrum is another way of saying People's War. The term regularization, means what Deng had stated in August 1980 at an enlarged Political Bureau conference: *nianqinghua* (making younger), *zhishihua* (increasing knowledge), and *zhuanyehua* (making professional). Depending on the time/space sequence, many of them would be positioned at where the party wanted them to go to. It follows that the CPC had not abandoned People's War, a military doctrine, which, before May 1953 was characterized by luring the enemy deep in so as to annihilate him through attrition. In late May 2004, the militia had again emphasized, in view of the inauguration of Chen Shui-bian as the 11th President of the Republic of China (ROC) on May 20, who is well known for his pro-Taiwan's *de jure* independence.[12] Paraphrasing Huang,[13] Mao's doctrine, People's War Versus Non-People's War is "old wine in the old bottle." Deng's can be seen as "new wine in the old bottle." And, Jiang's emphasis on high-technology reflects a refinement but basically it is "new wine in the old bottle but wrapped with cellophane." Thus, Chi said Internet war is still People's War, one which could paralyze the U.S. Department of Defense's super-computer system,[14] without having to fire a bullet. Similarly, in late 2003, it was also reported that the mainland, using the People's Armed Police Force (PAPF) (as opposed to the Chinese PLA) may just have to throw three electro-magnetic pulse (EMP/ *diancimaichongwuqi*) bombs in Taiwan's northern, central, and southern areas, thereby paralyzing the latter's C4ISR such as the command and control center, computer system, telecommuncation systems, finance and banking systems, etc., without even having to kill a Taiwan area resident. (Needless to say, we cannot preclude the use of neutron bombs or enhanced radiation weapon and high-power microwave [HMP] technology weapon). In a word, the Chinese PLA is at least psychologically ready to perform any of the three tasks as requested by the CPC.

We should also consider the Party (as Number 1), *Guojia* (as Number 3) [in general and Government in particular], and the Military (as Number 5) framework, plus others like the CPC and the *Guojia* framework and the CPC Versus the *Guojia* framework. The party is positioned at the left extreme in this fifth model, because it has supremacy over the *Guojia* and, in turn, the armed forces. To be sure, there should be unity in *zhijun* (governing, administrating or managing the armed forces) and *zhidang* (governing, administrating, or managing the CPC) after the separation of the party and *guojia*. In other words, to the CPC, it is necessary to first build or construct the *junduidang* (literally army-party, not party-army nor party's army) well, to be followed by building the military forces.[15]

There is also the sixth model, to wit, Politics and Military Versus Non-Politics and Military framework, which is called *tongyideduili* (the opposite of "the unity of opposites").[16] Again, 1 is Politics and 5 is Military. These two intertwined components, like the Party Commands the Gun and the Gun Commands the Party spectrum in the Party Commands the Gun and the Gun Commands the Party Versus the Non-Party Commands the Gun and the Gun Commands the Party framework, in Mandarin Chinese, are *bukefengedetongyi* (that which cannot be partitioned or carved up) or *duilidetongyi* (the unity of opposites, mutually complementary, not mutually exclusive by themselves, or complementary in opposition, like *Yin* and *Yang*). By the same token, Politics (or A) and Military Affairs (or E) in the Non-Politics and Military Affairs spectrum also go hand in hand. A non-military affair example could be educational. This kind of arrangement fit into what Shambaugh has described and explained concerning the Chinese PLA, that is, it has historically been organically "inextricably intertwined" with the CPC and, as a consequence, the *guojia*. In other words, a military figure who can or cannot play politics is decided by the person who has actual power and this person preferably should head the CPC's Central Committee. Thus, Guo and Cao even after the 16th CPC Congress could not have played politics, although they belonged to the Political Bureau. This kind of phenomenon can again cover the period before and after the creation of the PRC. If we were to include other spheres, we can rearrange the safe zone as: Political, 1; Military, 2; Economic, 3; Cultural, 4; and Social, 5.

A brief history is again in order. In August 1927, the Red Army was abruptly created. In December 1929, Mao, as leader of the Red Fourth Army presiding over the Gutian Conference, criticized the "purely military viewpoint"-the equivalent of Western military professionalism-by emphasizing the political role of the Red Army. In October 1944, Mao, as the CMC Chairman, expanded the role of the Red Army into the economic and cultural spheres. He wrote that in their work, the *zhandou* (war) comes first, then *shengchan* (production), then *gongzuo* (cultural work).[17] By saying that, he had, in effect, asked many, if not most, Chinese PLA officers and soldiers to perform such tasks. Needless to say, some talented officers and soldiers might have had to play several roles at the same time. Then, in February 1949, towards the end of the civil war on the mainland between the CPC and the ruling Nationalist Party of China (NPC or Kuomintang [KMT] for short), he further asserted the social affairs responsibility for the Chinese PLA, such as "organizing trade unions, mobilizing the youth, managing industry and commerce, running schools, newspapers, and broadcasting stations," adding "(i)n short, all urban problems, with which in the past our army cadres and fighters were unfamiliar, should from now on be shouldered by them."[18] In effect, Mao had assigned some Chinese PLA officers and soldiers to perform such tasks. Chong-Pin Lin wrote that "(i)t is worth noting these (Chinese) PLA social responsibilities prescribed by Mao would seem like a *déjà vu* four decades later immediately after the June 4, 1989 incident, when (Chinese) PLA soldiers took control of the government newspaper *Renmin Ribao* (People's Daily) and expanded indoctrinating classes for university students."[19]

The inevitable question is: How do we slot in the data presented above? It is not difficult. At time/space sequence 1, the Red Army was standing under both 1 and 2. (The Army can purely look at the Politics and Military Versus Non-politics and Military framework.) By that I mean, it was performing both political and military tasks. At time/space sequence 2, let us say, October 1944, the Chinese PLA officers and soldiers were spread out to cover 3 and 4 as well. And, in February 1949, some Chinese PLA officers and soldiers actually went up to 5, in performing their assigned tasks and required duties. Since the second half of 1957, especially after Lin Biao became the Defense Minister, he was gradually *tuchuzhengzhi* (putting politics in command). In December 1964, Lin Biao, for the first time, instructed the Chinese PLA to *tuchuzhengzhi* by ordering many troops to move to Number 1. He compressed military training from 60 to 40 per cent (another source said training fell below 30 per cent),[20] and he even slighted materialism and dialectics. Observations such as the Chinese PLA was becoming less political only fit into the later time/space sequences. When that took place, it simply meant that more military officers and soldiers had gone to Number 5. However, some still stayed at 1 or even 3. But, after Lin's death, Mao, in August and September 1971, instructed the Chinese PLA how to properly manage the Politics and Military as well as the Red and Expert relationships. Then, after Deng's re-emergence to center stage for the third time in July 1977, most Chinese PLA officers and soldiers returned to the barracks, because Deng had drastically reduced military representation in both central and provincial CPCs and government organs, and rid the Chinese PLA of socio-economic missions.[21] But, in summer 1998, when there were huge floods in many parts of the mainland, the Chinese PLA was called upon to perform non-military, counter-flooding duties. In any case, when we see less military leaders in the CMC, NPC, etc., it means that more of them are standing under 4 or 5 in the Politics and Military Versus Non-politics and Military framework. In sum, the Chinese PLA was never apolitical from the Red Army days up to now, unless the CMC were peopled by CPC members who do not have a whit of military background or connection. Still, once a miliary title is conferred on a civilian, the latter has to comply with the frameworks as mentioned in this study.

The seventh Red and Expert framework, which is *duilidetongyi*, still applies, so do military officer and soldier, *jun* (army) and (masses of) people, *jun* and *zheng* (administration), forging unity between the Chinese PLA and *youjun* (friendly army or forces), disintegrate the enemy, etc. If *jun* and (masses of) people can mingle as fish in water, so to speak, then the former would not have any enemy. In March 1980, Deng addressed an enlarged conference of the CMC's Central Committee, reiterating that "(i)n any case, political and ideological work in the army must be strengthened.... As for 'red and expert,' on no account must the 'red' aspect be discarded."[22] The problem with the Maoist era at the peak of the GPCR is that, since the mainstream economic line was at the nascent stage of Communism, Lin Biao in order to carry out Mao's policies stressed the Red aspect while slighting or discarding most of the things related to the Expert aspect, treating it as in the danger zone, instead of using the Red and Expert Versus Non-Red and Expert model. In other words, what Lin and, for that matter, the Gang of Four which consisted of, for example, Zhang Chunqiao who set up the *Geminweiyuanhui* (Revolutionary Committee) in Shanghai Municipal City in February 1967 and who was a First Political Commissar from May 1967 to October 1976 at the Nanjing Military Region as well as Shanghai Garrison, did was to replace the word *and* with the word *versus* in the same model.

When Chinese Communists talk about priority, they are, again, arranging them horizontally, not vertically, in their mind one by one. This means that the first model is equivalent to 1; the second dialectical framework, 2; the Party Commands the Gun Versus The Gun Commands the Party model and/or its variation is positioned at 3, which carried the most weight and received more attention than the other frameworks of thought and action, when it comes to the question of dealing with the Chinese PLA. Of course, there is also the model for Mao, Deng, and briefly for Ye, which can be positioned at 4. Since the Numbers can be increased beyond 5, there is no problem to arrange all the major, important frameworks as mentioned in this section accordingly into this eighth priority model.

There are other mechanisms which can help to control and guide the Chinese PLA's words and deeds. The first one is the way the CMC Chairman and Vice-chairmen is arranged or positioned. The chairman, of course, is Number 1, the vice-chairman perhaps is put at Number 5. If there are two or three vice-chairmen, then the first one could be 2 or 3 and so on and so forth in that order. On October 1, 1949, there were five Vice-Chairmen in the CMC, one of them was a KMT defector, Cheng Qian. This defector should be placed at 6, owing to the fact that there were six military figures in the spectrum. One thing certain is that they were all in the safe zone, arranged in terms of a spectrum, with 1 carrying the heaviest weight. This kind of arrangement is part of the CMC Chairman and Vice-Chairman/Chairmen Versus Non-CMC Chairman and Vice-Chairman/Chairmen model.

The second one is the organization of the PRC armed forces. They come in three (and later four) general departments (Headquarters of the General Staff, General Logistics Department, General Political Department, and General Armaments [or Equipment] Department which was created in April 1998), all services and arms (such as Second Artillery Force [or Strategic Rocket Force], Group Army, Airborne Troops, etc.), and military regions. The four general departments, peopled by about 100 staff, actually command the military under the CMC.[23] This means that, over the years, (forced) retirement, removing, reshuffling, rotating assignments, or the replacement of military commanders down to the regimental or lower level would be a standard operation. At the beginning of the War of Resistance Against Japan, the CPC only had 32,000 troops. After the outbreak of the Korean War, the Chinese PLA swelled to 6,260,000 troops, the largest number in its history. In July 2003, to be reiterated by Wen Jiabao, the Premier, in March 2004 at the Second Session of the Tenth NPC, the PRC announced that there will be another cut of 200,000 troops, the bulk of which belongs to the *lujun* (army). In other words, the number of Chinese PLA troops will be 2.3 million before

2005. During the GPCR, the CMC in January 1967 ordered that only units above the *jun* (corps), such as each Headquarters of the General Staff, General Political Department, General Logistics Department, Military Regions, Provincial Military Command, and the Chinese PLA Navy, might be involved in the struggle.[24] In November 1984, at an enlarged CMC meeting, Deng for the first time proposed a cut-back in the number of troops. After that, a study of cutting down one million troops was carried out. From late May to early June 1985, Deng at an enlarged CMC meeting formally announced the policy. Michael D. Swaine also pointed out that there is a high degree of control by the CMC over troop movements and deployment. A corps commander can only move a regiment, a division commander a battalion, a regimental command a company, and a battalion commander a platoon.[25] The political work system, which differs from capitalist countries' armed forces, consisting of the *dangweizhidu* (the CPC committee system in the armed forces), the *zhengzhiweiyuanzhidu* (the political commissar system, with each commissar enjoying seniority and authority over his or her military counterpart), and the *zhengzhijiguanzhidu* (political organ or office system) seem to work well on the whole. The commissars rely on, for example, the ninth Centralism (*jizhong*) Versus Democracy (*minzhu*) framework, as correctly pointed out by Ron Montaperto at an October 1995 hearing before the U.S. Congress. This dialectical model is quite different from the term *dangneiminzhu* (intra-party democracy) as put forward by Hu Jintao at the Third Plenum of the 16th Party Congress in October 2003. If there is no time during a battle, that such a dialectical model can be practised at a *pengtouhui* (brief meeting or literally knocking heads meeting).[26]

The third mechanism , as related to the above, is the party's frequent reliance on the Centralism Versus Democracy framework, although after the second half of 1957 the practice was disrupted. So, many of what the Chinese PLA has done can be intrepreted in its terms. In May 2004, the CMC for the first time issued a set of regulations to improve the work of the party in the armed forces. Set for trial implementation, the regulations represented an attempt to ensure a high degree of stability and unity. The framework is basically welcoming the military figures to voice their opinions before reaching a consensus or making a decision. This means that they can enter into the danger zone which is couched in terms of the Democracy spectrum for a period of time only to come back to the safe zone preferably at Number 1 later. On the eve of the November 1994

6th Asia-Pacific Economic Cooperation (APEC) Ministerial Meeting, Liu Huaqing, Zhang Zhen, Hong Xuezhi, and Qin bringing with them a letter signed by 80 generals urged Jiang Zemin not to succumb to American pressure. Later, the military brass apparently was satisfied that Jiang had stood firm at the APEC summit meeting.[27] As another example, just before Lee Teng-hui's trip to the United States in June 1995, the PRC armed forces were also very tough on Chairman Jiang, resulting in the latter's decision to conduct military exercises just before the ROC's first ever direct presidential election in the 10,000-year history of China in March 1996. To be sure, what the Chinese PLA did for having positioned themselves at Number 5, which is another way of saying conducting military exercises, was in between the framework of Not to Attack Versus To Attack. In other words, rounds of ammunication were shot, and nobody was hurt either in Taiwan or the mainland, or even a third party, because it is possible a foreign vessel passing by could be hit by a stray bomb. The Chinese characters for this kind of phenomenon is *budazhongyouda*, which is a mixture of Not to Attack and To Attack. This is similar to *junzhongyoudang* and *dangzhongyoujun*, which we will discuss later.

The fourth mechanism should also be noted. The CPC's tactics are flexible, changing according to time and space. For example, when Imperial Japan formally attacked the ROC on mainland China, the CPC regarded the former as *xindediren* (new enemy), whereas the *jiudediren* (old enemy), that is, the KMT Government armed forces, became *youjun*.[28] As another example, after the refusal by the then ruling party of the ROC to sign the *Guoneihepingxieding* (*zuihouxiuzhengan*) (Domestic Peace Agreement), Mao and Zhu De ordered the Red Army to cross the Changjiang (Long River) on April 20, 1949 at 8 pm. The ROC Government in Nanjing, which is the capital, began to collapse after that. Giving still another example, earlier in March 1949, Mao adopted three ways to handle the defeated troops: Tianjin, that is, the use of weapons to defeat the KMT troops; Beiping, to wit, the peaceful reorganization of the KMT troops; and Shuiyuan, namely, to keep the insurrectionary forces as they were and reorganize them at a later stage. The Chinese PLA also adopted the following general principle to co-opt the then ruling party troops, after October 1949: *tuanjie* (unite), *jiaoyu* (educate), *zhenqu* (win over), and *gaizhao* (remould).

The fifth one is that, at the *liandui* (or *lian* [company]) level, there are CPC branches. In each branch, there must be three or more CPC members. In October 1986 and July 1987, the General Political Department stipulated that there be 10 or more party members in each *liandui*. This type of *dangweizhi* (party committee system) can be dated back to September and October 1927, when Mao reorganized the troops at Sanwan Village, Yongxin County, Jiangxi Province.[29] Not all military officers and soldiers are CPC members. In 1997, for example, more than 5,000 high school graduates joined the CPLA, and, yet, CPC members only constituted 32 per cent. Stressing regularization and modernization in the context of a revolutionary army (*gemingjun*) can also enable the CPC to control the military forces. As a reminder, the 12th CPC Congress Political Report mentioned the three elements. As early as during *Tudigeminzhanzhengshiqi* (The Period of Agrarian Revolutionary War), Mao said, at the mature stage of the Red Army, it should gradually get rid of its guerrilla nature. As elaborated by Chong-pin Lin, *zhengguihua* "refers to the change of military style away from that of a guerilla force— loosely organized, poorly disciplined, ad hoc and adaptive in operation— to that of a standard army in the Chinese tradition."[30] This is a Dengist model for the army-building and its Maoist equivalent is Red and Expert (as opposed to Red Versus Expert later on especially during the GPCR), as mentioned earlier.

The sixth one has to do with the reinstatement of ranks in July 1988, which was abolished in May 1965, and it certainly can help to control the armed forces. From October 1983 to late 1986, the Chinese PLA tried to sort out three types of unwanted officers and soldiers. They were during the GPCR: 1) followers of Lin Biao and Jiang Qing; 2) under the heavy influence of *bangpai* (faction); and 3) engaged in *da* (beat), *za* (smash) or *qiang* (plunder). Needless to say, Hu Jintao, a victim of the GPCR at an early stage, would not adopt the old rank system, which was modelled after the Soviet Union's, which began in September 1955, and which was criticized for being "remnants of capitalist influences."[31] Several major promotions were carried out in the period from September 1988 to June 2004, totalling 96, out of which 15 of them were promoted by Deng. Right after the 16th Party Congress, the promotion announcement of ten generals was made. In December 2003, Jiang ordered a major reshuffle within the Chinese PLA army involving 24 generals, at least one of whom is known to have close links to Jiang and Zeng Qinghong, who is Jiang's closest ally and follower.[32] And, in June 2004, the rank of general was conferred on another 15 senior military officers, including Jiang Zemin's body-guard, You Xigui, in Zhongnanhai. Needless to say, the Hu Jintao core will think of making changes to reflect his military choice within the safe zone of dialectical frameworks once he comes out of the shadow of the Jiang Zemin core.

The seventh one is also unique. It is called *junzhongyoudang* and *dangzhongyoujun* (the army is in the CPC, and vice versa), which is another deep-rooted mechanism to control and guide the Chinese PLA. In Shiping Zheng's translation, it is an interlocking power-sharing relationship. One should not overlook the Chinese art of this cultivated *diaogui* (paradox as opposed to ambiguity), as opposed to the Western tradition of usually having clarity of intent and behavior.[33] To use the mechanism in dialectical terms, the CPC would penetrate into the armed forces and vice versa. For example, there are party members in the armed forces, just as there are Chinese PLA leaders serving in organs like the the Standing Committee of the CPC Political Bureau, NPC, etc., though the number of members fluctuate in response to prevailing political currents or tides and particular needs. This practice is also applied to *gong* (attack) and *fang* (defense). To the Chinese PLA, it is *gongzhongyoufang* and *fangzhongyougong*,[34] that is, there should be defense within attack and vice versa. *Dadatantan* (literally fight, fight as well as talk and talk) is the finest example.

Then comes the 8th mechanism. As reminded by Chong-pin Lin, the Chinese PLA also periodically practises the conventional method of self-criticism. However, this should be understood in term of Mao's *tuanjie-piping-tuanjie* (Forging Unity-Conducting Criticism-Forging Unity) for the party. This means that one begins at Number 1 but should move to E and then come back to 1 at time/space sequence (2) or a later sequence, when a consensus or a decision has been reached. *Zhualiangtou* and *daizhongjian* is another traditional, Maoist method, which says that one should sustain the advanced (represented by Number 1) and help the backward or those lagging behind (represented by 5) so as to bring the middle (or 3) along.[35]

The ninth mechanism has only become a tool lately. In June 1990, Jiang Zemin signed a military document, which for the first time included the *yifazhijun* (ruling the armed forces by law), which became a *zongfangzhen* (general principle) in the following year. Of course, it was Deng who was pushing Jiang to sign it. To be sure, recognizing that no one can be as charismatic or can hold actual power as Mao, Ye, and Deng, the laws, legal documents, as well as rules and regulations related to the Chinese PLA can also help to regulate the behavior of most officers and soldiers.[36] With the Long Marchers gone, it is extremely difficult to apply the framework for Mao, Ye, and Deng, that is, The Party Commands the Gun and the Gun Commands the Party Versus Non-the Party Commands the Gun and the Gun Commands the Party.[37] Jiang Zemin could not apply it until the 4th Plenum of the 14th CPC Congress in September 1994. For this reason, in less than three months as the CMC Chairman, Jiang had signed nine military statutes. This is unprecedented in the Chinese PLA history, according to a magazine in Hongkong. The CMC for the first time in March 1993 issued *lifaguize* (a rule stressing legislation). Thereafter, many laws notably the March 1997 *National Defense Law*, which clearly stated *yifazhijun* and the subordination of the military forces including the PAPF and others first to the CPC Constitution and then the PRC Constitution and which did not represent a separation of the CPC from the state and, therefore, the party from the Chinese PLA;[38] *Military Service Law* of the PRC; *Regulation on the Military Ranks of Chinese PLA Officers* (which stated, *inter alia*, that the CMC Chairman will neither receive a military rank nor the First Class or Grade of General); etc., came into being, and these army-building laws and legality-related decisions were promulgated by the 7th Session of the 8th NPC in May 1994. The *Garrison Law of Hong Kong Special Administrative Region* was approved at the 23rd meeting of the Standing Committee of the 8th NPC in December 1996.[39] In July 1998, the State Council for the first time made public the military legislative work or miliary legal system on the PRC's national defense and military affairs. Jiang Zemin also stated that in each military organization there must be lawyers who should be politically correct. As early as February 1985, the very first *faluguwenchu* (legal advisory panel) was created in the Chinese PLA Navy. In the year 2003 alone, courts at all levels handled 6,096 cases related to the military, including punishing those who had leaked military secrets.[40]

The next mechanism has to do with political correctness, which is another ethos of the Chinese PLA and it is important for the rank and file. On August 1, 2004, The PRC Minister of Defense, Cao, stressed that the Chinese PLA should unswervingly put ideological and political construction in the first place in all aspects of the construction of the army. In selecting the right officers and soldiers based on the correct mainstream economic line, the term *wuhusihai* (all corners of the country)[41] can serve as a reminder. This term is opposed to *santouzhuyi* (mountain-stronghold mentality), *zongpaizhuyi* (sectarianism or factionalism), and *xiaotuantizhuyi* (cliquism or small-group mentality).

This means that it does not matter where you come from, what your field army affiliation might be, or whether or not you have personal ties with a particular general or superior, an officer or soldier must obey the Party at all times. In April 1990, for example, a reshuffle of the seven miltiary regions took place, and it was done in that spirit. Thus, Chinese PLA analysts should not be misled by labels like the Sichuan clique, the Zhang Zhen and Zhang Wannian network, the Shandong network of senior officers who hailed from the Shandong Province, the Shanghai clique, and the New Shanghai clique that comprised of Hu Jintao, Zeng Qinghong, Wu Bangguo, etc. So, Chinese PLA analysts should not be surprised that Xu Shiyou has remained commander of the Nanjing Military Region[42] and Yang Dezhi of Jinan Military Region, respectively from March 1955 to December 1973 as well as Li Desheng who served at the Shengyang Military Region from October 1976 to June 1986. Mao stuck to this mechanism for a long period of time. However, as he became older, he failed to practise this principle, especially during the GPCR. Deng, after his third come back, reminded all the screening and review committee members to select the right military officers and soldiers for military promotion and appointment to participate in the NPC, for example. When the "Yang Family Generals," namely, the then CMC Vice-Chairman Yang Shangkun and especially his half-brother, Yang Baibing, who in November 1987 headed the Chinese PLA General Political Department, was no longer trusted by Deng in September 1992 or just before the 14th CPC Congress for having, without permission, discussed at a *pengtouhui* what should be done after Deng's death,[43] Jiang Zemin was more careful. To serve as a guide, in January 1967, Mao personally approved a Political Bureau *pengtouhui* at Zhongnanhai, the CPC Headquarters, where those who were for the GPCR struggled fiercely against those who were not, and a second one took place in the following month, in the course of which Lin Biao and Jiang Qing realized that the majority of leaders did not support the GPCR.[44] As another example, Chi, who was Yang Shangkun's protégé, had not been involved in the *pengtouhui* as called upon by Yang Baibing, thus Chi was able to retain his post as the Minister of Defense. Hu Jintao, who has only shelved the Maoist framework of Communism Versus Capitalism, will act similarly.

Then, there is the 11th mechanism. Periodically, political commissars will utilize nationalism or patriotism to the CPC's advantage, sometimes for the purpose of distracting some military officers and soldiers from discontent. For example, *China's National Defense* reported that by the end of 1994 the PRC still had over 100 pieces of land, totalling 160,000 square kilometers, and more than 2,000 kilometers of land borders under dispute with the Federation of Russia, Republic of Kazakhstan, Republic of Kyrgyzstan, Republic of Tajikistan, Republic of India (ROI), the Socialist Republic of Vietnam (SRV), and Kingdom of Bhutan, not to mention the South China Sea islands, islets, etc., continental shelves, exclusive economic zones, and ocean or maritime rights with both the Republic Korea (ROK) and the Democratic Republic of Korea (DROK), Japan, the Philippines (ROP), the Federation of Malaysia (FOM), Negara Brunei Darussalam, Republic of Indonesia (ROI), and the SRV.[45] As a second example, the party has tried to control the mass media. On October 8, 1976, less than two days after the arrest of the Gang of Four, Chi was asked to be in charge of *Renmin Ribao*. In October 1977, owing to the successful completion of a job, he was promoted to Deputy Chief of Headquarters of the General Staff to further clean up the Headquarters which was controlled first by Lin Biao's henchman, Huang Yongsheng, and later by the Gang of Four supporters.[46] As another example, they also glorified the brilliant deeds of the soldier, Lei Feng, who had actively spurred every revolutionary youth on or forward. Since April 1990, mainland China has sent military officers and soldiers wearing blue berets and helmets, including military observers, liaison officials and consultants, on United Nations (UN) peacekeeping operations abroad. In January 2002, the PRC formally participated in the Class-A stand-by arrangements mechanism for UN peacekeeping operations. Those who were sent were of the same profile as Lei. There are five other military heroes like Lei. In March 1989, a renovated Lei Museum was reopened in Hunan Province's Wangcheng County. If the mass media has failed to mention Lei Feng, it only means a temporary eclipse, meaning that, sometimes, if not Lei, then *Nanjinglushanghaobalian* (the good 8th Company on the Nanjing Road) or *Yinggutouliulian* (the hard-boned, dauntless, or steel-willed 6th Company) will be used as an advanced representative for propaganda and indoctrination purposes. When the time is ripe, Lei will appear again. His name will reappear in association with the Chinese PLA when the latter is engaged in peacekeeping operations (PKOs). Like Chinese nationalism or patriotism, Confucian virtues like *zhong* (loyalty) and *yi* (chivalric justice) will also be exploited to unify the officers and soldiers. Mao in December 1973, in the presence of all the military region commanders, even asked Xu to recite *Hongloumeng* (The Red Chamber) three times, so as to learn from General

Zhou Bo, who was under Liu Bang's leadership and who took care of everything after the latter's death.[47] In October 2003, Yang Liwei became the first Chinese *taikonnaut* (as opposed to the Soviet cosmonaut and the American astronaut) to go to outer space. Without his knowledge, he was promoted from lieutenant-colonel (*zhongxiao*) to colonel (*shangxiao*) before going to outer space. On December 7, 2003, Kyoto News mentioned his latest rank as senior colonel (*daxiao*).

The 12th mechanism is ironic. Sometimes foreign military and non-military figures may serve to increase the CPC and, for that matter, the Chinese PLA's bargaining chips. This is a boost to the morale of the Chinese PLA. Examples are many. After the collapse of the Soviet Union in December 1991, many Rusisan scientists and technicians were employed by the Chinese PLA research institutes, helping to build, among others, cruise missiles with a range of 1,800 miles and a circular error probability (CEP) or accuracy of 500 feet. As a second example, in July 1998, U.S. Senate Republican majority leader Trent Lott admitted that there were flaws in American export controls of sensitive technology, which had helped the Chinese PLA. Indeed, studies have also been published saying American friends are building the mainland's military might.[48] As a third example, the PRC was preparing to launch a small, underground nuclear test at its sprawling testing facility in Lop Nur in the western Xinjiang desert. In April 2001, a Chinese PLA F-8 jet fighter intercepted and collided with a large U.S. Navy's EP-3E surveillance plane, which was conducting a low-speed, reconnaissance, and electronic signals monitoring mission near the Chinese mainland coast. The crash caused damage to the American aircraft, forcing a rapid descent and an emergency landing on nearby Hainan Province. In dire circumstances, classified material aboard the U.S. spy plane was not entirely destroyed by the crew.[49]

Needless to say, there are other mechanisms. One thing is certain, that is, navigating within a series of dialectical frameworks does not mean that every single officer and soldier would stay within the safe zone all the time. Their mind could easily travel to the danger zone, followed by actions. Thus, over the years, there have been many serious incidents. When Mao was around, he could ask most of the Chinese PLA officers and soldiers to travel to the danger zone for a period of time and come back. This is because he had helped to create the PRC and he had the charisma to appeal to many Chinese and foreigners alike. When Deng was the paramount leader, he could also wield enormous power and influence over the course of national affairs in general and the Chinese PLA affairs in particular but he chose not to. During those times when he could not play a role similar to Mao's, he would consult with and rely on some senior, elder military officials.[50] And even with the promulgation of the *National Defense Law*, there should be some Chinese PLA officers and soldiers who have entered into the danger zone sometimes deliberately, and others, inadvertently. Let me point out some major incidents.

Deng said Mao used to seek truth from facts before the second half of 1957. Mao's personal edicts often disrupted, for example, the *wuhusihai* concept.[51]

Lin Biao during the GPCR said the Chinese PLA should not only control military power but party power as well (*bujinguanjunquan, haiyoudangquan*). He only stressed the prominence of politics, starting in December 1964, while neglecting the military aspect, as mentioned earlier. In October 1969, Deng and his wife, for example, were sent away to Xinjian County, Jiangxi Province for re-education. Just before that, Lin fabricated a Number One Order saying that owing to mounting tension between the PRC and the Soviet Union since March 1969, it had been necessary to evacuate them and others in order to step up combat readiness in the capital.[52] At the end of August 1977, investigations revealed that several thousand military officers had been involved in the Gang of Four activities, among them 32 per cent were military cadres, 52 per cent political cadres, with 14 per cent belonging to the General Logistics Department, and the rest were technical cadres.[53]

From June 24 to July 15, 1975, Deng at an enlarged CMC conference characterized the armed forces as "swollen or bloated (too many institutions), slack or lax (erroneous discipline and factionalism), arrogant or conceited (divorced from the masses), especially for having supported the *Sanzhiliangjun* [the task of "Three-support" and "Two-military" (back-up of the leftist masses, industrial production, agricultural production and support military control or supervision and military training, involving more than 2.8 million officers and soldiers from January 1967 to August 1972)], extravagant or extravagance (pursuit of a capitalist lifestyle), and lazy or inertia (decline of will power and failure to maintain one's integrity in one's later years)" as well as the military leadership as "*ruan* (feeble), *lan* (lazy), and *san* (undisciplined)." Ye made the concluding remarks. However, due to obstruction by the Gang of Four, the streamlining work came to a halt.

In February 1979, the PRC sought to teach the SRV a lesson. But, it turned out, after 15 days of battles, to be a Pyrrhic victory costing the Chinese Communist over 60,000 casualties, many times more than what the SRV army lost.[54]

In the winter of 1980, armed with a gun, a temporary worker, Hao Huaiming in Jize County, Hebei Province, turned up at an artillery regiment. He said he had a mission of creating a new PRC. Believing what Hao said, the political commissar of this regiment, Zhu Fuxiang, received him. Needless to say, the General Political Department regarded this incident as serious. So, the commissar was stripped of his party membership and relieved of his duties.

On and before the June 4, 1989 massacres in Beijing, more than one thousand military cars and 60 armoured vehicles, etc., were destroyed, and the 38th Group Army Commander Xu Qinxian, ordered by Deng in late April, was initially reluctant to enforce the martial law.[55] The origin of these crack troops can be traced to Lin Biao's Fourth Field Army. As a result of Deng's formal announcement of cutting the Chinese PLA by one million, all the field armies were reorganized as group armies by the end of 1985. After its involvement in the Korean War, Mao referred to it as a *wanshuijun* (Long Live Army). In August 1966 at the 11th Plenum of the 8th CPC Congress, Mao and Lin Biao ordered the movement of the 38th Group Army to Beijing from Baoding City, Hebei Province. And with Wang Dongxing's help, they forced Liu Shaoqi and Deng to compromise with Mao, Lin, and Zhou. To be sure, it possessed the best equipment, and it was to surround and safeguard the capital along with four other group armies together with forces such as the three divisions of armoured corps.[56] In September 1971, the Group Army sided with Mao, the result of which was the aborted coup by Lin Biao who fled to Outer Mongolia. In September 1976, it obeyed Ye's order to ignore the Gang of Four's instruction to move its troops from Baoding to the capital.[57] In 1999 alone, there were more than 2,200 cases of conflict of interest between the Chinese PLA and the masses.[58]

Jianan Military Region had a special mission. It was to assist other military regions during the war. In September 1997, four aircrew members, in two fighter-planes, deserted during training. They had planned to fly to either the ROK or Japan and then to seek political asylum in the United States. Before they were able to reach the high seas in Huang Sea, they were discovered and ordered to return to the base. Later, they were executed.[59]

Some Chinese PLA figures were under the influence of John F. Dulles' peaceful evolution, first enunciated in January 1953. According to Bo Ibo, who with others persuaded Deng to hold on to his CMC chairmanship and who later became an elder CPC leader,[60] Mao took the U.S. Secretary of State's words seriously. Yang Shangkun was said to have advocated the concept of *dangjun* (party-army) (as opposed to the Chinese PLA usage which is "people's army") or that the Chinese PLA should be *guojiahua* (making it part of the state), and this led to his loss of power in late 1992 and he had to step down from his PRC Chairmanship in March 1993. Jiang Zemin only spoke of loyalty of the armed forces to the party and the people.[61] Deng thought that, if the Chinese PLA were only to defend the country from a foreign attack, it would not be able to fulfill domestic duties.[62] And, from the party's perspective, advocating nationalization of the armed forces, which is one the three poisonous arrows, actually meant tearing up the unity among the proletariat class, the CPC, the socialist state, and the armed forces,[63] which can be arranged as follows: the class as 1; the party as 2; the state, 3; and the Chinese PLA and so on, 4 or 5.

ENDNOTES

1   The binary system in the computer system is a version of *Yin* and *Yang*.

2   This term was mentioned in my book (note 8, ch. 2). After its publication, I found in the website that a non-Chinese academic had also mentioned this term.

3   This would include the People's Republic of China (PRC) at the mature stage of Communism.

4   Jiang Zemin at the 16th National Congress Political Report said it was the party's target to make the entire nation, not just pockets of it, a well-off (*xiaogang*) society by 2020.

5   In retrospect and by applying Figure 1 and its sub-version or sub-framework, the Gang of Four's label for Deng was quite accurate.

6   In June 1992, Jiang Zemin mentioned this dialectical term for the first time. For a non-dialectical figure on the Chinese Communist economic development, see Minxin Pei, *From Reform to Revolution: The Demise of Communism in China and the Soviet Union* (Cambridge, MA: Harvard University Press, 1994), p. 19. For the Soviet economic development shown in a figure, see Robert V. Daniel, "Perestroika, the Post-Soviet Regime, and the Process of Revolution in Russia," *Problems of Post-Communism*, Vol. 46, No. 3 (May/June 1999), p. 27.

7   In June 1978, Deng hinted that he would rely on the Socialism (with Chinese Characteristics) Versus Capitalism framework, when he said that the functions, position and prestige of the political organs of the army

should be restored to the levels obstained in the days of Red Army (August 1927–July 1937), the 8th Route Army and New Fourth Army during the War of Resistance Against Japan (July 1937–August 1945), and the Field Armies during the Liberation War (August 1945–September 1949). Next is the Period from New Democracy to Socialism (October 1949 to December 1956). Then, there was the Period of the Beginning of the Overall Socialist Construction (January 1957 to April 1966). In September 1954, the National People's Congress held its first conference and created the Ministry of National Defense. Thereafter, it was called the *guofangjunshiqi* (National Defense Army Period). Chong-pin Lin followed up with this by saying Deng's 1978 talk was "a return to the pre-1949 past rather than a leap into the untrodden path into the future as many Western observers conceptualized PLA professionalization to be." Lin (note 9, ch. 2), p. 674.

8   *CT*, April 25, 1990, p. 7.

9   Wang (note 9, ch. 1), p. 56.

10   *Zhongguoguofangbao* (Beijing), June 25, 2001, p. 3. Zhang Guotao and Lin Biao were criticized for not adhereing to this dictum.

11   *Guanyuxinshiqijunduizhengzhigongzuodejueding* (Resolution on Political Work Over the New Era for the Army)(Beijing: Jiefangjunchubanshe, September 1987), p. 271.

12   *United Daily News* (hereinafter UDN)(Taipei), June 9, 2004, p. A13.

13   Huang (note 3, ch. 1), p. 14.

14   *Jingbaoyuekan* (Hongkong), April 1998, p. 43.

15   *Jiefangjunbao* (Beijing), August 30, 2000, p. 6. Scobell in his study of the June 1989 massacre posed the question: The People's army or the Party's Army? See note 6, ch. 2, pp. 165–167.

16   Lin (note 4, ch. 2), p. 56. It is possible to use the Politics Versus Military model. Another way of saying the same thing is Not to Attack Versus To Attack, depending on the context.

17   Cited in Lin (note 9, ch. 2), p. 661. However, the June 25, 2001 edition of *Zhongguoguofangbao* on page 3 mentioned that *gongzuodui* comes second and *shengchandui*, third.

18   *Ibid.*

19   *Ibid.*

20   Li and He (note 1, ch. 1), p. 260 and p. 216. It is because Lin fully understood what was on Mao's mind that the latter recommended the former to be his successor by putting down the former's name into the CPC Constitution in April 1969 at the 9th CPC Congress. See *Jiefangjunbao* (Beijing), December 18, 1998, p. 1.

21   Lin (note 9, ch. 2), pp. 661–662.

22   Quoted in *ibid.*, p. 674.

23   Shiping Zheng, "Party-miltary Relations," *EAI Background Brief*, No. 107, November 29, 2001, p. i and p. 3.

24   Li and He (note 7, ch. 1), p. 43. In early 1967, the mainland entered into the struggle for power phase. Jiang Qing *et. al.* wanted the Chinese PLA

to side with them. Kang Sheng said if the armed forces did not side with the leftists, the latter would have no power or *wujunzhiquan* (no military power). See pp. 226–229.

25   Cited in Bickford (note 7, ch. 2). See M. D. Swaine, *The Military & Political Succession in China* (Santa Monica, CA: the Rand Corporation, 1992). Chapter One. For four other points, see *UDN*, May 19, 1993, p. 10.

26   *Pengtouhui* was usually held at Zhongnanhai's Huairentang. Zhonghanhai is where the central CPC leadership compound in central Beijing is located. Beidaihe, a beach resort, is another place for *pengtouhui*. For other types of CMC meetings and conferences, see Cheung (note 6, ch. 1), pp. 71–72.

27   David L. Shambaugh, "The PLA in Transition," paper presented to the PLA Towards 2000 conference, as sponsored by the CAPS and *The China Quarterly*, Island Shangri-la Hotel, dated July 13–15, 1995, p. 4.

28   Junshilishiyanjiubu, *Zhongguorenminjiefangjundeqishinian* (70 Years of the Chinese PLA)(Beijing: Junshikexuechubanshe, July 1997), p. 159.

29   However, in November 1931, Wang Ming eliminated such a system. In May 1945, the system was re-instated above the regiment level.

30   Lin (note 9, ch. 2), p. 679.

31   Xiaoyu Chen, "The Nationalist Ideology of the Chinese Military," *Occasional Papers/Reprints Series in Contemporary Asian Studies*, No. 3, 1998, p. 19. After criticism and struggle, Hu later became a *xiaoyaopai* (literally a faction free from care or responsibility). See *Guangjiaojin* (Hongkong), February 1999, p. 19. Chi Maoji, a newspaper reporter, also mentioned *xiaoyaopai*. He first said those who were the targets of the GPCR *daji* (blow) and then those passive *shaoyaopai*. See *CT*, October 12, 1983, p. 2. Hu was born in December 1942 and joined the CPC in April 1964.

32   See http://www.taiwansecurity.org/ST/2004/ST-190104.htm. In the first half of 2003, reshuffles were made with regard to the navy and air force.

33   An exception is as follows. The term nation-state indicated its symbiotic relationship and combines the characteristics of both. It is defined by Anthony D. Smith as "a nation with *de facto* territorial sovereignty," meaning a nation may live within one or more state boundaries and a state may consist of one or more nations. Cited in Chen (note 31), pp. 4–5.

34   Lin (note 4, ch. 2), p. 56 and pp. 384–390.

35   *A New Chinese-English Dictionary* (Hongkong: Joint Publishing Co, Ltd., 1989), p. 1348 and Deng Liqun, ed., *Dangdaizhongguojunduidezhengzhigongzuo* (Contemporary Political Work of the Chinese Army)(Beijing: Dangdaizhongguochubanshe, June 1994), pp. 372–377.

36   For the highlights, see *Jiefangjunbao* (Beijing), December 20, 1998, p. 3 and *Zhongguoguofangbao* (hereinafter ZGGFB), March 10, 1999, p. 4.

37   Wang (note 9, ch. 1), p. 56.

38   Bickford (note 7, ch. 2), p. 21 and *Jiefangjunbao* (Beijing), July 2, 2001, p. 6.

39   Officers and soldiers in mufti or civilian clothings who committed crimes in Hongkong and Macao will be tried in the latter courts respectively. This law opened the barracks on the Stonecutters Island and Chek Chu to

the public to promote compatriots living in the former British colony to understand and to trust the garrison troops.

40 *Zhongguoguofangbao* (hereinafter ZGGFB)(Beijing), February 5, 2004, p. 1.

41 Literally, five (biggest) lakes, namely, Poyanghu, Dongtinghu, Hongzehu, Taihu, and Chaohu as well as four seas, namely, Bohai, Huanghai (Yellow Sea), Donghai (East Sea), and Nanhai (South China Sea) in China.

42 Xu, as early as January 1967, was a victim of the GPCR. See Li and He (note 7, ch. 1), p. 40. In March 1968, he set up a *Geminweiyuanhui* in Jiangsu Province. He was later transferred to Guangzhou Military Region in December 1975. He and other seven military region commanders were rotated by Mao's order at the same time, and this was the very first time in the Chinese PLA history.

43 *UDN*, November 14, 1992, p. 10. Ye and Hua called a Political Bureau meeting at Huairentang, making plans to arrest the Gang of Four. It turned out that not a single shot was fired. To be sure, the CMC's daily affairs are carried out at *Sanzuomen*, located at Beijing's Western Hills area.

44 However, Lin Biao and the Gang of Four got Mao's support. See Li and He (note 7, ch. 1), pp. 39–48. On January 19, 1967, the *pengtouhui* was held at *Jingxibingguan* (Western Beijing Guest House). See p. 40 and Jin and Xue (note 9, ch. 1), p. 22.

45 Cited in Chen (note 31), p. 43. The fourth one was issued in December 2002.

46 Li Guoqiang *et. al.*, *Zhonggongjunfangjiangling* (Hongkong: Wide Angle Press, May 1988), p. 143.

47 Jin and Xue (note 9, ch. 1), p. 31.

48 Richard D. Fisher, Jr., "How America's Friends are Building China's Military Power,"*The Heritage Backgrounder*, No. 1146, November 5, 1997, 27 pages.

49 *Straits Times* (hereinafter ST)(Singapore), April 10, 2001, p. A3 and http://www.taiwansecurity.org/CNN/2003/CNN-091203.htm (accessed September 15, 2003). It was not until November 2002 that the two sides resumed their military exchanges. On November 24, 2002, a U.S. destroyer called upon Qingdao. After the June 1989 Tiananmen incident, the American side put off its military exchanges with their counterpart, until November 1993 when a former high-ranking U.S. military official visited the mainland. In May 1995, Beijing again shelved the exchanges, in view of Lee Teng-hui's visit to the United States in the following month. When the PRC's embassy in Yugoslavia was bombed by U.S. missiles in May 1999, the exchanges were again put off.

50 In an intereview, General Secretary Hu Yaobang openly conceded, saying, that when Comrade Deng Xiaoping was in charge of the Chinese PLA, it was sufficient for him to say one sentence, but it took them [Hu and Premier Zhao Ziyang] five sentences. Their sentences also worked, but he had to utter only a single sentence. Cited in Ian Wilson and You Ji, "Leadership by 'Lines': China's Unresolved Succession," *Problems of Communism*, Vol. XXXIX (January–February 1990), p. 32. Zhao, on December 16, 1995, said, "in June 1989, only Deng had the great *qipo* (courage) to reverse the

course of events in mobilizing a big number of troops." See *CT*, December 5, 2004, p. A13.

51   In August 1996, Zhang Wannian in a speech to commemorate the 69th anniversary of the founding of the Chinese PLA also mentioned the same term. See Ling Haijian, *The Profile of New Prominent Military Chiefs in China*, (Hongkong: The Pacific Century Press, 1999), pp. 9–10.

52   *Ibid.*, p. 59. and Li and He (note 7, ch. 1), pp. 124–126.

53   Li and He (note 7, ch. 1).

54   Cited in Chen (note 31), p. 18.

55   *CT*, December 29, 1989, p. 7. According to Shambaugh, Jiang had quietly cleaned out those Chinese PLA officers and soldiers who were associated with the June 1989 massacre. See note 27, p. 7. Tang Jiaxuan said on March 5, 2001 that the Tiananmen Papers were fabricated. Xu was court-martialled and sentenced to a 10-year imprisonment. In July 1985, the field armies were reorganized as group armies. During the ROC on the mainland days, there were group armies. For example, in August and October 1937, the ROC Goverment's Military Committee reorganized the 1st, 2nd, and Fourth *Fangmian* (Front) Army as the 8th Route Army, which received another *fanhao* (designation) as the 18th Group Army, with no more than 20,000 troops. The 18th Group Army was under the command of Yan Xishan.

56   *Guangjiaojing* (Hongkong), June 1989, p. 37.

57   Lin Tong, "Evaluating the Party's Chinese PLA over the Last 40 Years," originally published in the October 1989 issue of *Mingpaoyuekan*.

58   *Cheng Ming* (Hongkong), August 2000, p. 19.

59   *UDN*, December 7, 1997, p. 9.

60   Li Guoqiang *et. al.*, *Zhonggongjunfangjiangling* (Hongkong: Wide Angle Press, May 1988), p. 63. Deng asked the armed forces not to talk about counter-peaceful evolution and counter-capitalism. See *UDN*, March 21, 1992, p. 9.

61   *Lianhezaobao* (Singapore), June 29, 1999, p. 16. A Chinese PLA watcher who used to live in the mainland, observed that following the reforms, it might be proper to label the *zhengdangjundui* (party-army) as having become highly professionalized. See Yiming, "Jiang Zemin's *Jingbing* (better troops) Way," *Lianhezaobao* (Singapore), March 16, 1998, p. 16. When the Red Army was coopted by the then ruling party, Mao insisted that it was still a *reminjundui* (people's army) under the CPC leadership.

62   Ling (note 5, ch. 2), pp. 364–365 and *CT*, November 18, 1992, p. 10. The June 25, 2001 edition of *Zhongguoguofangbao* on page 3 also mentioned two other erroneous thinking, namely, *feidanghua* (making the military separate from the CPC) and *feizhengzhihua* (de-politicizing the military).

63   *Jiefangjunbao* (Beijing), June 6, 2001, p. 1. Between June 1989 and 1992, Jiang had allowed the surfacing of such lefist notions as "countering peaceful evolution" and labelling every policy as either socialist or capitalist. See *Straits Times* (Singapore), January 16, 1999, p. 58.

CHAPTER 4

Comments and Major Observations

First, once fully understood, the relationship between the CPC and the Chinese PLA is not that complicated. One has to learn to simplify their relationship in terms of a series of dialectical models. This is because Hu and others in the CMC use the same dialectical, political language and they do not want to bother themselves with complicated, non-dialectical things. While Hu and Jiang Zemin may have heard of game theory, system theory, rational choice theory, etc. as well as models, theories, paradigms like corporatism; praetorianism;[1] professionalization model (or sometimes called the interest group model) which derives from Huntingtonian military professionalism and which is toward political quiescence[2] or Ellis Joffe's professionalism with Chinese characteristics;[3] (neo-) institutionalism; statism; patron-clientalism; inter-service resource competition; political socialization theory; technocracy theory; the nonrecursive simultaneous equations, and multiplicative causal model for analyzing the coalition behavior among the Chinese military elite model;[4] congruence model;[5] the anything is possible model for the study of Chinese politics, as constructed by Joffe;[6] etc. plus concepts like interlocking directorate at the central and provincial levels,[7] they certainly do not want to waste their time in using a foreign, non-dialectical language at (enlarged) CMC conferences, meetings, *pengtouhui*, etc., unless such a thing can be smoothly integrated into their frameworks.

Second, Jonathan Pollack said that "the study of Chinese military affairs has been politicized."[8] U.S. Senator Craig Thomas, who may not have realized that he was speaking dialectically when he remarked that the Chinese PLA since its conception "has had somewhat of a schizophrenic relationship with the party apparatus," adding that the military had gone "through cycles of favor and disfavor, as official policy has swung between the two poles."[9] In other words, the word schizophrenic should not be used, because it has a negative connotation.

To reiterate, a figure practising dialectics can think of many things at the same time. Shambaugh in a discussion paper prepared for the October 26–27, 2000 "Chinese Military Studies: A Conference on the State of the Field" at the National Defense University in Washington, D.C., said many Chinese PLA watchers fall back on inference, subjectivity, hunches, and even ideologically-driven and politically-motivated approaches. This paper, on the one hand, did not portray the Chinese PLA as a juggernaut or, in Alfred D. Wilhelm, Jr.'s description at an October 1995 congressional hearing, a puffer fish, which outsiders consider to be larger than life, that is, too large to be disturbed. On the other hand, this author is trying to decode and to decipher almost everything related to the CPC and the Chinese PLA. The series of frameworks can be repeatedly tested from now and in the future, until time/space sequence (n) for the CPC and the Chinese PLA is reached. This author sincerely pleads, without ideological bias, that only by so doing first can we then, as the next step, conduct a comparative analysis both dialecticaland non-dialectical.

Third, in a December 2000 interview, Bill Gertz, a noted national security reporter, said that, in the office of the Secretary of Defense, there were only three professionals who devoted full-time to PRC policy. But, nothing was said with regard to their understanding of dialectics. Chong-pin Lin, who is well versed in dialectics and who was a ROC Vice-Defense Minister, mentioned the dialectical unity only once in his paper, which was published in summer 1992, for example.[10] At the August 1992 Staunton Hill Conference, one participant said there was a distinction between *wen* (civil) and *wu* (military) in Chinese culture. There are temples to each, that is to say, a family might give one son to each. But, Chong-pin Lin added that there could be an effort to blend *wen* and *wu*, as exemplified by the character *bing* in his own given name, i.e., Pin, the translation of which is a blend of civil skills and martial prowess (*wenwushuangquan*), with the mythical Yellow Emperor as its personification in ancient China. What he said is dialectical. June Teufel Dreyer followed up by concurring with Chong-Pin Lin, saying it is misleading to sharply differentiate the two when talking about the CPC and the Chinese PLA experience, because, at least until recently, most high-ranking party members were actively engaged in military activities. Perhaps Chong-pin Lin has his own concern, that is, a paper employing a dialectical aproach may well be rejected by reviewers right away partly for the reason mentioned in the second point. What is missing in his paper is for us to see his dialectical models. In note 9, chapter 2, I cited his remarks. For instance, he said the Chinese PLA's "social responsibilities ... would seem *déjà vu* ... four decades later...." After reading this sentence, one might still be, as a Chinese would say, *banxinbanyi* (half-believing and half-doubting or not quite convinced). But, by looking at Figure 2, one should not have to face that kind of problem, simply because it is possible for the Chinese PLA to go back to the pre-PRC days or the ROC days on the mainland. To be sure, the Chinese Communists would not make it a secret that they are employing dialectics to play politics and conduct military affairs but they would not simplify and, more importantly, depict their words and deeds in terms of dialectical frameworks in figures for fear of revealing their closely guarded secrets.

Fourth, for a Chinese PLA student applying my version of dialectics, the train of thought means a series of frameworks, each with exactly the same logic and structure, etc. The properties differ, however, and each Number or Letter will be labelled differently. This person must learn to apply the crab motion and leap like a frog if and when necessary from one framework to another. More importantly, one should not associate a particular move at the previous time/space sequence or 10 or even 100 years ago with the next move at the next time/space sequence. Otherwise, one will be easily lost in the logic maze. The thought process of a non-dialectical, Chinese PLA student or scholar, is cause and effect, that is to say, linear. One example is pointed out by Shambaugh who argued that "since the mid-1990s, we may be witnessing increased military autonomy from the party-state in general, as well as nascent signs of increased *state* (i.e., government) control of the armed forces. This would suggest a more linear evolution from *symbiosis* (pre-1989) to *control* (post-1989) to *relative autonomy* (post-1997)."[11] Harlan W. Jencks, who promotes the professionalism thesis, is another. In the observation of one American academic, he is "highly teleological seeing a linear development directly linking military modernization with professionalism."[12] For someone who is applying dialectics, normatively speaking, it is linear, whereas, empirically speaking, it is *quxian* (curved) (see the four mainstream economic lines in Figure 2 again). Furthermore, the dialectical approach is both deductive and inductive. In any case, one should memorize by heart that a dialectical remark is just the opposite of a non-dialectical (usually linear) remark. If the two remarks somehow match, it only means that the dialectician has only, at best, accepted half-way.

Fifth, on two occasions, May 31 and June 16, 1989, Deng said Mao, Zhou, and Zhu De belonged to the first generation of CPC leaders.[13] Their leadership was formed after the Zunyi Conference. Hua lacks *zhongxinsixiang* (central thought) and, therefore, he did not qualify to be called the second tier leader. As for himself, he said he was playing a role in using the term core leadership in the minds of other party leaders. Deng also mentioned *jitimanyi* (collective satisfaction) and Jiang Zemin. When Mao and Deng were around, they and other premier military figures like Ye, for a brief period of time, could personally help to reinforce and monitor the application of those series of dialectical frameworks.[14] Joffe said that when the Chinese PLA "intervened en mass, this was because Mao or Deng had ordered it."[15] Not always. Mao had to rely on the support of Lin Biao when he tried to purge Peng and Huang Kecheng who was the CMC Secretary General in August 1959 and to remove Deng from power during the GPCR. For the record, the Fourth Field Army under Lin Biao's command was at least twice the strength of other field armies.[16] As Mao became older, he became romantic. He wanted to practise something that no other military leaders had done before, just like Pol Pot of Cambodia who had forcefully evacuated or executed all the unwanted people out of his desire to practise Communism in the capital. Hua, of course, was incapable of doing anything, although he was a political commissar.[17] By still standing under Number 1 after the death of Mao in the Communism Versus Capitalism model, he committed a grave mistake, at least symbolically, when he said that he would not emphasize production. But, his actions were not politically incorrect in terms of the other models. For example, Hua was able to become the CMC Chairman in October 1976, knowing that he had to adhere to the CPC Commands the Gun Versus the Gun Commands the CPC model, the Politics and Military Versus Non-Politics-and-Military framework, and other dialectical models. Deng was more sensible. In July 1977, he returned to the center political stage for the third time. In June 1981, Deng became the CMC Chairman. He would never venture into the danger zone, unless absolutely necessary. For example, he and others decided to *da* (attack) the student demonstrators in June 1989. To be sure, *Da* is part of the *Buda* (Not to Attack) Versus *Da* (Attack) model, the latter spectrum is equivalent to the danger zone. Similarly, it is a mistake to label Deng as the Gun,[18] in the Party Commands the Gun Versus the Gun Commands the Party framework, as if he were commanding the Party with a real gun barrel or ordering some Chinese PLA officers and soliders to point their guns at Deng's (potential) rivals. For this reason, Zhao was forced by Deng to step down, because it was inconceivable that a military figure was opposing the Party's policy when martial law was officially proclaimed on May 20, 1989. As a reminder, Zhao was a political commissar from November 1966 to May 1967 at the Guangzhou Military Region and from October 1975 to June 1980 at the Chengdu Military Region. In other words, he should have known better the rules and regulations of the dialectical games. Jiang Zemin had simply tried to execute the required tasks at the macro-level as demanded by Deng. Jiang was certainly grateful to Deng for not forcing him to step down as the General Secretary and other posts in between November 1989 and January 17, 1992. During that uncertain period, Jiang was standing under 3 in the Maoist *gangling*, to wit, Communism Versus Capitalism, which is the middle way, in the safe zone. So, what Jiang did, with the help of Liu Huaqing who belonged to the Second Field Army, Wang Ruilin who was Deng's political secretary for several decades, and Zeng Qinghong who liaisoned CPC leaders for Jiang, in the Chinese PLA system could be considered as returning a favor to Deng. For this reason, he was involved "in virutally every aspect of military affairs," including inspecting *liandui* and overseeing the purge of the Yang Shangkun-Yang Baibing network starting from October 1992.[19] When Jiang Zemin was confirmed as the leader in September 1994 at the 4th Plenum of the 14th CPC Congress, he took other initiatives, such as in January 1995.[20] In March 1995, he for the first time instructed the Chinese PLA and the PAPF to defend the regime.[21] And Hu Jintao's *lingdaobanzi* (leading group) from September 2004 is continuing Jiang's unfinished tasks.

When the National Defense Law was enacted in March 1997, it only meant that, with the demise of Deng, the month before, other elder Chinese Communist revolutionary leaders realized and acknowledged that personal stature such as prestige, record of politico-military achievements, and the network of supporters had helped to play a role. However, from March 1997, CPC leaders who did not enjoy the same stature as their revolutionary predecessors would have to use law to reinforce the execution of dialectical frameworks. That is to say, all the military officers and soldiers would have abided by the Rule by Law Politics and/or Rule of Law Politics lines in the very first dialectical model. The Rule by Law or Number 3 is preferred by the CPC, because it is still the ruling party, so every enacted law should be favorable to the party whereas Mao, Ye, and Deng, they could do the job by themselves. After September

1994, Jiang Zemin used the law to reinforce the execution of the dialectical models. Before that, he had to rely on Deng plus the laws related to military affairs. Beginning November 2002, Hu Jintao knew that he was standing under 1 and Jiang, 5 in the CPC Commands the Gun and the Gun Commands the CPC Versus the Non-CPC Commands the Gun and the Gun Commands the CPC model.

Sixth, is it possible to reverse the CPC Commands the Gun to read the Gun Commands the Party, the consequence of which becomes the Gun Commands the Party Versus the Party Commands the Gun? Dialectically speaking, this possibility cannot be ruled out. But, one must first construct another framework, that is, Normal Versus Abnormal, so as to figure out whether the CPC Commands the Gun is normal or abnormal for the party and the Chinese PLA. Given its long history, we can say that it is normal to have the CPC Commands the Gun, not its reverse. The same argument can be said with regard to other dialectical models as mentioned throughout the study.

Seventh, in November 1989, the Berlin Wall was breached, and the rest of the East European Communist countries fell apart, as if abandoning Communism.[22] In February 1990, to give the Soviet Union a lease on life, the ruling Communist Party was compelled by objective circumstances to amend its country's constitution stating that new political parties could be formed. Then, in December 1991, the Soviet Union collapsed. To be sure, the CPC has not allowed a multi-party system at the 16th CPC Congress. It has only permitted a *Shehuizhyyiminzhuzhi* (Systems of Socialist Democracy), which is 1 and which has been practised along with the *Duodanghezuozhi* (Multi-party Cooperation System), which is 5. In September 2004, the Third International Conference of Asian Political Parties (ICAPP) was, for the first time, held on the mainland, excluding Taiwan, Hongkong and Macao. In a word, so long as no new political party is allowed to compete against the ruling party for its position, the CPC will continue to sustain its ruling power status and control and guide the armed forces.

Eighth, as pointed out by You Ji, there is indeed room or autonomy for the CMC vis-a-vis the Party.[23] In the CPC's hierarchy, the CMC is under the Political Bureau. However, operationally, it is usually beyond the latter's reach. This long-established practice can be traced back to Mao, who deliberately separated the *guojia* and the military under the formula of *zhengzhijuyizheng* and *junweiyijun* (the realm of Political Bureau is *guojia* affairs and the CMC's, not only military affairs but *guojia* affairs as well). You added that Deng had maintained this kind of division, which allowed the paramount leader to prevent other CPC leaders from influencing the armed forces. In fact, the Chinese PLA reported its major affairs only to Deng throughout the 1980s. Jiang Zemin, like Deng, also prevented his Political Bureau colleagues from intruding into the affairs of the armed forces. Hu will be guided by the same line of action.

Ninth, with Mao's demise, there was no one to assume the CMC chairmanship, even though Mao had designated it in writing, Hua who was the State Council Premier from April 1976 to September 1980, as his successor. If one takes the Field Army approach[24] or another non-dialectical approach such as the institutional approach,[25] how does she or she describe and explicate (or explain) the gap in command? Chen Xilian, who was a relative of Mao and who belonged to the Second Field Army, was asked to take charge of the CMC's daily military affairs in February 1976, due to Ye's illness, and again on October 7, 1976 when Hua on the same day became the CPC Central Committee Chairman and CMC Chairman at the same time, up to June 1981. But, Chen, like Wang Dongxin who was in charge of the elite security force in Beijing and who ranked just one notch above him, was given the title of *Changwuweiyuan* (Member of Standing Committee of the Political Bureau).[26] He was the commander of Shengyang Military Region from October 1959 to December 1973 and of Beijing Military Region from December 1973 to January 1980. Chong-Pin Lin wrote that "[t]he pivotal factor in the downfall of the Gang of Four in October 1976 was that Beijing's military commanders, Wang Dongxing and Chen Xilian, switched loyalty to side with [Chinese] PLA marshals Ye, Xu Xiangqian, Nie Rongzhen and veteran [Chinese] PLA leader, Li Xiannian."[27] Li, for one, is politically conscious as to who opposes the tendency of being unwilling to do political work.[28] In other words, if and when, in a crisis, no one adhered to the Party Commands the Gun Versus the Gun Commands the Party model, the PRC would be in deeper trouble, as the Gang of Four could have called upon the Shanghai militia to take over the Communist regime. How would any field army help him to consolidate power? During the June 1989 crisis, it was advantageous to Deng that he had served in the Second (and Third Field, as one source indicated), Armies before the creation of the PRC, because he could rally support from many, if not most, officers and soldiers in those two armies. For the record, by early 1989, 43 per cent of the PRC's seven military regions had been placed under the command of generals once associated with the Second Field Army.[29] But, it makes no sense when the military officials whom he actually promoted belonged to the Fourth Field Army. Did it mean that this Army was against the CPC simply because Lin Biao was found guilty of plotting an assasination against Mao? To be sure, Minister Lin had failed to get support from the 38th Group Army, when he was attempting to assasinate Mao. If the non-dialecitcal analyst were to describe and explicate this command gap simply as an aberration, the cause and effect description and explanation would still be called into serious question.

10th, one observer said that a military figure must have the following three things before he or she can acquire military power: *zili* (record of service), *youjungong* (has performed military meritorious service), and *yourenshi* (has a network of personal connections).[30] Another study mentioned three inextricably linked conditions for admission to the power center: first, a network of personal ties; second, a solid power base, and, third, opportunity.[31] From this study, one should realize that the figure in question must first know where he or she should be positioned in a particular dialectical framework's safe zone. Otherwise, he or she is out for sure.

11th, Lin Biao, positioning himself at the nascent stage of Communism, in August 1966 on three occasions, indicated who should be selected as miltiary cadres. First, whether this figure was upholding the red flag of the Mao Thought. Second, did this figure put politics into command? And, third, did this figure have revolutionary *ganjin* (vigor)? Applying my frameworks, Minister Lin was looking at the Red Versus Expert model for the first criterion, the Politics Versus Miliary model for the second one, and the Communism Versus Capitalism model or the Men Versus Weapons model for the last criterion. In other words, all the three critieria were positioned at Number 1, if not its nascent stage.

12th, Ian Wilson and You Ji in a paper mentioned Chinese Communist leadership by "lines"[32] or strands. This is equivalent to the Chinese expression, *yitiaobian* (command like a continuous line in the safe zones of all the dialectical models). Applied to our study, most, if not all, leaders and their respective subordinates and/or supporters from top to bottom were working hand-in-hand by first correctly siding with a particular mainstream economic line.

13th, the Politics and Military Versus Non-Politics and Military framework could describe and explain the Chinese PLA's extramilitary roles including the economic construction role from the beginning up to now. If the Chinese PLA were positioned at Number 5, we could say that it is purely military. If it were positioned at 1 and/or 2 up to 2.5 (3 would be involving aspects of the military), it would be purely political, as Lin Biao was trying to do during the GPCR. At other times, the PRC armed forces could play both roles and the role in between them as well as whatever might be acceptable to the CMC.

14th, in December 1978, Deng launched the Four Modernizations—agriculture, industry, science and technology, and the fourth component—military. Which pillar came first made a big difference; the three of which constituted the Chinese PLA with Chinse characteristics, as coined by Yang Shangkun were:[33] revolutionization (as opposed to Deng's mere mention of revolutionary army), modernization, or regularization? Again, the one positioned on the extreme left or 1 would be the subject, which carried a special meaning or heavier weight. They could be arranged in many ways: 1, 2, and 3, respectively; 2, 3, and 1, respectively; 3, 2, and 1, respectively, 1, 3, and 2, respectively, etc. This is important, because the element that is placed at the left extreme or 1 is where the game will end up at time/space sequence (n). In this connection, Mao, Hua, Deng, Jiang Zemin, and Hu emphasized the lasting importance of political work in the Chinese PLA. Deng in June 1978 even said that "the functions, position and prestige of the political organs of the army should be restored to the levels obtained in the days of the Red Army, the War of Resistance Against Japan (1937–45) and the War of Liberation (1946–49)."[34] For this reason, in the Politics and Military safe zone or spectrum, this author mentioned Politics first, not Military and Politics. However, the data we collected might be contradictory to that of non-dialectical Chinese PLA watchers. As early as December 1942 in general and early 1942 in particular, the 8th Route Army and the New Fourth Army began its *jingbing* (streamlining of the military) policy.[35] In May 1953, the General Political Department mentioned regularization. Starting in the second half of the same year, the CMC decided to train the Chinese PLA along the regularization line, following the advanced experience of the Soviet armed forces. In August 1955, the then director of the General Political Department, Luo Ronghuan, commented that regularization should not go against or violate the principle of building up the People's Army, and, at the 8th CPC Congress, Peng and the new General Political Department director mentioned the term modernization.[36] In September 1981, three months after he became the CMC Chairman, Deng , before the Commanders, for the first time said, to quote him at length:

> We must build up our armed forces to be a powerful, modernized and regularized revolutionary army. We must adhere to the four cardinal principles, strengthen political and ideological work, and try to make the armed forces a model so far as carrying out the Party's line, principles (*fangzhen*)[37] and policies (*zhengce*) is concerned....
>
> We must further cement the army's relations with the civil authorities and the people....
>
> We must intensify the army's military and political training and further enhance its political consciousness and military capability. We must work hard to improve its ability to conduct combined operations involving the various services and arms under modern conditions.[38]

However, at other times, the order was reversed or changed. The January 25, 1982 edition of *Jiefangjunbao* on page 4 carried this headline: "Marching towards the goal of a modernized, regularized, revolutionary army." There were 12 major army events in 1981. Yang Shangkun first coined the word revolutionization in July 1986, saying "the Army should speed up its pace of revolutionization, modernization, and regularization."[39] In the late 1980s, the revolutionization element still appeared first in order.[40] Nontheless, dialectically speaking, this was possible and logical, because the CMC could think of 1 only at time/space sequence (3), both 1 and 2 at time/space sequence (10), the entire safe zone at time/space sequence (12), etc., whenever it felt appropriate to do so. In other words, to an outside, non-dialectical observer, what the CPC and the Chinese PLA did was illogical.

Because a new version of People's War was announced for the first time in May 1953, this author is of the view that revolutionization should be positioned at 1, modernization at 3, and regularization at 5. Article 29 of the December 1982 PRC Constitution mentioned the three elements in the following order: revolutionization, modernization, and regularization. To be sure, there is a sign in between the Chinese characters which is not a comma. It is what the Chinese called *dunhao*, which means "a sign for a shorter pause used *to set off items in a series* (emphasis added)."[41] In other words, one should look at or think about them together. In his important speech in December 1998, Jiang Zemin also put revolutionization in the first place. This is because before seizing state power, the Red Army was revoluationary. But, after October 1, 1949, it confronted the question of regularization and even modernization. Peng given his bitter Korean War experience advocated regularization. But, in May 1965, when Mao was at the 9th meeting of the 3rd NPC Congress, the military rank was abolished because he wanted to revolutionize the Chinese PLA by moving it to Number 1 in the Maoist *gangling*. So, logically, the three would be placed in the safe zone in the order that I mentioned. This kind of arrangement might also enable the CPC leaders to match the Men Versus Weapons framework or Men and Weapons Versus Non-Men and Weapons model, or even the People's War Versus Non-People's War model. In a word, they have the same structure but with each Number or Letter having a different concept respectively.

15th, when Jiang Zemin took over the CPC General Secretary position and months later, the CMC chairmanship, he commented that he was mentally not prepared for it (the former).[42] Yet, in February 2004, we see the following words written by Willy Wo-lap Lam, a Hongkong based reporter: The Chinese PLA "reports only to the Communist Party's dominant faction."[43] Although he had a little military connection, he did not know much about *junqing* (military situation). In any case, Jiang should be credited in July 1998 for daring to successfully do one thing that had been contrary to Deng's policy guidelines since the late 1970s: divestiture or ending of the commercial activites of the Chinese PLA and PAPF (plus judicial organs) five months later, with the PAPF being the most corrupt.[44] According to a March 1999 article in the monthly magazine *Shidai Chao*, published by *Renmin Ribao*, the Chinese PLA and PAPF had transferred 2,937 business enterprises to the state and closed a further 3,928 by an initial deadline of December 1998. Of those, 82 per cent had belonged to the General Logistics Department (GLD).[45] A second divestiture order designated August 1999 as the deadline. In October 1998, Hu in his capacity as a CPC Central Committee member was involved in the clearing up and processing of the transferred businesses. In May 2000, Hu declared that divestiture work was "basically completed" in March 2000 but admitted "shortcomings still exist."[46] In April 2004, *Asia Times* reported that many, if not most, of the Chinese PLA companies and enterprises were still in operation but under private management, which did not pay tax to the country.[47] This is possible, because a company can be located in the compound of a military headquarters. Of course, Jiang was able to do that due to the forthcoming Three Represents,[48] which were officially endorsed at the 16th CPC Congress, the first of which refers to the subject (*zhuti*), namely, workers, peasants, and the armed forces who are standing under 1 in the Socialism (with Chinese Characteristics) Versus Capitalism framework. (Some military scholars can be positioned at 3 or the second Represent). To eleboarate, Mao did not ask the armed forces to enter the realm of trade and profit-making.[49] Deng started moving in that direction as early as December 1977 and in his capacity as the CMC Vice-Chairman and Chinese PLA Chief-of-Staff, proposed, for example, training officers and soldiers with civilian job skills so that they would become *liangyong rencai* (dual purpose personnel), such that they could both fight battles and engage in socialist economic construction.[50] In June 1978 at the All Army Political Work Conference, he said each army unit should think about helping one or two adjacent communes and the nearby factories if there were any. Of course, Deng still had in mind the Chinese PLA's deeply rooted principle of living among the masses; like fishes in water. In April 1983, the Commission of Science, Technology, and Industry for National Defense (CSTIND) introduced the very first military technologies to civilian industries. In November 1984, the paramount leader again elaborated on his policy at a CMC seminar, mentioning the Chinese PLA Airforce, Navy, and CSTIND. In the following month, Yu Qiuli, the General Political Department director, mentioned the production of civilian goods. In the same month, Hong Xuezhi, the General Logistical Department director, urged the development of joint military-civilian enterprises in not only agriculture and industry but also in commerce. In February 1985, Yang Shangkun reiterated the same message at the divisional level of the Wuhan Military Region. On May 4, 1985, the joint order from the State Council and the CMC "affirms fully the necessity of the military to take part in production and business activities."[51] And, in summer, the concept "One Army, Two Systems" emerged. Nonetheless, Jiang played politics by agreeing to compensate the Chinese PLA's loss by offering it other things that they wanted, for example, increasing the annual defense budget. In November 1993, the CMC issued a central directive banning Chinese PLA units below the Group Army[52] level to do business, though it was not very successful until several years later.

16th, with Hua as his superior, Deng proposed the idea of having *liangyong rencai*, as noted above. Likewise, it does not matter whether Hu is the Vice-Chairman or the Chairman of the CMC. He would try to juggle those dialectical frameworks first to his Party's and second to the Chinese PLA's advantage.

17th, a Chinese writer living in the United States, who is for the nationalizing of the Chinese PLA, said figures like Deng and Yang Shangkun did not really believe in Communism but the gun barrel fetishism.[53] This is wrong, because one cannot just think of the Party Commands the Gun. As Mao said in April 1956 at the enlarged Political Bureau meeting, there are always two points at any point in time, now or 10,000 years from now. This means that, until the mature (as opposed to nascent and ascendant) stage of Communism or time/space sequence (n) in the second framework, that is, Communism Versus Capitalism, there will always be, at least, two points.

18th, in March 1973, Deng became the Vice-Premier of the State Council. It was Mao who invited Deng to come back. Mao said to Deng that he himself had done 70 per cent good things and 30 per cent bad things, adding you must be the same.[54] Of course, Deng could totally abandon things Maoist. This, in effect, is keeping the Maoist *gangling* or the Communism Versus Capitalism framework intact or frozen. Otherwise, everything including the party and the Chinese PLA would shatter and collapse, as Jiang Zemin mentioned in the 15th CPC Congress report. People's War (and, of course, active defense [military strategy]) are not dead. They will remain forever as key military features, as long as the CPC exists, even as an opposition party. When nuclear and non-nuclear disarmament has taken place throughout the world, all the armed forces will go back to the Men Versus Weapons model, standing under the former. In this connection, if Chinese PLA leaders periodically mention the People's War doctrine, what they do is to mention it in its entirety at a particular time/space sequence. For example, in early 1998, Chi at the National Defense University, a place for grooming generals, dialectically lectured People's War Under Modern Conditions.[55] After mentioning it, the leaders would move on to the next time/space sequence. They would reiterate the doctrine or they would mention something else in the safe zone. What they do does not pose a logical problem, for them, thanks to the existence of the spectrum which embraces variations. However, none of this would make sense to a Chinese PLA student or scholar who does not take a dialectical approach.

19th, The Chinese are fond of the following idiom: *juyifansan*. Translated, it is "learn (deduce) by analogy/draw inferences from one instance."[56] For example, one may use one fact to verify his or her argument. But, such a move can be easily negated by three other contrary facts. It has been the habit of Chinese PLA analysts to find fault with each approach, model, paradigm, or something else, by pointing out some contradictions. To be sure, the structure of our model can accommodate those approaches, models, paradigms, etc. which have Chinese characteristics. The reason for saying this is that 100 per cent professionalism does not really apply to the Chinese PLA. It must be mentioned in the context of the People's War or linked to revolutionization, modernization, and regularization, at least ideologically.

20th, when applying the frameworks, it is necessary to find out the background of those military officers and soldiers in question, so as to help us to determine where we can position each one of them in a chosen dialectical model. Liu Lunxian, born in December 1943 at a place which later became Shanghai Municipal City, was said to the youngest officer to be promoted in June 1993 to the rank of lieutenant-general. In November 1992, he served as the Deputy Commander of Nanjing Military Region, and was transferred to another military region in December 1993 but later in February 2000 became a deputy director of SMC's NPC Standing Committee. In any case, it is necessary to find out why did he not want to become a general. Since he is no longer a CPLA official, all those dialectical models not related to military affairs will not be applied to him.

The reason for engaging in this kind of further discussion is because Liu Jinsong, born in July 1933, has often been mentioned in the Chinese mass media.[57] For example, in December 1950, he joined the *Xinminzhuzhuyi* (New Democratic) Youth League, and, in February 1954, he became a party member. During the Vietnam War, he shot down three America fighter planes and damaged another one. In June 1985, he became the Commander of the Shengyang Military Region, a position in which he served until November 1992. Then, he was transferred to Lanzhou Military Region in November 1992 up to January 1996. Promoted by Deng, he was the youngest among the seven military regions. In June 1994, the grade of general was conferred on Liu by Jiang Zemin. Yet, one observer said he was played down by Jiang Zemin due to the reason that Liu was *yaoyan* (dazzled) during the Hu Yaobang and Zhao eras.[58] So, he only ended up being a Commandant at the Academy of Military Science. Was that really the case? May be another example can show that Jiang had his own bias. It has been reported that Jiang Zemin disliked Li Jijun who was promoted by both Yangs, because Li when serving as the Director of CMC's *Bangongting* (General Office) regarded CMC Chairman Jiang as a nobody.[59]

21st, under the September 1954 PRC Constitution, the PRC President commands the armed forces. In January 1975, the PRC Presidency was eliminated from the PRC Constitution. In other words, only the party chairman has that power. This is understandable because mainland China at that time was still in the nascent stage of Communism, whereby the country would not have disappeared so fast. No change was made in the February 1978 Constitution. In December 1982, the *guojia* CMC was created, resulting in *yigejigou, lianggepaizi* (one organization with two signs). This means that the chosen person must concurrently hold the party and the *guojia* CMC chairmanship. Otherwise, non-dialectical contradiction may emerge at meetings or other functions, domestic or international. So, Shambaugh said "ambiguity exists insofar as Jiang ... concurrently holds the offices of the President, [CPC] General Secretary, and CMC Chairman."[60] In September 1999, Hu became the CMC Vice-Chairman, and he did not replace CMC Chairman Jiang Zemin at the 16th CPC Congress. Therefore, a lot of discussion was made with regard to Jiang before and after the Congress.[61] Examples are many. First, Nan Li made the following technical and procedural observation on November 30, 2002. The Party Congress can only elect the General Secretary and the CPC CMC Chairman. If Hu had taken the party CMC chairmanship then, Jiang would have had to stay on as the PRC CMC Chairman until the NPC, which appoints the *guojia* CMC chairman in March 2003.[62] Li added that, to avoid the dilemma of having two CMC chairmanships with different figures, Jiang would stay as both the CPC and the PRC CMC Chairman until March 2003. Then, he would resign his party CMC Chairmanship at a CPC Central Committee plenum to be held right before the NPC, and hand over, in March, both the PRC CMC Chairmanship and the PRC President positions to Hu. Second, it would be interesting to find out whether Hu would get the CPC's CMC chairmanship. He would not have to be one, because, as General Secretary of the Party, Hu is placed above the party's CMC Chairman. The CPC comes first even as of today. That would resolve the problem of Hu being the PRC CMC Vice-Chairman and Jiang, being both the party and *guojia* CMC Chairman. Third, as the PRC President, it would be awkward for Hu to have elaborate sending-off and welcoming back ceremonies for Jiang who is Hu's superior, in both the CPC and *guojia's* CMC. if and when Jiang were to go abroad. But, this dilemma was resolved, when Hu undertook the prior scrapping off of such ceremonies.[63] Fourth, Hu said farewell to the first Chinese *taikonnaut* on

October 15, 2003, even though it was Jiang Zemin in September 1992 who had made the decision to send a *taikonnaut* to outer space. Many political observers wondered whether Jiang would steal the show, since he likes to show off at various diplomatic and social functions at home and abroad. Yet, he was only briefed on the 18th,[64] mainly because the launch of the Shenzhou (Divine Ship) Number 5, was not intended for any military purpose. In other words, the PRC wanted to send a peaceful message to foreign leaders just as it had done when it first tested its atomic bomb in October 1964, saying they need not worry about the Chinese achievement, as they had already stated in, for example, the July 1998 *China's National Defense*, regarding the issue of keeping outer space weapon-free. On November 4, 2003, Hu, with Jiang Zemin, sitting in the middle, posed for a group photograph with other academics at a conference for military schools held in Beijing.[65] As one observer in Beijing said, the framework for Hu in his first year as General Secretary was *Gan* (Perform) Versus *Bugan* (Not Perform).[66] Fifth, in March 2004, Xiong Guangkai, then a top ranking military official, said it was Jiang Zemin who coined the new term *xinjunshibiange* (new military change/reform) as opposed to *xinjunshigemin* (new military revolution) which was suggested by others.[67] This revelation suggested that Jiang Zemin was still pushing for military modernization, centering around the goal of building an information-oriented army and winning an information-based war by relying on scientific and technological progress. In other words, most of the generals whom he had promoted would enthusiastically obey his command. Sixth, in February 2004, Ching Cheong of the *Straits Times* (Singapore) wrote that Hu was taking no chances with Taiwan given the fact that the Taiwan area voters would be chosing their 11th President. Therefore, he set up an office at the military command headquarters at Yuquanshan (Jade Spring Mountain) which is located on Beijing's western outskirts and which can withstand a direct and major nuclear attack, so as to familiarize himself with war command preparations and operations.[68] Cheong continued by saying that Hu "cannot go there at will without the prior knowledge of" Jiang Zemin. This passage simply means that the time has not yet come for Jiang to report to Hu that (pre-emptive) military strikes must be taken in order to prevent some people in Taiwan from declaring *de jure* independence. Only by that time, would Hu be involved.

22nd, it is quite a mistake to just employ the term civil-military relations in the study of the Chinese PLA. As pointed out by Chong-pin

Lin, civil in the Western sense refers to the power-holders of the CPC.[69] Since *junzhongyoudang* and *dangzhongyoujun* is still working as the middle way or Number 5, the term should not be exclusively used in the foreseeable future. Otherwise, this incomplete term will mislead students of the Chinese PLA from the very beginning.

23rd, the Market Economy Line was publicized at the 15th CPC Congress. The SDS is a reflection of that. Hu Jintao in the October 1, 2003 National Day speech made a prominent call for its promotion. Needless to say, the party is not abandoning the multi-party cooperation system which is represented by Number 1. It is only emphasizing the middle road or Number 6, that is, SDS. What this means is that many non-CPC military officers and soldiers can hold important military posts so long as they still support the Four Cardinals, as spelt out by Deng and the *National Defense Law*. They, of course, include the ROC armed forces.

24th, this author does not deny the existence of *santouzhuyi* which according to the CPC is the breeding-ground for factionalism, nepotism, factions formed along the old field army, generational, territorial,[70] and service lines; cross-cutting coalitions or alliances, personality cliques at the uppermost levels of decision-making which have facilitated the earlier promotion of some *taizidang* (princelings) than others; cabals and the like in the military. Each number or letter can represent a faction. While the Chinese PLA as a whole has never threatened to replace the CPC, each faction can, indeed, help to decide the kind of Chinese Communists who are going to run the CPC.[71] The military figures who are promoted, rewarded, etc., may have attained their promotions and rewards by joining a particular faction. But, these military figures would first have had to pass periodically the tests of going through each dialectical framework. Only then might they form factions. Obviously, Yang Baibing did not meet the test in the Fall of 1992.[72] Accused of practising *zongpaizhuyi* or *santouzhuyi* by promoting most military figures only from his Beijing Military Region, he was not supposed to have *pengtouhui* without the permission of the party's CMC, to discuss issues pertaining to the post-Dengist era.[73]

25th, it does not matter whether new blood comes into the CMC and whether the CPC and the Chinese PLA elites had indeed been bifurcated.[74] This means that the organic, *huanhuanxiangkou* relationship between the party and the armed forces will remain even if the latter were no longer Communist or socialist. If the capitalist countries were to re-adopt Feudalism,[75] all the PRC military officers and soldiers will totally embrace Capitalism without fear of any punishment by the party. This is because the CPC and the Chinese PLA can still keep a distance from E which stands for Feudalism in the framework of Capitalism Versus Feudalism.

26th, even if the PRC were to become capitalist, the Chinese PLA will not be a (statist) national army, unless the CPC becomes an opposition party.[76] Dialectics can help to rationalize every word and deed of the two. The framework that it would use would be Socialism (with Chinese Characteristics) Versus Feudalism, with Capitalism in between serving as the middle way.

27th, there were many wrong observations or factual errors.[77] First, *guanxi* may not always work. He Long introduced a lady to Qin who later became the latter's wife. Qin was not He's subordinate. Yet, during the GPCR, both He and Qin were framed and persecuted. Second, one academic has pointed out that Wei Guoqing, like Deng, belonged to the Second Field Army. He frequently moved back and forth between political and military in the Politics and Military framework, and he opposed many of the economic, military, and social reforms as put forward by Deng.[78] According to a publication dated July 1968 in mainland China, the Chinese PLA in Guangxi Province, under Wei's order, killed many citizens. In June of that year, several thousand corpses were found in the waters off Hong Kong.[79] On August 26, 1968, he set up a *Geminweiyuanhui* in the Province. To elaborate, he, a minority,[80] was in June 1946 a Second Column Commander and a Political Commissar of the Shangdong Field Army, which was under the command of the Fourth New Army. A year later, his column was placed under the Huadong (East China) Field Army. In September 1948, he was a commander of Subei *Bingtuan* (regular force). In April 1949, Wei was a political commissar of the 10th *Bingtuan*, which was commanded by the Third Field Army. In a word, he was never under Deng. After October 1949, for example, he held the title of First Political Commissar at the Guangzhou Military Region from November 1966 to January 1980. From March 1977 to June 1982, he also headed the General Political Department. At the 12th CPC Congress, Wei was one of the 27 Political Bureau members but not considered by a Japanese academic as belonging to the Deng faction.[81] As a third example, Chi was predicted by the October 1997 issue of *Guangjiaojingyuekan*, a Hongkong magazine, on page 17 as a possible candidate for the State Council's Vice-Premier. But, this did not turn out to be true. And fourth, Jiang Zemin was, as it turned out, not a transient or transitional figure of the third echelon leadership.

ENDNOTES

1   This refers to a situation if and when the legitimate government owing to, for example, ideological bankrupcy, is taken over by armed forces, as in the case of the CPLA replacing the CPC. Bickford (note 10), pp. 39–41.

2   It covers the functional and technical specialization, esprit de corps, career-service, meritocratic promotions, and other non-extramilitary dimensions. Samuel P. Hingtington's 1957 book, *The Soldier and the State*, is a classic in Western literature on civil-military relations. Specifically, expertise, responsibility, and corporateness are Huntington's three principal criteria. See also Bickford (note 7, ch. 2), p. 9.

3   Ellis Joffe, "Party-Army Relations in China: Retrospect and Prospect," paper presented to The PLA Towards 2000 conference, July 13–15, 1995, Island Shangri-la Hotel, Hongkong, as sponsored by the Chinese Council of Advanced Policy Studies (CAPS) and *The China Quarterly*. To Shambaugh, professionalism encompasses doctrine, command and control, as well as tactics and training. See note 27, p. 8. At the Enlarged Conference of the CMC held from May to June 1985, Deng told the Chinese PLA that it must no longer prepare to fight "*zhaoda, dada, dahezhanzheng* (an early war, major war, and nuclear war)" and, instead of "*dazhan* (major war) or *zhongtizhan* (total war)," the Chinese PLA should prepare for "*youxian zhanzheng* (limited war) or *jubu zhanzheng* (local war)." *Guangjiaojing* (Honkong) in the June 2000 issue on page 19 mentioned *zhiyejunren* (professional soldier). You Ji mentioned "the sense of professionalism in soldiers" in one of his publications. See You Ji, "Can Hu Jintao also Rein in the PLA? (II)" *EAI Background Brief No. 114* (February 19, 2002), p. 11.

4   See William Pang-yu Ting's June 1979 paper, as published in *American Political Science Review*, as cited in Bickford (note 7, ch. 2), p. 12.

5   This model is put forward by William Odom, a professional soldier, who sees the CPC and the CPLA as basically being in agreement with little or no conflict between them. The military is "an administrative arm of the Party, not something separate from and competing with it." Cited in Bickford (note 7, ch. 2), p. 22.

6   Fourth Annual Conference on China's People's Liberation Army, August 1993, Staunton Hill, Virginia, as sponsored by the American Enterprise Institute, p. 41. Indeed, that is possible. For example, Taiwan signed a contract with France in August 1991 to buy some warships from France. A rebate of more than US$500 million was involved. Some of the money went to Taiwan, and some of it even went to mainland China. Beijing was not informed of the signing of the agreement until later. According to Qian Qichen, the then PRC Vice-Premier, in November 1992, France again signed a contract to sell 60 military airplanes to Taiwan. Again, Beijing was not informed until later on.

7   The jargon itself is foreign to the CPC and the CPLA. Basically, it is, for example, Provincial First Secretaries serving as political commissars of military districts and military commanders serving on provincial party committees. See *ibid.*, p. 19.

8   Jonathan Pollack, "CAPS and the Study of the PLA: A Review Essay," paper presented to the CAPS-Rand PLA Conference, July 8–11, 1999, Radisson Barcelo Hotel, Washington, D.C.

9   *The Growth and Role of the Chinese Military*, hearing before the Subcommittee on East Asian and Pacific Affairs of the Committee on Foreign Relations, United States Senate, 104th Congress, First Session, dated October 11–12, 1995, p. 1.

10   Lin (note 9, ch. 2), p. 668. He also used such dialectical terms as personal and non-personal. See p. 676.

11   Shambaugh (note 2, ch. 1), p. 6.

12   Bickford (note 7, ch. 2), p. 10.

13   *UDN*, July 20, 1989, p. 3.

14   The Red Army differs from the Soviet armed forces. See Mark von Hagen, *Soldiers of the Proletarian Dictatorship: The Red Army and the Soviet Socialist State, 1917–1930* (Ithaca, New York: Cornell University Press, 1990).

15   Joffe (note 1, ch. 2), p. 17.

16   Lin (note 9, ch. 2), p. 661.

17   It was mistake for Wang (note 9, ch. 1 in page 58) to say that Hua had no foundation in the Chinese PLA.

18   Cited in *ibid.*, p. 680. See also *Central Daily News* (hereinafter CDN), October 6, 1987, op-ed.

19   Ling (note 5, ch. 2), p. 315 and Shambaugh (note 27), p. 7. The younger Yang was given the title of Member of Politcal Bureau at the 14th CPC Congress but without any power.

20   Ling (note 5, ch. 2), p. 333.

21   *Ibid.*, pp. 334–335.

22   From the Communist point of view, he or she can always dialectically rationalize the phenomenon by saying Communism can come back as shown in Figure 2.

23   You Ji, "Jiang Zemin's Art of Controlling the PLA (I)," *EAI Bcakground Brief No. 113* (February 19, 2002), p. 2 and p. 4.

24   To Bickford, this one "can be called a Rasputin-like theory as neither the dearth of supporting evidence nor evidence to the contrary seems able to kill it. The main evidence to support its validity is that most Chinese believe it to be true." See note 1, ch. 2, p. 36.

25   Lin was right in saying that the purely institutional approach tends to de-emphasize personal relations (and loyalty). So, when Deng only had the CMC chairmanship, a curious, if not absurd scenario surfaces from an institutional point of view: the gun, that is, Deng, in this context commands not only the state (headed by Yang Shangkun) and also the CPC

(represented by Zhao Ziyang). See Lin (note 9, ch. 2), pp. 680–681. It is wrong to label Deng as the Gun in the danger zone.

26 *Guangjiaojingyuekan* (Hong Kong), April 1990, p. 90.

27 Lin (note 9, ch. 2), p. 661.

28 *Ibid.*, p. 675.

29 *Ibid.*, p. 677.

30 *CT*, December 16, 1992, p. 11.

31 Eu Chooi Yip and Ziying Zou, "Power Struggle After Deng," *IEAP Background Brief, No. 17* (October 14, 1971), p. 5.

32 Wilson and Ji (note 50, ch. 3), pp. 28–44. They pointed out that the CPC practices leadership by lines. The top leadership group is divided into those of the first line who manage the day-to-day work of the CPC, including formulation of some policies , and the second line leaders who are those involved only in major strategic and policy issues.

33 Lin (note 4, ch. 2), pp. 240–241.

34 Quoted in Lin (note 9, ch. 2), p. 674.

35 *Junshilishiyanjiubu* (note 28, ch. 3), p. 227.

36 During the GPCR, the term modernization was also mentioned. See Xu Caihou, *Dangdaizhongguojunduidezhengzhigongzuo (Shang)* (Political Work of the Chinese Army)(Book One)(Beijing: Dangdaizhongguochubanshe, June 1994), pp. 46–47 and p. 66. On May 29, 1950, Mao said "China should build a powerful *guofangjun* (national defense army)." Cited in *Jiefangjunbao* (Beijing), July 2, 2001, p. 7.

37 Shambaugh translated it as policy direction. See note 2, ch. 1, p. 6.

38 Cited in Lin (note 9, ch. 2), pp. 662–663. This means that the CPLA has to absorb, reduplicate, digest, and master advanced technology.

39 *Ibid.*, p. 684. A February 1, 1983 edition of *Hongqi* (Red Flag)'s editorial on page 7 first mentioned modernization to be followed by regularization.

40 Lin (note 9, ch. 2), p. 664.

41 *A New Chinese-English Dictionary* (note 35, ch. 3), p. 255.

42 *Guangjiaojingyuekan* (Hongkong), April 1990, p. 90.

43 See http://taiwansecurity.org/CNN/2004/CNN-060204.htm (accessed February 6, 2004).

44 *CT*, August 4, 1998, p. 15. It is not possible to know the exact number of companies and enterprises run by the Chinese PLA. A system exists whereby reinvestment of profits for further creation of other companies and enterprises is possible.

45 *Far Eastern Economic Review* (hereinafter FEER), July 13, 2000, p. 15.

46 *Ibid.*, p. 14.

47 See *CT*, April 8, 2004, p. A13.

48 According to a critic of Jiang, Three Represents is nothing new, because Communist International Movement in the 20th Century mentioned such a thing. See *Hong Kong Economic Journal* (Hong Kong), April 19, 2001, p. 14.

49   Lin (note 9, ch. 2), p. 665.

50   *Ibid.*, pp. 664–666.

51   Quoted in *Straits Times* (Singapore), November 26, 1998, p. 54.

52   According to Shambaugh, each group army has about 50,000–70,000 ground force troops which is divided into three divisions. Now, the operational units are the brigades with 15,000 officers and soldiers. See Shambaugh (note 27), p. 10 and the October 29, 2002 edition of *Straits Times*, Internet edition. According to him, the central directive's date is November 1994. According to Tai Ming Cheung's talk at the Mainland Affairs Council (MAC) in Taipei on January 6, 1998, it is November 1993. Two years ago, there was another round to *qingli* (liquidate) and *zhengdun* (consolidate) businesses and enterprises belonging to the armed forces. In early 1980s, no more than 5 per cent of the troops can engage in businesses and enterprises. But, in reality, 30 per cent of the armed forces were doing that.

53   *Xinbao* (Hong Kong Economic Journal), April 19, 2001, p. 14.

54   Deng humbly said he should be 50-50. See *Central Daily News* (hereinafter CDN)(Taipei), February 21, 1997, p. 5.

55   *Jingbao* (Hongkong), April 1998, pp. 42–43.

56   *A New Chinese-English Dictionary* (note 35, ch. 3), p. 553.

57   When attending the 4th International Symposium on Sun Tzu's Art of War in Beijing from October 18 to 22, 1998, I had the honor to sit with him at the same table for lunch. See also note 46, ch. 3, pp. 160–162.

58   *CT*, December 24, 1997, p. 9 and *Qianshaoyuekan* (*The Front-line*)(Hongkong), April 1998, p. 22.

59   *Qianshaoyuekan* (*The Front-line*)(Hongkong), April 1998, p. 22. It has a staff of between 200 and 300 and it is located in Sanzuomen, near Zhongnanhai in central Beijing. See Tai Ming Cheung (note 6, ch. 1), pp. 69–71.

60   Shambaugh (note 2, ch. 1), p. 10.

61   See, for example, James Mulvenon, "The PLA and the 16th Party Congress: Jiang Controls the Gun?" *China Leadership Monitor* (U.S.), No. 5, December 2002. But, Pollack wrote "[t]here seems an undeniable fascination (especially among journalists) with assessments of the 'who's up and who's down' sort, since it is readily marketable to editors and readership alike.)," adding Chinese PLA " studies are far better served by institutional analysis rather than seeking to divine elite-level political outcomes." See note 8, p. 13. A PRC general said there would not be two power centers. Jiang Zemin in his capacity as the CMC Chairman will discuss things related to military with Hu Jintao. The Chinese PLA will obey whatever the decision has been made by the the CMC. In other words, Jiang does not have to hide himself. See the March 5, 2003 edition online: http://www.chineseworld.com/publish/today/11_0900.4w/m/4wmp(030305)01_tb.htm.

62   See http://www.straitstimes.com/sg/commentary/story/0,4386,15794,00.html (accessed November 30, 2002).

63   See http://taiwansecurity.org/Reu/2003/Reuters-151103.htm (accessed November 17, 2003).

64   See http://www.zaobao.com/special/newspapers/2003/10/others271003w.html (accessed October 28, 2003). Jiang did talked to the *taikonnaut*, when the latter was in outer space. The very first such talk in human history was made on July 21, 1969.

65   See http://www.worldjournal/com/wj-ch-news.php?nt_seq_id=866546 &sc_seq_id=? (accessed November 5, 2003).

66   See http://www.udn.com/news/world/wor1/1510128.shtml (accessed August 18, 2003).

67   See http://lw9fd.law9.hotmail.com.msn.com/cgi-bin/getmsg?msg =MSG1078967056.25&mfs=&_HMaction=move&to (accessed March 10, 2004).

68   See http://taiwansecurity.org/ST/2004/ST-220204.htm.

69   Lin (note 9, ch. 2), p. 680.

70   For example, the Sichuan *bangpai* (faction) under Deng and the Shanghai *bangpai* under Jiang Zemin. The Chiang Kai-shek *bangpai* is another example.

71   Bickford (note 7, ch. 2), p. 25.

72   In July 1992, Yang Baiping, with Deng's permission, spoke about the CPLA's mission of *baojiahuhang* (protect Deng's way of reform and guard his inspection tour). See the July 29, 1992 edition of *Reminribao* (Beijing) and *CT*, July 30, 1992, p. 11. On September 22, 1971, Huang Yongsheng admitted that he committed a *zongpaizhuyi* mistake. He was with Lin Biao.

73   From mid-October to late November 1992, the large-scale *diaodong* (transfer) for the first time in the Chinese PLA history took place, according to *Wen Hui Pao* (Hongkong). See *CT*, December 16, 1992, p. 11. A 50-member special committee was set up by Jiang to investigae the past activities of both Yangs. See Srikanth Kondapalli, "Structural Reorganisation of the PLA: Issues and Problems," *Strategic Analysis*, Vol. XVIII, No. 11 (1996), p. 1489. Mao only rotated eight military region commanders. Willy Wo-lap Lam argued that Deng and his colleagues perceived that the Yangs were simply too powerful and ambitious, as they had placed their supporters in key posts. See his book, *China After Deng Xiaoping* (Hong Kong: Professional Consultants, Ltd., 1995), pp. 211–216. You Ji also said that Deng was fearful that Yang Baibing would form a second power center. Challenging Jiang Zemin. But, this should not be the main reason. Otherwise, Deng would have prevented even the younger Yang from holding another post, that of member of the Political Bureau, after the 14th CPC Congress. To be sure, this post did not give Yang Baibing power. For a report defending Yang Baibing, see *CT*, April 23, 1993, mainland China section.

74   Shambaugh (note 2, ch. 1), p. 3.

75   Dialectically speaking, this possibility can never be ruled out, because those capitalist countries may suffer from, for example, natural disasters, meaning that a lot of their territory might be destroyed with a heavy toll on lives.

76   This point is raised by Shambaugh (note 2, ch. 1), pp. 6–10

77   Richard D. Fisher, Jr., at the October 26–27, 2000 conference sponsored by The National Defense University Center for the Study of Chinese Military Affairs, "Chinese Military Studies: A Conference on the State of the Field," said a 1995 RAND study contradicted the June 2000 congressionally mandated report by the U.S. Department of Defense, the latter of which stated that "after 2005 ... if current trends continue, the balance of air power across the Taiwan Strait could begin to shift in China's favor...." In the *American Annual Report on the Military Power of the PLA of China* for the fiscal year 1998, which was released to the Congress, it was stated that it will take 10 more years for the mainland to launch a space shuttle. See *CT*, January 3, 1999, p. 14. Yet, in October 2003, Yang Liwei became the first Chinese astronaut to accomplish that feat.

78   Cited in Bickford (note 7, ch. 2), p. 12. A newsreporter, Yu Yu-lin, said Wei was against reform. See *CT*, May 3, 1992, p. 3.

79   Lin (note 57, ch. 3).

80   Zheng Yi, *Jieyanbuduitanmi* (Probing the Troops Under Martial Law), (Hongkong: Mingchuangchubanshe, April 1990), p. 198.

81   *Huanghouribao* (New York), March 2, 1995, p. 2.

Chapter **5**

Closing Remarks

In this study, this author has attempted to decode and decipher the relationship between the party and the Chinese PLA, to unravel its many puzzles, or to come out of its politico-military mazes. This author has argued that it is the dialectical frameworks which keep the CPC and the Chinese PLA together, not necessarily Mao, Ye (for less than one month after Mao's death), and Deng. On many issues, Jiang retained the actual military power for several years but he still had to rely on laws to reinforce the models. Hu will do likewise. So will his successors. What they have done was to ensure that the models worked well. To make up for the demise of Mao and Deng, it is the laws, especially the *National Defense Law*, which have been performing that function. So it is that both Jiang and Hu have come to rely on the March 1997 Law to map out the movements for the party and the military forces.

Having said this, this author wishes to point out several things. First, this author is very confident that he has presented almost all the major dialectical models and non-fragmented insights. If so, the study of the Chinese PLA should no longer be an enigmatic and frustrating field of research. Second, in this chapter, I have cited many times Chong-Pin Lin's 1992 research paper. But, he did not present a model or a series of dialectical frameworks. Wang Xinyang and Haijian Ling are two others, who have adopted the dialectical approach. Lin even said that the reason that the Party can command the Chinese PLA is due to the execution of a series of *yuanze* ([guiding] principles) and *zhidu* (system/institution), such as observing the Centralism Versus Democracy framework.[1] In other words, my writing has made contribution to the CPC and the Chinese PLA literature and challenged the military professionalism/professionalization model, which some Chinese PLA analysts regard as dominant.[2] Third, new proposals which do not fit into the existing frameworks will not be accepted by the party. This was true when the Soviet military advisors were assisting the Chinese PLA between 1955 and 1957. Liu Bocheng commanded the Second Field Army. He also graduated from a Soviet military academy. But, he has still insisted on maintaining the Chinese characteristics for the armed forces.[3] This is also true today. For example, a member of Jiang Zemin's brain trust, Wang Huning, proposed that a civilian be the Minister of Defense, to set up a joint chief of staff like the one in the United States, and to add a provision in the Constitution stipulating that the President of the PRC, General Secretary, and the CMC Chairman must be the same figure. But, these proposals were rejected by Jiang.[4] In May 2004, Liu Yazhou, who is the political commissar of the Chengdu Military Region's airforce said the Soviet way of fighting wars should be abandoned.[5]

ENDNOTES

1   Ling (note 5, ch. 2), p. 336.

2   Bickford (note 7, ch. 2), p. 3.

3   Jin Ji, *Confederation: China's Best Solution* (Hong Kong: Pai Shing Cultural Enterprise, April 1992), pp. 32–33. Peng criticized Liu's as outdated. The former preferred to learn from the Soviet experience. Due to such a conflict, the latter chose not to manage military affairs.

4   *UDN*, June 14, 1997, p. 9.

5   *CT*, June 1, 2004, p. A13.

II

A Macro-Level Perspective

CHINA, China, and china: A Dialectical *CHINA* at Time/space Sequence (n)?

CHAPTER 6

Background

There are many political scientists who are well-versed in models[1] and theories. To be able to have a better academic standing, they would try to construct a model or come up with a theory by themselves. Of course, they would spell out the structures and properties of their models and theories and apply them in their description, explanation, and prediction (or inference) of certain or chosen political phenomena. There are also some political scientists and non-political scientists who do not or have not yet realized the usefulness, power, and purpose of applying models and theories.

It is possible for us to categorize models and theories as either dialectical or non-dialectical, not just either normative or empirical, because a dialectical model/theory is both normative and empirical. What I am saying is that the methodology, therefore, is strikingly different between the two approaches.

Most political scientists in the West, especially the United States, have been non-dialectically trained. To many of them, dialectics is abstruse. To other social scientists, they have argued that, with the demise of the Communist camp headed by the Soviet Union in December 1991, dialectics is already dead. There are still some academics who, several years ago, alerted me that dialectics has been "out" for some two decades. Those who think this way have not fully understood what dialectics is all about, for dialectics can not only rationalize everything from the birth of humankind to its extinction but decode and decipher Chinese (Communist) politics as well, as Camilla Lowenhelm, a non-Chinese academic, has, for instance, identified two basic concepts in Chinese (political) culture-dialectics and collectivism.

In the Spring and Autumn Period (770–475 B.C.), the proper noun *Zhongguo* (Middle Kingdom, The Multitude of Great States, All Under Heaven, or China in the conventional Western usage) was coined, and, to Confucius, it was the entire world.[2] In this study, *Zhongguo* shall mean the period before the *Xinhai* Revolution of October 10, 1911 or the creation of the Republic of China (ROC) in January 1912.

To most political scientists in the West, *Zhongguo*, at least on the appearance of this proper noun, is *Zhongguo*, be it in the past, present, or future. In other words, the conventional way of writing this proper noun—China—would not give them a second thought, that is, as to whether it is possible to change the size, font, etc., of *Zhongguo*, so as to precisely distinguish the differences of each phase, stage, and so on of its progressive or non-progressive development. In short, these political scientists are only thinking about a non-dialectical *Zhongguo*.

Two types of China can be said to exist:[3] dialectical and non-dialectical. Unless otherwise stated, the use of the proper noun China in this study will indicate the dialectical China, whereas *Zhongguo* is non-dialectical. For the purpose of this book, another way of saying *Zhongguo* is a non-dialectical China. Since this author takes a dialectical approach, whenever the proper noun China is used, it means a dialectical China, which comes in terms of a spectrum as I will introduce it later on. So, readers are advised to remember that a dialectical China is just the opposite of a non-dialectical China or simply *Zhongguo*. China Versus *Zhongguo* is its dialectical equation or formula.

In the study of a non-dialectical China, most authors, on the one hand, do not apply a model or theory. To many serious academics, they are called pseudo-scientists.[4] There are always exceptions, of course. Merle Goldman and Andrew J. Nathan, for example, have been searching for an appropriate model for the People's Republic of China (PRC) since its creation.[5] They, in their writing, mentioned the Soviet, Stalinist model and Maoist models of heavy industrial autarky. For example, the "Maoist model was characterized by a distinctive mentality, involving the personality cult of Mao [Zedong], asceticism and self-denial, the definition of human value in political terms, and the valorization of cruelty in the service of class struggle."

On the other hand, some social scientists like G. William Skinner, who are aware of dialectics, are concerned with the structure or structural features of *Zhongguo* history. Hence, Skinner came up with a dynastic-cycle model and mentioned such terms like "the dialectic of dynastic strength" and "the dialectical challenge."[6]

One might ask whether political scientists who do care whether the study of a non-dialectical China is based on a model or theory, have been successful? The answer is: hardly. Describing the "East Asian model" which appeared on page 309 of their book, Goldman and Nathan wrote, concerning Deng Xiaoping that he "began the reforms without blueprints or models...."[7] They were definitely wrong! In other words, readers were told that there were models for the PRC from October 1, 1949 to late 1978; yet, there were none after late 1978 for a period of time. That is to say, the authors are still searching for a model, akin to the "East Asian model," from late 1978, with the hiatus in mind, to the present. But, can the authors' "East Asian model" incorporate the period from October 1, 1949 to late 1978? The answer is: certainly not. This means that there are problems with their study, at least in terms of logic. What about the hiatus between late 1978 and the period immediately after that? Again, something is missing. In other words, they should think of a new model, which can describe and explain or cover the entire period from October 1, 1949 up to now, if not including the future as well. In this connection, is the "East Asian model" non-dialectical? Yes, it could be. It is necessary to ask this question because East Asia includes Southeast Asia, not just Northeast Asia. It is very doubtful that most Southeast Asian political figures apply dialectics. Besides, it would be difficult to accommodate all the contradictions within one non-dialectical, East Asian framework. It follows, then, that when there is already confusion, it can only beget further confusion, to say the least.

This is a study of a dialectical China, which incorporates CHINA, China, and china. It also includes other versions, due to the existence of, as we shall see later, other numbers and letters. The progressive dynamics is moving from the right to the left. This is what Zheng Bijian, who is a close aide to Hu Jintao, the mainland leader since the 16th Party Congress, in October/November 2003 at the third Boao Forum for Asia said about the *heping jueqi* (literally emerging precipitously in a peaceful way) theory (as opposed to the China threat and other related theories), that is, "China's only choice is to strive to rise, more importantly, to strive for peaceful rise." By "other numbers or letters," is meant that in between CHINA and China, for example, there could be some other precise ways of dialectically writing them in order, for example, "CHINA," CHINa, CHIna, and CHina, each in this spectrum reflecting a certain stage of the normative development. Of course, things do not move or progress normatively or smoothly, that is, from the right to the left. For this reason, the time/space sequence element has been added to show the empirical, tactical or micro-level moves. In any case, one should always expect decay, reverses, twists and turns, zigs and zags, ups and downs, etc., from time/space sequence (1) to time/space sequence (n).

October 1, 1949, the day the PRC was founded, is a good starting point for this study. But, aspects of ancient, non-dialectical China and the Republican era will also be touched upon. This is because some historical facts could still be applied and be relevant at present and in the future, until the demise of the dialectical China.

ENDNOTES

1   The word is used interchangeably with framework (of thought and action).

2   See http://www.worldjournal.com/wj-forum-news.php?nt_seq_id=920075. China originated from the Chengdu area of Sichuan Province, because it is related to silk. See http://www.mpnews.com/content.cfm?newsid =200211110856ca10851a (accessed November 11, 2002). According to the mainland China academics, the concept dragon originated in the Liaohe *liuyu* (valley or [river] basin). See *China Times* (hereinafter CT)(Taipei), February 21, 2004, p. A13. To Wang Gungwu, China can also be *Zhonghua*. See his book, *The Chinese Way: China's Position in International Relations* (Oslo: Scandinavian University Press, 1995), p. 12. He said the proper noun China is foreign to Chinese people. The Chinese characters for *Zhongguo* has existed since ancient times. Talk given by Wang, dated April 24, 2001 at the East Asian Institute (EAI), National University of Singapore (NUS). According to W. D. White, China and Chinese were used by the West in around the year 1700. At that time, China was still strong. See *Lianhezaobao* (hereinafter LHZB)(Singapore), November 22, 1998, p. 4. According to researchers, using mitochondrial DNA-genetic material in a cell that is passed down unchanged from mother to child, modern Chinese like all human beings living today descended from sub-Saharan Africans or they dispersed "out of Africa" 100,000 to 200,000 years ago. See *Straits Times* (hereinafter ST)(Singapore), September 30, 1998, p. 21 and December 8, 2000, p. 26. Adda B. Bozeman wrote that "… the Chinese regarded China as the sole world state and the center of all humanity." See his book, *Politics and Culture in International History* (Princeton, NJ: Princeton University Press, 1960), p. 133. Many Chinese cultural relics were unearthed. Chinese authorities were trying to preserve them. But, due to economic development, some of the relics had to be torn down, so

the transliteration pronunciation for China became 拆呐. See *United Daily News* (hereinafter UDN)(Taipei), January 29, 2001, p. 13. Another one is 氣餒 or 支那 as mentioned by a mainland China diplomat. See *Sin Chew Daily* (Malaysia), February 13, 2003, p. 1. A PRC-government-funded study has pushed back the dates of *Zhongguo*'s earliest dynasties, shedding light on the origins of Chinese civilization and adding fuel to a controversy over the influence of Chinese Communist politics on scholarship. The study documents the emergency of early Chinese kingdoms from the prehistoric New Stone Age and edge *Zhongguo*'s verifiable history to more than 4,000 years ago—a 1,200-year jump. The project's stated mission was to fix dates for three dynasties: the half-documented Zhou, the shadowy Shang, and the myth-shrouded Xia. Davis

Nivison, a retired Stanford University academic, said: "Establishing the Xia as history, not legend, authenticated history that rivals Babylonia or Egypt." He added: "Still, I think, they're all wrong." See *ST*, November 11, 2000, p. A9. According to PRC archaeologists, Sanxia of Changjiang is the cradle of Chinese civilization. People have been living there more than 100,000 years ago. See *LHZB*, October 27, 2000, p. 2. In January 2002, it was reported that Indian archaeologists had discovered an older city, which was built in 7,500 B.C. The previous discovery was dated 4,000 years earlier.

3   According to a mainland China academic, the proper noun China originated in Chengdu area, Sichuan Province. See http://www.mpinews.com/content.cfm?newsid=200211110856ca10851a, dated November 11, 2002.

4   See, for example, Hans Kuijper, "Is Sinology a Science?" *China Report* (India and United States), Vol. 36, No. 3 (July–September 2000), pp. 331–354. See also his updated and revised website: http://www.soas.ac.uk/eacs.

5   Merle Goldman and Andrew J. Nathan, "Searching for the Appropriate Model for the People's Republic of China" in Merle Goldman and Andrew Gordon, eds., *Historical Perspectives on Contemporary East Asia* (Cambridge, MA: Harvard University Press, 2000), pp. 297–320.

6   G. William Skinner, "Presidential Address: The Structure of Chinese History," *Journal of Asian Studies* (hereinafter JAS)(U.S.), Vol. XLIV, No. 2 (February 1985), pp. 281 and 289.

7   They are wrong, because Deng had a series of dialectical models in mind and practises according to these frameworks. p. 310.

CHAPTER 7

Presenting the Model

We are all interested in social sciences. But, we are confronted with a myriad of contradictory phenomena in politics, economic affairs, society, etc. For example, in October 1993, the then ROC President Lee Teng-hui said the reason why the country wants to purchase weapons from abroad was to safeguard Taiwan people's life, properties, and national security. He added that Taipei would only buy defensive weapons, not offensive weapons.[1] In April 2001, American President George W. Bush, Jr. personally approved the sale of eight diesel submarines to the ROC. Taipei was certainly elated. If Germany and Holland are reluctant to sell those submarines to the ROC, the latter is thinking of building them or assembling the parts in southern Taiwan. But, how would it rationalize the fact that, for years, Taipei has wanted to buy them? Moreover, submarines, conventional or nuclear, are offensive weapons, according to the American definition or standard. In a word, how do we describe, explain, and interpret them logically, systematically, and coherently, preferably within one framework?

According to one astronomer in Hongkong, China, our civilization has one more hundred years to sustain itself. It would be an elephantine task to study human words and deeds since the dawn of humanity to the day when they become extinct. Hence, one question inevitably comes to our mind: How do we compress the phenomena into a manageable proportion or simplify them into a model or theory? This calls for methodological aptitude, knack, or skill. If many people accept a particular model or theory over a long period of time, the model or theory becomes a school of thought and action and even a paradigm.

The most skilful social scientist with an aptitude, knack or skill relies on only one dot/point[2] to conduct research. Unless one is well-versed in model or theory, he or she would not dare do that. It takes time to put forward a new, rigorous model or theory. One may even have to fight an uphill fight, before gaining acceptance by generations of academics. To be certain, the discipline of political science is already littered with abandoned models and theories, which failed to last beyond a decade or two. The Eastonian theory has been criticized, and Samuel P. Huntington's clash of seven or eight civilizations theory has been challenged in many quarters. Having witnessed the September 11, 2001 attacks by some middle-class Moslem activists/terrorists in the United States, the rational choice theory, which has been in vogue for some two decades already, can be seriously called into question.[3]

ROC President Chen Shui-bian, who is a member of the Democratic Progressive Party (DPP), for example, mentioned the Eaves theory (*wuyan lilun*) on the first day of the 21st century to describe and explain the relations between Taiwan and mainland China.[4] Decades ago, a West German scholar said that, in the *Dachtheorie* (Roof/Housetop Theory [*wuding lilun*]), West Germany and East Germany exist. This theory was endorsed by an editorial writer of the *United Daily News* (UDN) in Taipei, and James C. Soong, the March 2000 presidential candidate in Taiwan, also advocated the adoption of a Roof/Housetop Theory for both Taiwan and mainland China.[5] The Kuomintang (KMT) chairman, Lien Chan, also mentioned the word Roof/Housetop in July 2001.[6] If one has fully understood what a theory is, a dot/point can actually refer to the theory itself. To Chen, the Eaves theory is a dot/point.

Mao, speaking of the 10 relationships in April 1956, said that at present, there are two dots/points/extremes and, in the future, there will still be two dots/points/extremes. He added that, in ancient, non-dialectical China or *Zhongguo*, *Yin* and *Yang* constituted the two dots/points/extremes. There is a plethora of examples given by Mao in using the two dots/points/extremes: The Third World Versus The First World;[7] The Party (referring to the Communist Party of China [CPC]) Commands the Gun" Versus "The Gun Commands the Party; Red Versus Expert;[8] One Versus Many (*yi yu duo*), Not to Attack Versus To Attack, and so on and so forth. Applied at the personal level, we have, for example, the Mao Versus Chiang Kai-shek framework, because Mao once said that he wanted to show two Suns to his arch-rival, Chiang, the latter of whom said there can be only one ruler under heaven, namely, himself. In Mao's mind, one sun refers to himself and the other, Chiang.

Here, a word must be added. When we see the word versus, one should immediately think of dialectics, seething with contradiction, struggle, conflict, tension, competition, etc. But, some dialecticians would say The Third World *and* The First World. The word *and* in the previous sentence in Mandarin Chinese is *yu*. By using this Chinese character *yu*, it means both The Third World and the The First World, and the dialectician would immediately think about its opposite, that is, Non-The Third World and the First World. By way of analogy, in the mainstream literatureof international organization (i.o.), the latter could refer to the management of peace and tranquillity through a world, global or international body, whereas international organizations (in plural) simply refer to the world or international bodies, such as the United Nations (UN), the North Atlantic Treaty Organization (NATO), and World Trade Organization (WTO).

Some people rely on three dots/points to conduct research. John Wong, an economist at the National University of Singapore (NUS), for example, proceeds by distinguishing between what is the subject (*zhuti*) and the object (*keti*) in a given situation or universe. To Wong, there is a third dot/point in between the subject and the object, namely, action. (See Figure 3) To distinguish it from the left extreme word and the right extreme word, we shall blacken the word, which refers to action.

This is because action must be taken by the subject and/or the object in their relationship flow, so as to move on and to arrive at something else. But, to Chen and Mao, action is taken for granted and, therefore, they would not mention it.

Deng, like many other Chinese, relies on four dots/points. He wants to be more thoughtful, so that other people would not miss what he is trying to drive at. Some 3,100 years ago, the *Yin* and *Yang* plus the Five Elements (*wuxing*) doctrine was developed. According to another source, *Fengshui* (geomancy or relationship between human beings and their environment) can be dated back to more than 5,000 years. Most Chinese superficially or on surface know what they are and stand for. On top of *Yin* and *Yang* as well as the Five Elements, there is *Ren* (human being). Roof/Housetop or Eaves is another way of referring to the top. In other words, *Ren* equals to *Yin* and *Yang*. Another way of dialectically saying the same thing is that *Yin* is part of *Ren*, just as *Yang* is part of *Ren*. So, if you were a male, you would put *Yang* on the left extreme and *Yin*, on the

FIGURE 3

Subject	Action	Object

right extreme. Similarly, if you were a female, you would position yourself on the left extreme and place *Yang* on the right extreme. In other words, you cannot just think of yourself as either male or female, because aspects of you are both male and female throughout your life. For example, your teacher may ask you to play a role of a female on stage. When you as a male are doing that, you are a "female" for that period of time, however short. After the show is over, you go back to yourself, the original you or the male. To reconcile *Yin* and *Yang* or to bring about harmony to *Yin* and *Yang*, you would rely on the Five Elements (to wit, metal, wood, water, fire, and earth to which the ancient Chinese scholars attributed the origin of the physical world), which refer to actions taken by the person (which could be done with the help of others) positioned on the left extreme and/or the person on the right extreme. (See Figure 4)

There are many similar frameworks set up by Deng. (See Figure 5) The major difference is that *Yin* and *Yang* plus the Five Elements stress harmony, whereas Deng's frameworks, applied to politics, include other things such as contradictions, struggle, etc. A word must be added. To Deng and other dialecticians who think alike, their frameworks also can be converted or transformed into a harmonious one at a given time/ space sequence. The finest examples are that of contradiction between the enemy and ourselves (*diwomaodun*) and contradictions among the people (*renminneibumaodun*). They are regarded as in the safe zone. Hence, the word and (as opposed to versus) is used.

FIGURE 4

	Ren **Five Elements**	
Yin	**Five Elements**	*Yang*
	or	
	Ren	
Yang	**Five Elements**	*Yin*

FIGURE 5

	Yige Zhongxin	
Sige Jianchi	***Fan Fubai Yundong***	*Gaigekaifang*

Yige Zhongxin, in English, is "One Center." It constitutes the Roof/ Housetop or Eaves. This dot/point refers to the catch phrase, economic construction. *Sige Jianchi* at the left extreme refers to the Four Insistences, such as adhering to Marxism, Leninism, and Mao Zedong Thought. *Fan Fubai Yundong* is the action, which must be taken to reconcile the left and right extremes and to eventually bring about the disappearance of the right extreme by elimination, cooptation, etc. Its English translation is To Conduct Anti-corruption Campaigns.[9] And *Gaigekaifang*, positioned on the right extreme, stands for Reform and Opening to the Outside World. Because it is positioned on the right extreme, it has bad, negative, etc., connotations. Indeed, after opening to the outside world, the mainland has been peopled by corrupt officials, businessmen, etc., and the society plagued by social ills. So, anti-corruption campaigns are aimed at reconciling the two extremes. They are still going on till this day.

My model, on the surface, is a little bit more complicated but less abstract and abstruse, and it will be introduced later. But, once understood, it is easy as writing A, B, and C, and one should find it easier to understand than other versions as noted above and elsewhere in figures.[10]

There is ample evidence to show that Chinese (Communist) leaders apply one version of dialectics or another, at least they have such a proclivity toward dialectics. We can name some well-known names: Mao Zedong, Zhou Enlai,[11] Deng Xiaoping, Zhang Xueliang,[12] Jiang Zemin, Hu Jintao,[13] Chiang Ching-kuo, Lee Teng-hui, Chen Shui-bian (perhaps with the help of his advisors),[14] and so on. Dr. Sun Yat-sen, the great precursor of revolution or the great pioneer of the Chinese democratic revolution, according to a mainland China academic, *sometimes* applies dialectics.[15] As a matter of fact, most Chinese idioms should be understood in terms of dialectics.

As a political figure, sooner or later, one has to apply dialectics. This is because one cannot be a man/woman of principle in the political arena *all* the time, without being contradictory. If one's words and deeds do not match, the political figure can be easily criticized in the legislative branch/parliament/congress/diet or by the media. Whether we write contradictorily or non-contradictorily is important, because we are in academia, where scholarship, to me, comes in the following order: logic, contribution, whether your writing is closer to reality, whether or not you have access to first-hand information, etc. If one cannot convince logically oneself, how can he or she expect to convince others?

To package oneself as logical, systematic, and coherent, a political figure, who is in between a statesman and a politician, will inevitably or sooner or later rely on dialectics, which, to many people who do not understand dialectics fully, is related to sophistry. Otherwise, he or she cannot survive. Chiang Kai-shek lost the Chinese civil war, because he failed to apply dialectics. But, in February 1951, Chiang instructed not himself but the KMT members who were trained at the Yangming Institution of National Revolution and Development (YINRD) and military cadres at the Fu Hsin Kang (Political Warfare) College (FHKC) to study Hegelian dialectics and practice it, so as to counter Chinese Communists.[16] Nonetheless, he still lost to Mao when the PRC entered into the UN in Fall 1971, because he insisted on the principle that a great man cannot brook his rival (*hanzei bu liangli*) in that important world body. In other words, if Mao were Chiang and he were to be put into the latter's shoes, he would have accepted a Two-China arrangement and deceived himself as having only made a tactical or temporary move. Another option would be to accept two seats under the One China principle. This would mean that, when the situation reverted to Mao's favor, he, without a second thought, would switch back to his original principle, of representing the sole, legitimate China.

Each of all the Chinese (Communist) political figures probably has his or her own version of dialectics. Lee, for example, said he relied on the *Yin* and *Yang* plus the Five Elements to govern the ROC on Taiwan. Hu, the chosen successor of Jiang, is certainly well-versed in dialectics, as, since May 2000, he has been preaching about the Three Represents (*Sange Daibiao*) important thought, which must be understood in terms of dialectics, especially the framework of Communism Versus Capitalism and its variants, such as Socialism (with [distinct] Chinese Characteristics) Versus Capitalism. The jargon said the party represents the interests of advanced social production forces, advanced culture, and the majority of the Chinese people. Moreover, Hu, after becoming the new PRC President and/or the CPC General-Secretary in late 2002, would, as he has said on numerous occasions, be creative in putting forward theories, so as to advance the party's interests by mingling with the majority Chinese people. When I explain the four economic lines/tracks from October 1949 up to December 2004, readers will understand what I am talking about.

Having made these remarks, we are in a position to introduce our dialectical model.[17] It is a paradigm in mainland China, Taiwan, Hongkong, and Macao, simply because the Chinese have (subconsciously) been taught dialectically from an early age. Most, if not all, Chinese idioms are constructed dialectically.

One paradigmatic way of simplifying complex, ever-changing, and ever-dynamic reality for a long period of time is to perceive or to present reality in terms of two dots/points (*liangdianlun*) or, to be more precise, two extremes, at any time/space sequence before the last one. The two dots/points/extremes, in parallel, are depicted below:

●   ●

But, these two dots/points/extremes are originally derived from one dot/point,[18] which is another way of referring to as the Roof/Housetop or Eaves.

●

That is to say, the extreme at the left is part of the above original dot/point, just as the other extreme at the right is also part of the original dot/point. In other words, if the original dot/point equals to 100, the left extreme dot/point could be 75 or 51, while the right extreme dot/point, 25 or 49 respectively. Or, if the original dot/point is 1, the left extreme dot/point could be .75 or .51, while the right extreme dot/point, .25 or .49 respectively. In this connection, there is a distance between the two dots/points/extremes. There is a reason for having the distance, as we shall see later.

To facilitate later discussion, I shall label the left dot/point/extreme as Number 1 and the right dot/point/extreme as Letter E.[19] Another way of depicting the two dots/points/extremes is shown in Figure 6.

Each dot/point/extreme refers to something, be it a concept, a phrase, a sentence, a label, a symbol (which does not necessarily have any meaning but could just reflect something or represent something else). Each point in the two-dot system is just the opposite of the other dot/point/extreme (or, as one other possibility, it could be the dot/point half-way between two other extremes). If there are many issues which

FIGURE 6

1	E

need to be dealt with or (re)solved, many working frameworks or sets of two dots/points/extremes can be created or employed, linking each other. Players can manipulate or play a lot of games at once, by moving sideways like crabs within the framework of each game (or set of two dots/points/extremes) and by making leaps like frogs from one framework to another one at any time/space sequence. By "moving sideways like crabs," I mean the movement of a politico-military figure (or a political entity, political party, country, etc.) within the framework in any of the following manners: staying at or sticking to the left dot/point/extreme (or 1) or the right dot/point/extreme (or E); moving to the edge of the safe zone or 5 (which comes in terms of a spectrum or which extends from the left extreme to the center-point between the two dots/points/extremes) of a framework or a set of two dots/points/extremes; moving to the edge of the danger zone or A (which comes in terms of a spectrum or which extends from the right extreme to the centre-point between the two dots/points/extremes) of a framework or a set of two dots/points/extremes; staying at a dot/point/extreme in between the left dot/point/extreme and the centre-point or staying in between the centre-point and the right dot/point/extreme; etc. However, the politico-military figure ought to concentrate on one primary game (working framework or set of two dots/points/extremes) at a time/space sequence to enhance the figure's ability to be logical, systematic, and coherent in what he or she does and says. There should be one primary dialectical framework of thought and action at any time/space sequence. Choosing the right framework is very important. Failing to do that even by dialectical players would be disastrous.[20] If one framework does not fit into a particular time/space sequence, another can. In between them, one may have to construct another framework, so as to link them up. So, a dialectician, like a frog, would constantly leap from one framework to another. To an outsider who does not understand dialectics, he or she will certainly be confused, saying the politico-military figure is illogical, unsystematic, and incoherent in what he or she does or says.

A politico-military figure may also make use of the frameworks (games or sets of two dots/points/extremes) to perform any one of the following functions: rationalization and self-protection, control and guidance, as well as struggle. The term rationalization means that whenever one does and says something, it is done within the safe zone, preferably positioned at 1. Because it is safe, one can protect himself or herself from unnecessary criticism while control means that the politico-military figure will make sure that his or her (potential) enemy falls within the framework. Guidance is necessary, because some politico-military figures may deviate and enter into the danger zone. Thus, efforts must be made to bring them back to the safe zone. And struggle is obvious. The subject wants to eliminate, co-opt, or absorb the object, and vice versa, hence the tension, friction, conflict, etc.

Even more important still, the politico-military figure should preferably attempt to stay at the left dot/point/extreme at all time/space sequences or at least within the safe zone (which always refers to the spectrum made up of Numbers ranging from the left dot/point/extreme to the center-point of the framework or 5). In this context, the safe zone is the opposite of the danger zone (which refers to the spectrum made up of Letters ranging from the right dot/point/extreme up to the center-point of the framework or A). It is always possible that, due to circumstances beyond his or her control, the politico-military figure may voluntarily or involuntarily venture into the danger zone for a period of time. However, in order to justify what he or she is doing and saying, he or she will attempt to rearrange the two dots/points/extremes, so that their actions can be seen as still taking place within the safe zone. That is to say, the politico-military figure will attempt to make the original centre-point or 5 into the new left dot/point/extreme or 1 with the right dot/point/extreme or E remaining in the same place. All games end when they reach the time/space sequence (n), in which the final and conclusive crab-like/sideways move takes place.

In order to help readers to acquire a better visual understanding of what has been said in the preceding paragraphs, I shall depict the working framework or the set of Numbers and Letters plus the time and space elements in Figure 7.[21]

Numbers 2, 3, 4, and 5 are each a variation/synonym[22] of Number 1 which is the left extreme. For example, we can have CHINA as 1,

FIGURE 7

<pre>   1 2 3 4 5 A B C D E
time/space sequence (1)
time/space sequence (2)
....
time/space sequence (n)</pre>

"CHINA" as 2, CHINa as 3, CHIna as 4, and China as 5. Similarly, Letters A, B, C, and D are, again, each a variation/synonym of Letter E, which is the right extreme. We can refer to china as E. But, for D, it could be written in a different font so as to show that a slight difference exists, for example, china. There could also be more than just 5 numbers and 5 letters, if one chooses to. But, it is not really necessary, because, the dialectician would not burden himself or herself with too many things. In a word, dialectics appears to be complicated at first but actually it is not. Within each Number or Letter, there is room for manoeuvre (or change) from right or the nascent (or primary) stage to the ascendant stage, and to left, the mature stage. The Numbers can be conceived as one dot/point/extreme or *zheng* (thesis), and the Letters, another dot/point/extreme or *fan* (anti-thesis).

In the face of constant change, a dynamic, operational concept (or what the Chinese Communists called *fangzhen*) is needed to reconcile the two dots/points/extremes or to eventually bring about the disappearance of the right extreme by elimination, cooptation, absorption, etc. Another way of saying this concept is action. Conducting anti-corruption campaigns is one example of possible actions. Having three links and four exchanges (*santongsiliu*), such as shipping link between mainland China and Taiwan after January 1, 1979 is another example. Such a concept/action must work in favor of the left extreme.

To summarize the description and explanation above, Number 1 represents the left dot/point/extreme. Numbers 1 to 5 constitutes the safe zone/spectrum. Number 5 refers to the edge of the safe zone (which touches the framework center-point). Letter E is the right dot/point/extreme. Letters A to E fall into the danger zone/spectrum. Letter A refers to the edge of the danger zone (which also touches the framework centre-point). In a nutshell, Number 1 and Letter E are simply the two dots/points/extremes (*liangdianlun*) I referred to earlier.

A politico-military figure or a dialectical player can rely on a series of dialectical models or any model at any time/space sequence. But, it is not necessary for us to dwell on all of them. Otherwise, we are only burdening ourselves. Indeed, there is no such need. Besides, readers may be confused. One primary dialectical model stands out at any time/space sequence, in order to understand what I am going to describe, explain, and infer. This means that all the other models, such as the CHINA, China, and china framework and the Communism Versus Capitalism framework are relatively less important. Of course, there are still other less important dialectical models.

The primary model that we have to enter into is the Rule of Law Politics (under Socialism with Chinese Characteristics)[23] Versus the Rule of Men Politics or the Rule of Personality (*renzhi* [*qua* E]) (under Socialism with Chinese Characteristics). The former one is positioned at 1, and the latter, E. At 5, it is called the Rule of Dialectical Politics.[24] The framework could be expanded to become Rule by Virtue (*dezhi* [*qua* 1]) Versus the Rules of Men Politics, the Rule by Virtue Versus the Rule of Dialectical Politics (*bianzheng zhengzhi*), and so on and so forth. There is always politics, for the simple reason that decisions must be made by at least a few people even when tangible and intangible resources are plenty.

Under the "Rule of Law Politics," when anyone is involved in money matters he or she should position himself or herself at 1. Punishment will follow, if they failed to observe the relevant laws. It is easy to identify these people. They must know the law related to finance, banking, foreign exchange, etc. Those who serve the party and the military and, yet deal with money matters, have equally to obey the relevant laws. So, they still have to position themselves at 1. Of course, they must also adhere to other frameworks, which are applicable to the military. By Rule of Men Politics, it is meant that the ruler governs the state or country according to his or her liking or whim. In the morning, the ruler may promote someone to the rank of general. In the afternoon, the same ruler may order the same general to be executed. The Rule of Dialectical Politics is a combination of both the Rule of Law Politics and the Rule of Men Politics. In other words, even if one or a few people were making the decision, they would not discard or ignore certain existing laws, domestic, international, interplanetary, intercelestial or interterrestial. In between the Rule of Law Politics and the Rule of Dialectical Politics, we have the Rule by Law Politics (*fazhi* [legal system] or *yifa* or 3). By Rule by Law Politics, we mean the CPC makes use of the law or its superior position at the National People's Congress (NPC) and other related bodies for the sake of advancing its own interest and to sustain its ruling power status, whereas, in Rule of Law Politics, it is possible for a non-CPC party to emerge as the ruling party. Because there are laws in the PRC from the very beginning, it is a mistake to say that Chinese Communist politics is the Rule of Men Politics, because even Mao had to adhere to some CPC laws, PRC laws, and (socialist) international laws sometimes. On the other hand, if we were to talk about dynasties in *Zhongguo*, the

Rule of Men Politics is probably a very accurate description most of the time, since there were not many laws at that time.

In this study, if the PRC were to juxtapose a totalitarian or authoritarian rule, the way dialectical players play dialectical games would be quite different. By authoritarian rule, adverbs could also be added, such as fragmented or sporadic. From October 1, 1949 to the downfall of Hua Guofeng, we can say that mainland China was under totalitarianism. Almost everything was controlled and monitored, and almost everyone had to rely on the work unit (*danwei*) for survival. To eat, one needed coupons in exchange for food. Most people learned to adhere to or comply with the Rule of Dialectical Politics, whereas the political figures practised the Rule of Men Politics or close to E. The PRC entered into an authoritarian system, when Deng in the late 1970s started economic reform. More and more people moved themselves into the safe zone. And when Deng went to southern mainland China in January and February 1992 to give symbolic emphasis to the economic line of Market Economy (as opposed to Socialism with Chinese Characteristics), most people were asked to gradually position themselves at 1, 2, and 3 in the framework of the Rule of Law Politics Versus the Rule of Men Politics by September 1997 when the 15th National Congress of the CPC was held. As for political figures, they can still stand at 5, until such time when the Rule of Law Politics in the framework of the Rule by Virtue Versus the Rule of Dialectical Politics became the mainstream. In a word, throughout the study, the Rule of Dialectical Politics is considered the mainstream for the political figures, so long as the party is in power or in existence. But, a word must be added. Conducting public opinion polls becomes more important, so as to find out, if possible, the behavioural pattern of mainland China residents, if not elsewhere. After that, we can still position them accordingly within each framework in terms of certain numbers or letters.

After entry into the first framework, readers have to understand that a myriad of dialectical frameworks exists in the order they appear at a particular time/space sequence, and they are all positioned at Number 5. The foremost one is CHINA Versus china, which is another way of saying Non-China Threat Versus China Threat. We shall discuss where the PRC stands in terms of this foremost framework ideologically and politically (which is also closely related to things like diplomacy, military affairs, etc.). In other words, when the Rule of Dialectical Politics is no longer mainstream, that is, when it has become E, there is no urgent need to discuss CHINA, China, and china. It is safe to say that the Rule of Dialectical Politics will continued to be played within the 21st century for the simple reason that dialectics has five functions which can be put into three categories and they help political figures to rationalize without fear of being criticized.

In the paragraphs below, I shall try to discuss what a dialectical China is. It is depicted in terms of four dots/points in the following figure:

Whenever we see *CHINA*, Roof/Housetop or Eaves should appear top-most in our minds. They are equivalent to each other. Next, the positive, if not better, aspects of the Han (206 B.C.– A.D. 221) and Tang (A.D. 618–907) Dynasties (*hantangshengshi* [the golden age of Han and Tang]) plus the positive experience of other dynasties as well as the ROC and PRC should surface. They would emerge at time/space sequence (n) of the framework, which could be 1,000 or 10,000 years from now. In other words, the Han and Tang Dynasties plus the positive experience of other dynasties as well as the ROC and PRC could be positioned at 1, but they are not yet equivalent to *CHINA* before time/space sequence (n), because it is possible to regard the positive aspects of these dynasties only as in their nascent or ascendant stages of CHINA.

CHINA is a *Pax Sinica*, a world united harmoniously by the ties of universal love, humanitarian sentiment, peaceful intention, enlightened virtue,[25] etc. No one should ever think about it as being imperialistic, expansionist, or hegemonic. Napoleon Bonaparte once perceived that *Zhongguo*'s awakening would "shake the world," and the world would be sorry.[26] However, the non-Chinese would embrace CHINA voluntarily. When we think and conceive about *CHINA*, we should associate *CHINA* with concepts like what a Singapore-based academic, Shee Poon Kim, has mentioned: the Javanese (or Indonesian) concept of *Musyawarah* (consultation), *Mufakat* (consensus), compromise, coordination, cooperation, communitarianism, and coexistence.[27] In ancient *Zhongguo* days, intermarriage and tribute-presenting practices with vassal states were carried out so as to live harmony with nearby regions. And, during

FIGURE 8

	CHINA	
CHINA	China	china

---

the military heydays of the Han (206 B.C.–A.D. 220) and Tang dynasties, the Chinese people did not instigate a war.

CHINA should not be conceived of as being hierarchical, unlike, for example, the period before the 17th century, whereby relations between *Zhongguo* and Korea, for example, were patterned on the family relationship of father and son.[28] Sometimes, ROC political figures like Lee Teng-hui regard the Taiwan and the mainland relationship as that of father and son.

CHINA is a success. Examples of this might be drawn from the past. We can cite some examples. The first one that comes into my mind is Kublai Khan. He was a Mongolian. But, he was mesmerized by things *Zhongguo* or *Zhonghua*. So, he was sinicized and established the *Yuan* Dynasty, which lasted from 1280 to 1368. There are other interesting examples. As pointed out by Lillian Craig Harris, "[t]he late 10th century Arab geographer and traveller Al-Muqaddasi referred to the Red Sea as 'the sea of China' and his near contemporary the Arab historian Tabari (d.923) boasted that, 'there is no obstacle between us and China; everything on the sea can come to us on it.'"[29] There are other modern examples. Abraham Lincoln appointed Anson Burlingame as the first Minister to the Qing Dyansty (A.D. 1616–1911). Burlingame was instructed to cooperate with other foreign powers in assuring equal economic opportunity for all but he became such a sinophile that he started to represent Chinese interests rather than American interests to such an extent that, upon Burlingame's retirement in 1867, the Qing Dynasty appointed him "Imperial Envoy" to the Western world.[30] In the early 20th century, Paul Reinsch was Woodrow Wilson's "evangelical Christian" ambassador. Like Burlingame, Reinsch came to serve Chinese interests. When the ROC students protested the June 1919 Versailles Treaty decision to give the former German concessions in Shandong Province to Imperial Japan, he resigned his ambassadorship and joined the student protest.[31] K.M. Schipper, a French expert on Daoism, said passing down Chinese culture is a matter of world importance. In February 2002, Indonesian President Megawati Sukarnoputri announced that the 2003 Chinese Lunar New Year will be celebrated as an official holiday in the world's largest Muslim-populated nation. In February 2004, K. Rupert Murdoch of the News Corporation, speaking at the Asia Foundation in New York City, said parents in the West should encourage their children to learn Chinese history, culture, and language. And, on July 4, 2004, Ted C. Fishman, in a

New York Times (NYT) article entitled "The Chinese Century", pointed out that "[b]y having changed itself, China is changing the world."

CHINA means worldwide and global as well as interplanetary/inter-celestial/inter-terrestrial. The migration of Chinese people to other places in the world and other outer space bodies helps to spread *CHINESENESS*. There are Chinese all over the world by now.[32] Before the end of 2006 or in early 2007, Chinese *taikonnaut* (as opposed to Soviet cosmonaut and American astronaut) can orbit the Moon, for example. Between the first and 11th century, the Chinese population had doubled to 50 million. By early 19th century, the figure was about 400 million.[33] In mid-19th century, there were 430 million Chinese people. Until the 19th century, we have witnessed many Chinese people in large numbers migrating to foreign lands. *Huaqiao* (Overseas Chinese) became a term of popular usage in the late 19th century. How this came about can be traced back to the Southern Song Dynasty (1127–1279 A.D.). There was a marked shift of the economic center from the north to the south.[34] This meant that more people were migrating to the south, especially to the coastal areas. Later, this migration of the Chinese extended overseas, for one reason or another. In 1860, there were 35,000 Chinese working as coolies in the United States.[35] In 1870, the number had increased to 62,000.[36] And, in 1880, there were about 110,000 Chinese.[37]

There were economical and non-economical reasons impelling the Chinese to leave their country. Some Chinese had fled their motherland, because they were desperados, outlaws, and fugitives.[38] Others were prisoners of war. There were also some Chinese who had left *Zhongguo*, because of economic dislocation, famine, flood, etc. From the very beginning once overseas, people from the same locality would congregate, forming clans and guilds (*bang*), such as Guangdong *bang*, Chaozhou *bang*, Hakka *bang*, etc.

We have to also consider other planets, because, in November 1999, the PRC launched its first unmanned spacecraft, the *Shenzhou* (Divine Ship), from the Gobi Desert of Gansu Province. In October 2003, Yang Liwei became the first Chinese citizen to go to outer-space. The PRC is also planning to set up something similar to the International Space Station (ISS). At time/space sequence (n) in the framework of CHINA Versus china, all the Chinese people in this world and on other outer-space bodies would be politically tied to each other, upholding the *CHINA* qualities. If the Chinese cannot do it in 1,000 years, they can reach the *CHINA* goal 10,000 years from now. In any case, that is the Chinese ideal.

"china" is quite similar to what David L. Shambaugh has posited: an isolationist hegemon.[39] It basically has feudalistic characteristics.[40] European intellectuals would consider china as despotic, feudal, and stagnant.[41] It is insular, self-absorbed, and prides what it has only for itself; china could also be internally aggressive, brutal, merciless, bloody, self-deceiving, lacking respect for human rights, etc. In a famous essay written in the early 1700s, Fang Bao divided Chinese history into two periods—the 2,000 years before the Warring States and the unification of the empire, and the 2,000 years after the Warring States. He at the same time warned that the more recent two millennia had seen far more slaughters and endless military turmoil than at any period prior to this.[42] Michael D. Swaine and Ashley J. Tellis compiled from two other academics regarding campaigns taken by various dynasties from the Qing onwards[43] While it is not clear what is meant by the term campaign as it could be in the form of a punitive action, military action, battle, war, and so on, they all occurred within mainland China and its neighbours. Campaign in Chinese could also just be *yundong* (a political movement or drive) without bloodshed. From 1902 to 1911, there were more than 1,300 rebellions by the ordinary people in mainland China, on average once in every 2.5 days.[44] On record, the KMT killed many CPC members. The April 1927 massacre of CPC members is one of the pertinent examples. The CPC also killed many (reactionary or anti-revolutionary) people after seizing state power, in the name of revolution.[45] There was also the Nanjing massacre by Imperial Japan from December 13, 1937 which lasted for more than a month, as documented, for example, in the German Federal Archives, which were publicized in the February 1991 issue of *Outlook*, a Chinese weekly magazine.[46]

"china" also reflects weaknesses, and portrayed as it is by European America's media and theatrical performances.[47] For example, the Portuguese first sailed to Guangdong Province with Christian missionaries in between summer 1513 and early 1514.[48] In the Fall of 1517, eight armed Portuguese ships entered into Zhujiangkou's Tumen Island and fired canons. In 1601, the first Dutch ship went to Guangzhou. The first British ship hired by the Portuguese went to *Zhongguo* in 1635. Two years later, four British naval vessels sailed to Zhuhai and bombarded the Human fort. From 1840 to 1945, foreign imperial powers, namely, the United Kingdom, Russia, Japan, Germany, France, the United States,[49] Italy, and Austria-Hungary had invaded *Zhongguo* and later the dialectical China 84 times, involving more than 1,860 ships and 470,000 troops. According to Hu Sheng, the Qing Dynasty, for example, after the Opium War, which lasted from April 1840 to August 1842, resembled a giant at its last gasp.[50] During the War of Resistance against the Japanese Aggression in 1937–1945, 30 to 35 million Chinese people were reported to have lost their lives.

"china" is also associated with many unequal treaties, secret agreements, and foreign debts. We can provide some evidence. The very first unequal treaty was the *Nanjing Treaty* of July 24, 1842 between the British Empire and the Qing Dynasty.[51] Public Concession (*gonggong zujie*), meaning International Concession/International Settlement (*guojide zujie*), in Shanghai developed first in 1843. It was like a state within a state (*guozhongzhiguo*), because the legislative body, police, jails, as well as city administration, and tax administration were all under foreign hands. Chinese army and policemen cannot enter into this state within the state.[52] In addition, the coastal areas, such as important ports in Changjiang and Zhujiang as well as customs area were under the control of foreign powers. In 1844, the British Royal Navy's China Station was established. In March 1896, Li Hongzhang signed a secret agreement with Russia's Czar, allowing, *inter alia*, Russia to build a railroad from Heilongjiang Province to Haishenwei via Jilin. In exchange, he received a bribe of 500,000 taels of silver (*yinzi*).[53] History should be of some guide to our knowledge. Between 1839 and 1900, *Zhongguo* under the Qing Dynasty had to pay indemnities to foreign powers in the wars that it lost. After the Opium War, Great Britain exacted 21 million taels from it. After the Sino-Japanese War of 1894–1895, Imperial Japan ultimately received an indemnity of 230 million taels, and the Qing Dynasty had to borrow money from other foreign businessmen.[54] And, then, only five years later, after the Boxer Rebellion fiasco, the eight allied foreign powers received a financial settlement of 450 million taels. And, at the time of the Xinhai Revolution of October 1911, China's foreign debt amounted to a staggering 900 million taels.[55]

It is also perceived that after becoming a member economy of the WTO, many mainland China state-owned enterprises (SOEs) would close their doors and the mainland would be peopled by the unemployed and flooded with foreign goods and services. Some people are also worried that someday India may replace the mainland as an economic powerhouse.

Some Chinese people also seek independence or try to break away from the China proper. The British considered instigating Zhang Zhidong to make Hunan and Hubei Provinces independent and also instigated Li Hongzhang to make Guangdong and Guangxi Provinces independent as well.[56] There were other officials who had sought to use the barbarians to check the barbarians, thinking that, by so doing to create benefit for *Zhongguo*.

In the "middle" of CHINA and china is China or Number 5. It is a modern and contemporary term, closely associated with Western concepts like sovereignty, jurisdiction, and so on. China is different from the dialectical China, which should be understood in terms of a spectrum in that the former is a part of the whole process, whereas the latter reflects the whole process. To paraphrase Wang Gungwu, China is considered a hybrid, a strange creature, combining CHINA and china. This means only parts of it are dressed in modern, Western, and contemporary clothes.[57] Chinese officials only have the concept of *Tianxia* (Mandate of the Heaven or universal empire in Prasenjit Duara's translation), which is not exactly a state, because *Zhongguo* does not have a boundary (*jiangyu* or *bianjie*) (which is not the exact translation for *guanwai*). For this reason, international law was almost foreign to *Zhongguo* until the mid-19th century. Lin Zexu, prior to the Opium War, translated a book on international law. The only boundary, as pointed out by Wang, was the ocean.[58] *Zhongguo* has a geographical boundary, and it has to emphasize it, due to the existence of sovereignty, which is imposed by the West. For example, in March 2001, the State Oceanic Administration (SOA) reminded all the map-makers about the June 1998 notice, which said they should include the four archipelagos plus the U-shaped line in the South China Sea (SCS) in the Chinese maps.[59]

To be sure, Beijing feels quite uncomfortable about those foreign concepts, which are imposed upon this China. Yet, to live on, it has to adjust itself to embrace those concepts for a period of time, however long. After taking over Beijing in January 1949, the Chinese People's Liberation Army (PLA) deliberately walked through *Dongjiaomin* lane, which was an extraterritorial symbol of Western imperialism. When China moved on to become CHINA, there would be less emphasis on those Western terms, because international law would not be emphasized as much.

CHINA is cultural, a civilization-state (as opposed to nation-state). It symbolizes rejuvenation built on its historic past and historical roots. Anything appearing before the emergence of CHINA could be the past and historical. CHINA is possible, as British historian Arnold J. Toynbee predicted that 21st century is the Chinese century.[60] It is possible that the process may take longer. To repeat, CHINA has no geographic boundary. At least, it does not really emphasize it. Even if CHINA still has an astonishingly long land border—more than 22,000 kilometers — and a coastline which stretches over 18,000 kilometers in all, it prefers not to think about or to stress it, unless other foreign powers invade and rule it. CHINA, couched from the initial stage to mature stage, still has a long way to go before becoming **CHINA**, which would theoretically appear at the time/space sequence (n) or the mature stage of CHINA. Alexander Woodside, an expert on Chinese emperorship, pointed out that no one in *Zhongguo* could have imagined a "state" as being more than an extension of the personal authority at the "forbidden center" of the empire.[61]

When dialectical China has reached the initial stage of CHINA, CHINA would be an extension of all the Chinese people at the center of human beings. It would be free of foreign exploitation as well as imperialistic, expansionist, and hegemonic pressures. It would not suffer from an arrangement like the Versailles Treaty of April 30, 1919. Of course, CHINA could still have alien modes of thought and styles of life, just as the Chinese had absorbed Buddhism and later transformed it into a Chinese-version of Buddhism. But, it is the dialectical Chineseness that prevails or outshines other foreign things. Here, Zhang Zhidong's "Chinese learning as the basic structure, Western learning for use (which is a repository of skills and techniques which China could select and adapt those most useful for it)" should ring a bell.

CHINA is certainly tied to globalization, that is, the spread of positive Chinese values. Both are ideals, and both of them are possible, given time. Under CHINA, many enduring Chinese values would be globalized, such as Chinese philosophy, Chinese language and writing,[62] Chinese cuisine,[63] Shaolin martial art, etc. In the West, there is one product, Coca Cola, the Chinese ideographs of which could be literally translated as "Right for Your Mouth, Right for Your Happiness," and it has already been successfully globalized and drank by almost everyone on Earth, if not on other outer space bodies.

CHINA is also associated with Dr. Sun Yat-sen's notion of *shijiedatong* (Universal Harmony in the World).[64] Actually, there is not much difference between *shijiedatong* and Communism or Utopia. The reason for writing in a different way is mainly due to ideology. If one were a member of the KMT, one would say *shijiedatong*. If one believes in Marxism, then he or she would prefer to use the word Communism or Utopia. And, to a capitalist, globalization is properly the right concept.

There are many other ways of saying the same thing about CHINA Versus china, depending on the situation. Thus, the following frameworks should be of interest to readers:

The Kingly Way of the Sage King (*Wangdao*) Versus
The Way of the Feudal Lord (who is associated with military conquest and hegemony) (*Baodao*);

Peace and Development (or Peaceful Development) Versus
Non-Peace-and Development (or Non-Peaceful Development)

Peaceful Ascendancy/Rise Versus Non-peaceful Ascendancy/Rise;

Non-China Threat Versus China Threat;

Good Versus Bad;[65]

Wealthy and Powerful (*fuqiang*) Versus Not Wealthy and Powerful;

"*CHINA* Has Stood Up" Versus "CHINA, China, or china Has Not Stood Up;"[66]

"*Yitiaolong* (A Dragon)" Versus "*Yitiaochong* (An Insect);"[67]

"Global" Versus "Local"/United the Whole World in Confucian Harmony Versus Closing the Door and be the Emperor (*guanqimenlaizuohuangdi*);

Praise (*bao*) Versus Blame (*bian*), etc.

Some non-Chinese academics are also aware of these kind of parallel arrangements prevalent in Chinese thinking. James R. Townsend, for example, wrote: "Historically, Chinese saw the possession or non-possession of Chinese culture as the mark of civilization or barbarism...."[68] In other words, possession is related to civilization, whereas non-possession, barbarism. Applying this author's framework, Possession Versus Non-possession can be set up. In this connection, another framework would be Civilization Versus Barbarism. It is difficult to quantify all of the frameworks. But, a few words can be said about some of the important, parallel frameworks.

Wealth and power, in the framework of Wealth and Power Versus Non-Wealth and Power, are the national goals put forward by Chinese (Communist) political figures. They are considered good. They should be placed at the left extreme. It takes time for china and China to reach that stage. Even if the CHINA stage were reached at stage at time/space sequence (1), it would still have a long way to go before time/space sequence (n). At time/space sequence (n), CHINA becomes **CHINA**. Needless to say, should decay set in, **CHINA** may revert back to CHINA, China, and even china. This framework is another way of saying the "**CHINA** Has Stood Up" Versus "CHINA, China, or china Has Not (Yet) Stood Up" framework. Only at time/space sequence (n), can **CHINA** appear, meaning that mainland China, Taiwan, Hongkong, and Macao as well as **CHINESE** entities elsewhere such as those on the Moon or Mars have finally stood up. It is another way of saying that it would have achieved the status of being a real Dragon in the A Dragon Versus An Insect framework. So, it was accurate for Goldman and Nathan to equate what Mao said on October 1, 1949 at the Tiananmen (Gate of Heavenly Peace) in Beijing as a "bold promise."[69] That is to say, when Mao was making that remark, he and some Chinese jumped to the ideal **CHINA** at that specific time/space sequence. But, seconds later, he went back to China by being more pragmatic, realizing that there is a lot of work to do, for example, getting recognized by other countries in the world. Besides, the Chinese situation differs from situations in other countries. Needless to say, **CHINA** may not come to pass, because, in February 2000, it was reported that Earth will encounter a catastrophe in 500 million years' time, and CHINA could be destroyed by comet, asteroid, etc. or submerged under the sea. Hence, the sub-title of Part II ends with a question mark.

It should be clear by now that China is simply a mixture of Good and Bad. CHINA reflects wealth and power. Therefore, it is good to be CHINA. Naturally, it is difficult to be perfect before time/space sequence (n).

It is necessary to go back to *Zhongguo* history, for there is continuity and change in CHINA, China, and china.[70] This is because some of the past glorious records will provide additional confidence to the Chinese people which they can further apply to the days when **CHINA** arrives, in the same way that they apply the thoughts of Confucius and Mencius, because their core values are timeless and beyond the constraint of space. For this reason, in summer 1996, Jiang instructed cadres to study *Zhongguo*'s place in modern and contemporary *Zhongguo* history and world history, in addition to the CPC history.[71] Perhaps he had in mind what Samuel P. Huntington, in an interview with a Japanese newspaper, had observed about the 21st century being that of the Chinese era.[72]

There are strong reasons arguing that **CHINA** will not be aggressive, imperialistic, expansionist, etc. First, **CHINA** would be cultural at the mature stage, possessing plenty of tangible and intangible resources. There is a political force, which hold Chinese people together at home and abroad. It is not what Dr. Sun Yat-sen had described the Chinese people as a tray of loose sand or what Francis L. K. Hsu had said, that is, the Chinese people "are like a heap of yellow clay which adhere to each other too well in small clumps but fail to unite in bigger and more powerful clusters."[73] The Chinese did not have a firm concept of state or in Prasenjit Duara's translation fatherland (*guo*) until the May 4, 1919 movement.[74] Kung-chuan Hsiao wrote the following words: *Zhongguo* "had no knowledge of international law and international relations, in their strictly modern sense, until the latter part of the nineteenth century." Furthermore, its Confucian and Mohist sages discovered the great truth that it does not pay and it is never right to wage an aggressive war against any state. Hsiao continued by saying, "[a] virtuous king could rectify the mind and win the hearts of the people entirely through the influences of education or his own exemplary conduct." "So great was the moral force thus exerted that even persons living in the remotest regions would willingly place themselves under his rule."[75] In a word, the framework of The Kingly Way of the Sage King Versus The Way of the Feudal Lord captures the essence of Confucian thought. The former concretely embodies the principle of human-heartedness, and the latter, a government by means of force and in the interest of the ruler. For centuries, soldiers have been considered the lowest rung of Chinese society, so goes the saying good men do not become soldiers.[76] Imperial Japan's invasion of China further woke up many Chinese intellectuals. It was not until October 1949 that Beijing began to thoroughly indoctrinate the Chinese people regarding nationalism/patriotism.

Second, since ancient *Zhongguo*, the Chinese, on the whole, have not engaged in foreign adventures in taking land that is far away.[77] During the PRC era, the position of Beijing had always been: "We will not attack unless we are attacked—if we were attacked, we will certainly counterattack." Wang Gungwu pointed out that *Zhongguo* does not have a history of being an expansionist power.[78] Chinese emperors think continentally, trying to hold on to *Zhongyuan* (the Central Plains of *Zhongguo*). So, they are more idealistic. The ordinary people think about the Changjiang (Chang River), the Great Wall of China (*Changcheng*), Huangshan (Huang Mountain), and Huanghe (Huang River).[79] The emperors prefer setting up tributary systems in which the relationships were "largely unsystematic and unenforceable"[80] and engage in tribute trade (*chaogong maoyi*). Ensure all nations live together peacefully (*Xiehewanbang*) is the leading principle, with universal or great harmony under heaven (*Tianxiadatong*) as the ideal goal.[81] Traditionally, Chinese emperors and heroes since Sui Dynasty (A.D. 581–618) and Tang Dynasty were only interested in taking Central Plains of *Zhongguo* or *Zhongyuan*. He who takes the *Zhongyuan* gets the *Tianxia*. Civil war between the KMT and the CPC also began in the central plains in June 1946.[82] This simply means that the majority of Chinese people is only good at infighting.[83] To this day, this argument still applies in the context of mainland China, Taiwan, Hong Kong, and Macao, although Lee Tenghui in January 1995 put forward a new slogan saying Taiwan is the neo-*Zhongyuan* (as opposed to the old *Zhongyuan*) or, as some mainland China academics labelled Sichuan Province as "a neo-*Zhongyuan*-area" since its valley/(river) basin and its eastern part are located in central China, and not the Central Plains, which are very different from southern and western Sichuan.[84] It is due to infighting, according to the observation of Wang Zuorong, that a dynasty waxes and wanes.[85] In this connection, Confucian teachings taught that it is a shame if one were to migrate to a foreign land, because such an act meant a lack of respect and betrayal of one's ancestors. Wang Gungwu also pointed out another reason, that is, a Chinese would be considered a criminal for if he left *Zhongguo* without official permission.[86]

Third, in January 2000, *Xinhuashe* (the New China News Agency) reported that the first Chinese map of the world (*Wanguo Dadi Quantu*) was recently discovered at Shijiazhuang City, Hebei Province.[87] The date of the map was October 1845.[88] Before that there were only two foreign world maps, depicting *Zhongguo*. The first one was by an Italian preacher, who drew up the map in 1584. He wanted to please the Ming Dynasty (A.D. 1368–1644), which regarded itself as the center and, therefore, the Italian put *Zhongguo* in the middle of the map. Over the last 400 and more years, *Zhongguo* has been put in the middle of a Chinese map.[89]

And the other map was made by a Belgian in 1674. From this, it is possible to infer that Chinese were like Admiral Zheng He had no plans to take foreign lands. Otherwise, they would have drawn maps to facilitate their imperialist and expansionist voyage at sea or on land by way of taking the Silk Road.

Fourth, *Zhongguo* invented four things, among them, gunpowder and compass. As early as the 9th century in the late Tang Dynasty, gunpowder had been invented not by people seeking better weapons in warfare but by alchemists seeking the elixir of immortality. Gunpowder was invented around third century B.C. Around 1040, the true gunpowder formula was first published, and in the second half of the 10th Century, it was applied to military purpose. Only in the second half of the 13th century, did gunpowder pass on to Europe. And the "Arabs learned of saltpetre (potassium nitrite) around the end of the thirteenth century when they were introduced to it as 'Chinese snow' and began to use rockets which they called 'Chinese arrows.'"[90] Later in 1580, General Qi Jiguang of the Ming Dyansty invented land mines. His achievement was 300 years earlier than the Europeans'.[91]

From the first century to the 15th century, *Zhongguo*'s scientific achievements, overall speaking, were ahead of the West's.[92] Out of about 300 scientific achievements, the Chinese had more than 170 of them.[93] In the period from the Qin Dynasty (221–206 B.C.) to the Northern and Southern Dynasties (A.D. 420–550), *Zhongguo* had developed relatively complete systems of mathematics, astronomy, medical science, agriculture, metallurgy, textile, chemistry, architecture, and communications. Scientific and cultural exchanges through the Silk Road in succeeding Tang and Song Dynasties further helped *Zhongguo* to flourish.[94] The Chinese were already solving cubic equations in the 13th century, which the Western counterpart was not able to until the 19th century.[95] In terms of military technology, *Zhongguo* was still leading in the early 15th century. However, *Zhongguo* did not take foreign lands far away, unlike the Europeans.

Fifth, in November 2002 and September 2003, it was reported that Chinese archaeologists had unearthed a most ancient 5.6-meter long, wooden boat dating back at least 7,600 or 7,700 years in Xiaoshan City's Kuahuqiao (bridge) of Zhejiang Province.[96] Zheng He's voyages from July 1405 to March 1433 to other countries further testified to *Zhongguo*'s non-aggressive stance. He sailed in ships with multi-masts. On the last voyage, these ships bore names such as "Pure Harmony,"

"Lasting Tranquility," and "Kind Repose," reflecting the continued mission for keeping peace. And, three days after Zheng's last voyage, the Ming Dynasty dropped the scheme of utilizing the ocean from a strategic point of view (*jinglue haiyang*) and prohibited civilians from going out to sea to trade with foreigners. Louise Levathes' book has a picture showing how big Zheng's treasure ship (*baochuan*) was (300 feet and even 400 feet long) as compared to Columbus' St. Maria (85 feet) or Vasco da Gama's 85 to 100-foot vessels.[97] Zheng encountered pirates in the Straits of Malacca, for example. They had to engage in battles. The book mentioned that Zheng's warships "had an array of many so-called fire weapons. By the mid-16th century military treatises were describing two to three hundred incendiary weapons. *Fei tian pen tong* (sky-flying tubes) sent a spray of gunpowder and flaming bits of paper to set fire to the enemy's sails, while *huo yao tong* (gunpowder buckets) and *huo zhuan* (fire bricks) were compact gunpowder-and-paper grenades soaked in poison. Half of the men on later Ming warships were specialists in deploying such explosives…."[98] In the years immediately following the seventh expedition of the treasure fleet of the dragon throne, "Chinese sea power seemed as secure as ever," "a dozen countries came to pay tribute to the emperor," and plans for the treasure ships existed until the 1477.[99] In a word, Zheng could have conquered many foreign lands, from Taiwan to the Persian Gulf and distant Africa, *Zhongguo*'s El Dorado, if he had had such an ambition, as observed by Levathes, *Zhongguo* "could have become the great colonial power, a hundred years before the great age of European exploration and expansion." Indeed, in March 2002, Gavin Menzies, a former British submarine commanding officer and an amateur historian, revealed what he found.[100] That is to say, according to Menzies, Zheng was the first person to have circumnavigated the world in March 1421, beating the Portuguese navigator Ferdinand Magellan by about a century, and America, ahead of Columbus by 70 years. However, instead the Ming Dynasty closed its door to international intercourse (*biguanzishou*), "resulting in the rapid demise of its navy and the loss of its technological and scientific edge over Europe."[101] The main reason was to ward off foreign military and economic invasion and to maintain Chinese sovereignty.[102] In 1685, the Qing Dynasty lifted its sea prohibition. It opened Guangzhou, Zhangzhou, Ningbo, and Yuntaishan (which is nearby Liangyungang today).[103] In 1759, it closed the latter three ports.

A. T. Mahan's work on sea power appeared in May 1888. The Qing Dyansty before 1865 did not have a steam navy.[104] In June 1866, the first shipyard was created at Fuzhou City, Fujian Province.[105] In August 1881, two naval ships of the Qing Dynasty for the first time sailed overseas. In October 1888, *Zhongguo*'s first new navy—Northern Navy (Beiyanghaijun)—was legalized, meaning that it was in existence before that time. In the year 1891, it was ranked top 10 in the world, according to a Western naval yearbook.[106] In the 1860s, except for opium, none of the foreign powers could sell a lot of their products.[107] In other words, *Zhongguo* enjoyed a surplus in its foreign exchange. From the 1870s up to the Sino-Japanese War, foreign powers could only increase a little over 33 per cent. In the year 1872, there were 343 foreign enterprises and the total number of their people was 3,673. In the year 1892, there were 579 foreign enterprises. The total number of foreigners living in *Zhongguo* was 9,945.

Jumping to January 2000, the then Deputy Chairman of the Central Military Commission (CMC) of the CPC, Chi Haotian, reiterated that the Chinese PLA would not be deployed outside of the PRC nor set up military bases abroad.[108] In May 2002, a fleet of two Chinese PLA ships began its four-month cruise around the world's three oceans (*huanqiu*) for the first time, and the first country among the 10 that it visited was Singapore. The ships also sailed to the United States and Russia and through the Panama and Suez canals. Yet, we did not see any military conflicts between them and other countries.

In 111 B.C., Annam (Pacified South, a name resented by the local people), comprising most of central Vietnam, was "invaded" by the Chinese. In 1407/1408, the Ming Dynasty reoccupied Annam, until the conquest by the French in the 19th century. The reason is that it was unruly and unfriendly.[109] Because the Chinese carried out such an "invasion," we can position that dynasty at that particular time/space sequence at china. However, it should be noted that in the primary and secondary schools of Vietnam, there is a lesson, saying the Vietnamese should take back Fujian, Guangdong, and Guangxi Provinces of China.[110] What this means is that the ancestors of the Vietnamese people once lived in mainland China. So, can we use the term the *Zhongguo* invasion? It is highly questionable. In any case, viewed at the macro-level, dialectical China has both a positive and a negative record. But, on the whole, it is more accurate to say that the Chinese dynasties were more preoccupied with keeping the throne in the Central Plains than eyeing foreign land.

In sum, ***CHINA*** and CHINA is different from, for example, China and china. One should not mix them up, because each possesses different connotations, implications, and so on. However, there is no guarantee that **CHINA** would appear, even one billion years from now, because, as mentioned earlier, an asteroid, for example, may hit CHINA, generating *tsunami*, or ocean waves caused by seismic activity and eventually destroy CHINA.[111] In February 2004, it was predicted that, should nothing be done to stop pumping subterranean or ground water, the entire Shanghai Municipal City could be submerged under water 600 years from now, thereby becoming *xiahai* (literally below the sea, which is just the opposite of *shanghai*).[112] In May 2004, according to a study by the Chinese Academy of Sciences (CAS), by 2050, as a result of global warming, the shrinking of the Yulong Snow Mountain glacier (*bingchuan*) in southwestern Yunnan Province may put at least 300 million Chinese people at risk.[113]

ENDNOTES

1   *Taiwan Hsin Wen Daily News* (hereinafter THWDN)(Kaohsiung, Taiwan), October 2, 1993, p. 1.

2   The word pole can also be used. Applying quantum physics, any person in outer space can view Earth and every imaginable phenomenon that comes with it as a dot/point. B. J. Habibie became the Indonesian President in May 1998. Thereafter, he referred to Singapore as a tiny red dot. Singapore's Prime Minister Goh Chok Tong in March 2001 said the tiny red dot will get tinier in terms of its population as compared to its bigger neighbours. See *ST*, March 28, 2001, p. 4. In April 2001, Singapore's Trade and Industry Minister George Yeo urged the Singaporeans to think "Big Singapore," not small Singapore. He continued by saying, if managed well, Singapore can be larger than what it is geographically and in terms of population. The mindset must be changed. See *ST*, April 30, 2001, p. 3.

3   Gordon Hyden mentioned "… the imperialist aspirations of rational choice." See his article, "Africanists' Contributions to Political Science," *PS: Political Science and Politics* (hereinafter PS), Vol. XXXIV, No. 4 (December 2001), p. 797.

4   See *CT*, January 1, 2001, p. 2 and *UDN*, January 9, 2001, p. 2. The English translation for *wuyan* should be eaves. But, the word roof or housetop (*wuding*) was used. See *Taiwan News* (hereinafter TN)(Taipei), January 1, 2001, p. 1. Some Democratic Progressive Party (DPP) members understand dialectics. See, for example, *UDN*, October 22, 1997, p. 2. Yang Jiemian, a mainland China academic, said the Chinese people usually think about principle first to be followed by *juti* (concrete/specific). See his book, *Houlengzhanshiqidezhongmeiguanxi: Waijiaozhengcebijiaoyanjiu* (Sino-American Relations in the Post-Cold War: A Comparative Study of Foreign Policy)(Shanghai: Shanghairenminchubanshe, November 2000), pp. 254–255. Beijing's "One China" principle is the Roof/Housetop. According to Zhou Mingwei in January 2002, it is "the most typical and pragmatic Chinese wisdom." One Middle East academic said dialectic materialism

presents the best method for studying the Arab politics. Cited in Nasr M. Arif, *Western Political Science in a Non-Western Context* (Lanham, MD: University Press of America, 2001), p. 30.

5   *UDN*, March 23, 1998, p. 2 and August 28, 2000, p. 2, http://www.chineseworld.com...oday/11_0900.4wtp(010327)02_tb.htm (accessed March 27, 2001), and the June 1, 2002 issue of *UDN* and *China Times* (hereinafter CT)(Taipei).

6   *UDN*, July 4, 2001. p. 4. According to HU Zhongxin, Chen Shui-bian's version of dialectics is "conflict, compromise, and progress." See his *LHZB* article published on August 22, 2003. In October 2003, Lien in the United States again mentioned it but reversed the order by first mentioning the One China as referring to the ROC. See *CT*, October 22, 2003, p. A4.

7   In July 1957, Mao said the American imperialism is, from the strategic perspective, a paper tiger. But, tactically, we must respect it.

8   Mao mentioned this in January 1958.

9   The first "Strike Hard/Severe Strike" crime sweep campaign was carried out in August 1983 and ended in January 1987. The second was launched in April 1996 and the third one, April 2001. In February 2004, the CPC started anti-corruption campaign against the *zhidu* (system) as opposed to *quanli* (power) in the past. In July 1979, Criminal Law and Criminal Procedure Law were adopted by the 5th National People's Congress.

10   Jiang Cunqi, "Zhonggong Wenwu Guanxi Di Bianzheng Jiangou (Civil-Military Relationship in Chinese Communists' Dialectical Construction)," *Cross-Strait Interflow Prospect Foundation Paper No.5* (hereinafter CSIPFP)(Taipei), May 1998, 32 pp.

11   In January 1958, Zhou was empowered by the CPC to manage Changjiang (Chang River). In late February and early March of that year, he brought along experts and others to Changjiang, including the Three Gorges site. He encouraged them to speak up and to defend their views. At the end, he particularly reminded the people concerned to take care of the following seven dialectical relationships: long-range perspective/the future and short term/the immediate future; the trunk stream/mainstream and tributary/affluent; upper, middle, and lower reaches; large-sized or large-typed, middle-sized or middle-typed, and small-sized or small-typed (or *da, zhong, xiao xing*); anti-flooding, electrical power generating, as well as irrigation and navigation; hydroelectric power and thermal power; and electrical power generating and electrical power consuming. See Long Pingping and Zhang Ning, editors, *Mao Zedong, Zhou Enlai, et. al.: The Gist of Their Philosophical Thought* (Beijing: Gaodengjiaoyuchubanshe, January 1990), pp. 82–83. In December 2001, mainland Chinese scientists using scientific instruments found out that Changjiang only has 6,211.3 kilometers, not 6,300 as commonly known. Nevertheless, the river is still the third longest in the world. If we were to talk about the railroad, *chang* (long), *da* (big), and *zong* (weight) are the dialectical concepts to consider. As to the World Trade Organization, *li* (advantages) and *bi* (disadvantages) form a framework.

12   According to *Beijing Ribao*, he said he is a Communist. He attempted twice to join the party. See http://lw9fd.law9.hotmail.msn.com.com/cgi-bin/getmsg?msg=MSG1073109436.17&mfs=&+HMaction=... (accessed January 2004).

13   *UDN*, September 30, 1996, p. 9.

14   One DPP legislator, Shen Fuxiong, applies dialectics. See *CT*, July 4, 2001, p. 15. Lee Teng-hui, when he was young, read books applying dialectics. See http://www.chineseworld.com/publish/today/11_0900.4w/t/4wtp(021108)_tb.htm (accessed November 8, 2002).

15   Jueyuan Wang, *Dialectics and its Application*, reprinted edition (Taipei: Pamir Shudian, December 1963), p. 3. See also the chapter on Sun in Zuohua Yang and Feng Zhang, eds., *Bianzhengfashilungao* (History and Exposition of Dialectics)(Yujiashan, Wuchang: Huazhongligongdaxuechubanshe, February 1993).

16   *Ibid.*, p. 1. See also Yushan Zhou, "Study and Assessment by Mr. Jiang Zhongzheng on Materialistic Dialectics," *Studies in Communism* (hereinafter SIC)(Taipei), Vol. 9, No. 6 (June 15, 1983), pp. 39–42.

17   See my books, *Bicoastal China: A Dialectical, Paradigmatic Analysis* (New York: Nova Science Publishers, 1999) and *The Crab and Frog Motion Paradigm Shift: Decoding and Deciphering Taipei and Beijing's Dialectical Politics* (Lanham, MD: University Press of America, 2002). To Chris M. Sciabarra, dialectics is "the art of context keeping" or what I called the art of anticipating the opposite development and he defined it as a value-free and purely "methodological orientation." See his book, *Total Freedom: Toward a Dialectical Libertarianism* (University Park, PA: Pennsylvania State University Press, 2000). See also Douglas Walton, *One-sided Arguments: A Dialectical Analysis* (New York: State University of New York Press, 1999).

18   If we look at Earth from outer space, it is possible to see what is going on since the beginning of human beings as one dot. This is quantum physics.

19   In September 1994, I constructed my version of dialectical model. In October 2003, I realized that Chinese Communists like to mention three things at a time. For this reason, it is easier to slot in data if I were to use only five numbers and five letters. In June 2004, I read an article exactly saying the same thing. See Li Yong Yan, "China, as easy as one two *three*," *Asia Times* (Hongkong), http://www.atimes.com/atimes/china/ff12ad03.html (accessed June 12, 2004). Another finding is that, in between two dialectical frameworks, it is always possible to set up another framework to connect their logic.

20   See *Zhongguo mianxiang ershiyi shiji de ruokan zhanlue wenti* (China Facing the 21st Century: Some Strategic Problems)(Beijing: Zhonggong Zhognyang Dangxiao Chubanshe, May 2000), p. 9.

21   Many academics are unaware what they are doing is typically Chinese. See, for example, Steven F. Jackson, "Introduction: A Typology for Stability and Instability in China" in David L. Shambaugh, ed., *Is China Unstable?* (New York: M.E. Sharpe, 2000), Chapter 1. Jackson's "Stability Typology" comes in terms of a spectrum: Hyper-stability—Stability—Instability.

22   In religion, they could be called *fenshen* (spare time to attend to something else or disengage oneself to [inf]), and Number 1 would be *benzun* (the revered or esteemed). The same thing speaks for A, B, C, D, and E which are *fenshen*, and F is *benzun*. One good example is as follows: Dr. Sun Yat-sen is 1, whereas Wang Bingzhang could be 2, 3, 4, or 5 because a reporter said many people adore Dr. Wang and referred to Wang as "Contemporary Sun Yat-sen." Wang in November 1982 published the inaugural issue of *China Spring*. See *China Times* (hereinafter CT), March 28, 1998, p. 9.

23   In March 1996, at the closing ceremony of the annual session of the National People's Congress, Qiao Shi formally proposed to "rule the country in accordance with law, and build a legally institutionalized socialist country."

24   This concept was first conceived in September 1994 when I built a dialectical framework of thought and action. None of the Chinese Communists have put forward this concept. But, Deng Xiaoping said something which is very close to this concept. See *Zhonggongshiwudawenjianxuexijianghua* (Learning the Documents from the 15th National Congress of the CPC)(Beijing: Zhonggongdangshi-chubanshe, September 1997), pp. 116–117.

25   Kung-chuang Hsiao, "The Chinese Philosophy of War: The Traditionalists' Arguments" in Joel Larus, ed., *Comparative World Politics* (Belmont, CA.: Wadsworth Publishing Co., 1964), p. 153 and p. 158. *Pax Sinica* is unlike *Pax Romana* which had its foundation in military power.

26   See one of the chapters in my edited book, *The Chinese PLA's Perception of an Invasion of Taiwan* (New York: Contemporary U.S.-Asia Research Institute, 1996) and *Newsweek: The International News Magazine*, February 18, 2002, p. 13. But, some academics and experts argued that the French leader did not make such a remark, because the French already had the following expression: *n'éveillez pas le lion qui dort*. See http://www.zaobao.cm/y/yl502-240504.html (accessed May 24, 2004).

27   Shee Poon Kim, "Is China a Threat to the Asia-Pacific Region?" in Wang Gungwu and John Wong, eds., *China's Political Economy* (Singapore: Singapore University Press and World Scientific, 1998), p. 356. Gregory Clark, a former Australian diplomat and author of *The Fear of China* (Melbourne: Lansdowne Publishing, 1967), asked the question: China a Threat? See his article in *ST* (Singapore), April 2, 1999, p. 68. See also his article, "Stop Demonising China," *ibid.*, June 25, 1998, p. 36.

28   There are five traditional, fundamental human relationships: those between husband and wife, father and son, older and younger brother, friend and friend, as well as sovereign and minister (or subject). To Li Guoding of Taiwan, he added the sixth relationship, namely, the group and oneself. David L. Shambaugh also posited the hierarchical hegemon. See his article, "Chinese Hegemony Over East Asia by 2015?" *Korean Journal of Defense Analysis* (hereinafter KJDA)(R.O.K.), Vol. IX, No. 1 (Summer 1997), pp. 17–20. To Harlan Jencks, in the context of *Zhongguo*, "'Hegemony' is understood as the ability to act in East Asia without constraint." See his article, "China's Defense Buildup: A Threat to the Region?" paper presented at the Fourth International Conference on CPLA Affairs, as

sponsored by the Chinese Council for Advanced Policy Studies (CAPS), June 26–28, 1992, p. 4.

29   Lillian Craig Harris, *China Considers the Middle East* (London: I. B. Tauris & Co. Ltd., 1993), p. 17.

30   David B. Chan, "The China Syndrome," in Jonathan Goldstein, Jerry Israel, and Hilary Conroy, eds., *America Views China* (Bethlehem, PA.: Lehigh University Press, 1991), p. 185 and *China: U.S. Policy Since 1945* (hereinafter China)(Washington, D.C.: Congressional Quarterly, 1980), p. 76.

31   *Ibid.*

32   See, for example, Wang Gungwu, *China and the Chinese Overseas* (Singapore: Times Academic Press, 1991), Francis L. K. Hsu and Hendrick Serrie, *The Overseas Chinese: Ethnicity in National* Context (Lanham, MD.: University Press of America, 1998), Chen Bisheng, *Shijiehuaqiaorenjianshi* (Xiamen, Fujian: Xiamendaxuechubanshe, August 1991), and Ignatius Wibowo, "Exit, Voice, and Loyalty: Indonesian Chinese After the Fall of Soeharto," *Sojourn: Journal of Social Issues in Southeast Asia* (hereinafter Sojourn)(Singapore), Vol. 16, No. 1 (April 2001), pp. 125–146. In April 1955, the following document was signed: *Treaty Between the PRC and the Republic of Indonesia Concerning the Question of Dual Nationality* and it entered into force in January 1960. In October 1965, the Indonesian Government prosecuted overseas Chinese in that country. From October 10 to November 28, 1965, the PRC dispatched a vessel to take back more than 2,000 overseas Chinese in Indonesia. In April 1969, Jarkata unilaterally abrogated this treaty. See Liu Lufeng *et. al.*, eds., *Zhonghuarenmingongheguo-yaoshilu* (Important Events of the People's Republic of China)(Shandong: Shandongrenminchubanshe, August 1989), p. 344. In May 1999, Indonesian President B. J. Habibie issued a presidential instruction allowing the teaching of Chinese. After liberating the south, the Socialist Republic of Vietnam (SRV) prosecuted overseas Chinese in Vietnam. The Committee Against Genocide by Vietnam (CAGV) was set up at 44 East Broadway, New York City, N.Y. 10002, U.S. See its advertisement in *Xingdaoribao* (hereinafter XDRB)(New York), July 11, 1979, p. 12 and the *New York Times* (hereinafter NYT), July 13, 1979, p. A7. The American Refugee Committee also advertised in the *NYK*, February 18, 1979, p. 20E. See also the U.S. Peace Council's advertisement in *ibid.*, June 24, 1979, the page after the columns and the Committee to Rescue Indochinese Refugees' advertisement in *ibid.*, July 13, 1979, p. A9. In early 1979, Hanoi began its anti-Chinese movement in the country. According to Leo Suryadinata's 1997 data, there are about 432,000,000 ethnic Chinese living in Southeast Asia, representing about 4.7 per cent of the total population in that region. Many overseas Chinese have helped their motherland. For example, Yao Shiong Shio of the Philippines advised Chiang Kai-shek in the late 1940s on how to make the country better by upgrading higher education, increasing export, and making plastic products. Yao's love for the ROC was unquestionable. He often said his love for the country is not for sale. Conversation with one his daughters, dated November 22, and December 1, 2001.

33   *LHZB*, October 25, 1998, p. 4.

34   Chen (note 32), p. 17.

35   Hu Sheng, *Cong yapian zhanzheng dao wo-si yundong* (From the Opium War to the May 4th Movement)(Beijing: Renminchubanshe, June 1981), p. 391. In 1850s, there was the gold rush in America.

36   In November 1871, 19 Chinese were killed by American whites in Los Angeles, California. A monument was erected 130 years later. See http://www.chinesewolrd.com/publish/today/17_0900.4t/4tt(011118)01_tb.htm (accessed November 16, 2001).

37   In May 1882, the U.S. Congress passed the Chinese Exclusion Act, saying Chinese labourers may endanger certain localities in the U.S. territory. In 1920, there were only 60,000 Chinese. In December 1943, as a result of the wartime alliance between the United States and the ROC, the Chinese Exclusion Repeal Act was passed. In 1950, there were 120,000 Chinese. From October 1965, Chinese and other races can immigrate to the United States in terms of a quota. In 1980, the Chinese constituted about 0.4 per cent of the U.S. population. By 2000, the percentage had increased to 1 per cent. There are not many Chinese in North Dakota and Wyoming. California has the most Chinese population, followed by New York, Hawaii, Texas, and New Jersey.

38   Chen (note 32), pp. 6–9.

39   Shambaugh (note 28), pp. 7–28.

40   *Zhongguo* had 2,300 or 2,400 years of feudalism. See Hu (note 35), p. 1.

41   See Timothy Brook and Gregory Blue, eds., *China and Historical Capitalism: Genealogies of Sinological Knowledge* (Cambridge, UK: Cambridge University Press, 1999).

42   Frederick Wakeman, Jr. "1839: The Proscenium of Late Imperial China" in *Perspectives on Modern China: Four Anniversaries*, edited by Kenneth Lieberthal, Joyce Kallgren, Roderick MacFarquhar, and Frederic Wakeman, Jr., *Perspectives on Modern China* (New York: M. E. Sharpe, 1991), p. 7.

43   Michael D. Swaine and Ashley J. Tellis, *Interpreting China's Grand Strategy: Past, Present, and Future* (CA: RAND Corporation, 2000), p. 48. To them, Venice, Portugal, Netherlands, Great Britain, and the United States at one time or another are the hegemons. See *ibid.*, p. 219.

44   Cited in Guojiajiaoweigaoxiaoshehuikexuefazhanyanjiuzhongxinzuzhi, compiler, *Zhongwailishiwentibarentan* (Conversation Regarding Chinese and Foreign History Among the Eight People)(Beijing: Zhonggongzhongyangdangxiaochubanshe, March 1998), p. 59.

45   See the late 1999 book, *Yigegemingdexingcunzhe* by Zengzhi, cited in http://star2001.net/liberty/4-17f.htm (accessed April 17, 2001).

46   For the account by a German businessman, John Rabe, see *China News* (hereinafter CN)(Taipei), December 14, 1996, p. 1 and *CT*, December 14, 1996, p. 9. For the account by Minnit Vautrin, an American teacher, see *Guangjiaojing* (hereinafter GJJ)(Hongkong), December 2000, pp. 78–81. In December 1998, the Tokyo High Court ruled that soldiers named in

the wartime diary, *Nanking Massacre Experienced by a Drafted Soldier—My Nanking Platoon* (1987) by Shiro Azuma, about the 1937 massacre cannot be brought to trial. *ST*, December 25, 1998, p. 21. The concept comfort women first surfaced in March 1932 in Shanghai.

47   Examples are the *Orphan of China* in 1767 and *The Chinese Must Go* in 1879. In the 20th Century, we see the films of Dr. Fu Manchu and Charlie Chan. *Yellow face* and its companion, *Yellow Peril*, are a racial body branding and they reaffirmed whiteness as the supreme attainment. See David Wellman, "Minstrel Shows, Affirmative Action Talk, and Angry White Men: Making Racial Otherness in the 1990s," in *id., Displacing Whiteness: Essays in Social and Cultural Criticism* (Durham, North Carolina: Duke University Press, 1997), pp. 312–313. Some observers say that, in Indonesia, 3 per cent of the Chinese population controlled almost 70 per cent of the economy. But, others like Faisal Basri of the University of Indonesia pointed out this is false. See *ST*, October 30, 1998, p. 31. Habibie said there are about eight to 10 million Chinese in Indonesia and "[i]t is absurd that the ethnic Chinese, who make up 3 per cent of the population, are controlling 90 per cent of the economy." See *ibid.*, June 15, 1998, p. 32 and February 23, 1999, p. 1. Jusuf Wanandi wrote: Suharto "was not interested in bringing the Chinese Indonesians into politics, the civil service or public life. He treated them like concubines to be enjoyed but not recognized." See *ibid*, August 3, 1998, p. 36.

48   Qing Tian and Huo Xiaoyong, eds., *Zhonghuahaiquanshilun* (On China's Historical Sea Power)(Beijing: Guofangdaxuechubanshe, July 2000), p. 136.

49   According to *Instances of Use of United States Forces Abroad, 1798–1993* (Washington, D.C.: Congressional Research Service, Library of Congress, October 7, 1993), we were told that in 1843, "[s]ailors and marines from the *St. Louis* were landed after a clash between Americans and Chinese at the trading post in" Guangdong.

50   Hu (note 35), p. 430.

51   In June 1840, British navel vessels blockaded Guangzhou. From the British Empire to *Zhongguo*, it would take at least four months by sea at that time. From India to *Zhongguo*, it would take at least one month.

52   Zhao Jin *et. al.Beipinghepingjiefangqianhou* (Before and After Beiping's Peaceful Liberation)(Beijing: Zhongguoshudian, March 1999), p. 82. The lane is called Dong (as in east) jiao (as in jiaotong) and min (as in minguo).

53   Hu (note 35), p. 435.

54   *Ibid.*, pp. 437–438.

55   Tu Wei-ming, "The Enlightenment Mentality and the Chinese Intellectual Dilemma," in Lieberthal *et. al.* (note 42), pp. 128–129. Another source said, after 1894/1895, the Qing Dynasty had to pay Imperial Japan 200 million taels. See *Straits Review* (hereinafter SR)(Taipei), January 1, 2001, p. 1. For another figure, see also Guojiajiaoweigaoxiaoshehui-kexuefazhanyanjiuzhongxinzuzhi (note 44), p. 96. According to Wu Tianwei, a Chinese-American historian, it was mainly due to Qing Dynasty's payment to Imperial Japan that China became poor and lagging behind. The amount paid was 29 million taels. See *UDN*, April 27, 1999, p. 13.

56   Hu (note 35), p. 626.

57   Wang (note 2), p. 18.

58   *LHZB*, July 26, 1998, p. 10. But, according to *Zhongguorenminjiefangjunguan-shouce* (The Handbook for the Chinese People's Liberation Army)(The Army Volume)(Qingdao: Qingdaochubanshe, June 1991) on p. 2, after the birth of Xia, which is about more than 4,000 years ago, boundary gradually developed.

59   *China Ocean News* (hereinafter CON)(Beijing), March 27, 2001, p. 1. During the Cultural Revolution, a stamp did not include the four island groups. The newly edited "Sanzijing" did not include the seas of the motherland. And the Chinese Century Forum failed to have the waters belonging to China.

60   Cited in *Hong Kong Economic Journal* (hereinafter HKEJ)(Hongkong), March 5, 2001, p. 9. In Patrick Buchanan's book, *The Death of the West*, the author wrote: "In 1960, people of European ancestry were one-fourth of the world's population; in 2000, they were one-sixth; in 2050, they will be one-tenth. These are the statistics of a vanishing race." Cited in http://www.straitstimes.com.sg/analysis/story/0,1870,99906.oo,html, dated January 30, 2002. In January 2002, it was reported that the number of Japanese will start decline from 2006. By 2050, Japan will have its least number of people.

61   Wakeman, Jr. (note 42), p. 1.

62   The December 1982 Constitution of the PRC stipulates that the usage of Mandarin Chinese. A British cultural association said by the mid-21st century, the number of people speaking Chinese would be placed first, to be followed by Indian, Arabic, and English. See *CT*, October 23, 1997, p. 10. An archaeologist in mainland China pointed out that Chinese characters were 1,500 years older than Egyptian hieroglyphics. The origins of Chinese characters can be traced to the Peigang Culture some 7,000 to 8,000 years ago. Egyptian hieroglyphics are thought to be 5,500 years old. See *ST*, November 16, 1998, p. 19. The first Beijing Man skull was discovered in December 1931 at Zhoukoudian.

63   Sushi is a Japanese food. But, its origin was from the Han Dynasty. See *See Hua Daily News* (hereinafter SHDN)(Malaysia), No. 48, July 11, 2002, the New Women section, p. 13.

64   Tianxiayijia is a synonym of *shijiedatong*. The *fanwen* is vasudhaivakutumbakam.

65   John W. Lewis wrote an article, "Casting China as the Bad Guy a Mistake," and it was first published in the *NYT* and reprinted in *ST*, June 6, 2001, p. 22.

66   Another way of saying the same thing is Rise Versus Fall.

67   One author mentioned that Hong Kong is a contemporary insect, whereas *Zhongguo*, a pre-contemporary dragon. See *HKEJ*, November 9, 2000, p. 8.

68   James R. Townsend, "Reflections on the Opening of China" in Lieberthal *et. al.* (note 42), p. 407.

69 Goldman and Nathan (note 5, ch. 6), p. 297.

70 Achim Mittag, "Historical Consciousness in China: Some Notes on Six Theses on Chinese Historiography and Historical Thought" in Paul van der Velde and Alex McKay, eds., *New Developments in Asian Studies* (London: Kegan Paul International, 1998), pp. 47–76.

71 See Guojiajiaoweigaoxiaoshehuikexuefazhanyanjiuzhongxinzuzhi (note 44). A U.S.-based academic, Xu Zhuoyun, said in recent years, Chinese culture in the world has been increasingly marginalized. See *UDN*, December 16, 2000, p. 2.

72 *CT*, January 28, 2001, p. 8.

73 Francis L.K. Hsu, "Opportunity & Cultural Differences," *Journal of Overseas Chinese Studies* (hereinafter JOCS)(Taipei), No. 1 (June 1989), pp. 25–26.

74 To Dr. Sun Yat-sen, there are five criteria to form a nation: blood/race, language, custom, religion, and livelihood.

75 Hsiao (note 25), pp. 153–154 and p. 157.

76 Morton H. Fried, "The Chinese Philosophy of War: A Dissenter's Hypothesis" in Larus (note 25), p. 159.

77 One may debate on neighboring lands, especially Vietnam.

78 So, to him, this is one of the myths. The other two myths are: Chinese in Indonesia own 70 per cent of its wealth. The reality is that the 70 per cent refers narrowly to corporate wealth, not Indonesia's wealth. This myth contributes to perceptions of anti-Chinese racism and revives concerns for future Sino-Indonesian relations. The third myth is Greater *Zhongguo* includes 55 million overseas Chinese. This is damaging because, "[t]he grouping comes close to a racist definition of Chinese that verges on calling upon the Chinese to act together in the interest of a larger Greater China." To Wang, the reality is that "[t]he figure is rounded off after adding 27 million Hong Kongers and Taiwanese to 25 million Chinese abroad. This confluence of all Chinese in some seamless web or network created the myth." Wang also said when the three myths become one, they form a mega-myth that prevents economic virtues alone from turning mainland China into the good guy on the block, but actually makes the mainland's courting of countries in Southeast Asia, for example, all the more threatening. See *ST*, May 10, 1999, p. 15.

79 Zhang Haiping, *Zhongguohaichuan* (China's Sea Power)(Beijing: Renminribaochubanshe, December 1998), p. 299.

80 Wang (note 2, ch. 6), p. 58.

81 Another characteristic is that the Chinese people attach great importance on coordination (*xiezuo*) when its comes to production style. This is different from other empires. See The Mirror Post Editorial Department, ed., *Jiang Zemin Yunchouweiwo* (Jiang Zemin Mapping Out Strategies Inside a Commander's Tent)(Hongkong: The Mirror Post Cultural Enterprises Co., October 1999), p. 302.

82 *CT*, August 28, 1993, p. 11. In November 1945, the ROC and the United States agreed on a plan to attack the area controlled by the CPC.

83   Vincent W. Xiao, former Vice-Premier of the ROC, said, when he was a diplomat, his superior had told him that even the ROC diplomats were very good at in-fighting. See *UDN*, April 13, 1999, p. 5. When the first attempt to rejoin the UN had failed, Lee Teng-hui urged the Taiwan people not to fight against each other but to unite themselves. See *THWDN*, October 2, 1993, p. 1. Members of the China Democratic Party (CDP) had also engaged in-fighting, for example, when Wei Jingsheng was testifying at a House hearing in Washington, D.C., another pro-democracy activist, Wang Xizhe, protested. See *LHZB*, January 10, 1999, p. 2; *UDN*, January 10, 1999, p. 13; and *ST*, January 17, 1999, p. 40.

84   Tang Aimin, *Dazhenghe* (The Big Integration)(Beijing: Zhongguojingjichubanshe, February 2000), p. 375. One Chinese-Malaysian soothsayer, with a doctoral degree, predicted that Chongqing could become another capital for mainland China. See *Haowaizhoubao* (Special Weekly), No. 53, January 28, 2002, pp. 24–26.

85   *UDN*, April 29, 1998, p. 4. Wang, who speaks what is on his mind, headed the Control *Yuan* (branch).

86   Wang (note 2, ch. 6), p. 55.

87   http://www.chinatimes.com.tw/news/papers/online/china/c8911270.htm (accessed January 12, 2000). From December 27, 2001 to January 26, 2002, for a month, a display of several thousand maps related to China was carried out in Hongkong. See http://www.udnnews.com/NEWS/FOCUSNEWS/ TAIWAN-CHINA/683787.shtml (accessed January 27, 2002).

88   According to Gavin Menzies, Zheng He from 1421 to 1423 had already come up with an embryonic map of the world.

89   *Ta Kung Pao* (hereinafter TKP)(Hongkong), May 25, 2000, p. A3. A mainland China academic pointed out that *Zhongguo* is placed at 150 degrees East Longitude. If *Zhongguo* were to be placed in the center, it should be at 105 degrees East Longitude. See *ibid.* In May 1999, a high ranking official of the ROC's Ministry of Interior said Nanjing is still the capital of the ROC and the official map still includes Outer Mongolia, because the National Assembly has not yet relinquished it. See *CT*, May 21, 1999, p. 9.

90   Harris (note 29), p. 25.

91   *THWDN*, March 7, 1997, p. 40.

92   *Zhongguo Guofang Bao* (hereinafter ZGGFB)(Beijing), May 7, 1999, p. 3 and May 21, 1999, p. 3. Joseph Needham during World War II formulated his problem in terms of the negative question of "why modern science had not developed in China but only in Europe?" But, he soon expanded his inquiries with the more positive formulation of "why was Chinese civilization much *more* efficient than occidental in gaining natural knowledge and in applying it to practical human needs" prior to the 16th century. Needham argued in his 18-volume *Science and Civilisation in China* (SCC) that the difference was due to the fact that *Zhongguo* did not have a full development of capitalism, an European concept. See Brook and Blue (note 46), p. ix. However, one other reason as pointed out by a professor in Beijing is that, in ancient China, natural sciences (as opposed to eight-legged essays) were not tested.

93 Zhonggongzhognyangzhuzhibuketizhu, *Zhongguodiaochabaogao: 2000–2001* (Beijing: Central Compilation & Translation Press, May 2001), p. 6. A mathematics professor at the National University of Singapore, Lan Lirong, who received the Kenneth O. May Medal, said that the Chinese in 475 B.C. already had the concepts from 1 to 9; they also knew addition, subtraction, multiplication, and division. The concept 0 was first discovered by the Indians after 600 A.D. But, the Chinese already had such a concept before that time, by regarding the space in between a bamboo and another bamboo as 0. See *SHDN*, July 8, 2002, p. C4.

94 http://english.peopledaily.com.cn/200007/10/eng20000710_45087.html.

95 *ST*, August 27, 1999, p. 42.

96 English people's daily.com.cn/200211/21/eng20021121_107216.shhtml, dated November 24, 2002. The U.K. discovered a wooden oar used 7,500 years ago, but failed to find any boat remains.

97 Louise Levathes, *When China Ruled the Seas* (New York: Simon & Schuster, 1994), pp. 20–21. For comparison between Zheng's and Columbus' voyages, see also Nanjing Zheng He Study Association of China, *Zouxianghaiyangdezhongguoren* (Chinese: Heading For the Sea)(Beijing: Haichaochubanshe, April 1996), p. 169 and Roderich Ptak, *China's Seaborne Trade with South and Southeast Asia (1200–1750)* (U.K.: Variorum and Ashgate, 1999). Columbus explored America four times between 1492 and 1504. From November 16–17, 2002, the National Cheng-kung University in Tainan City, Taiwan, ROC held an International Symposium on Cheng Ho's Great Voyage. See http://www.ncku.edu.tw/~history/chinese/sailing.htm. See also http://www.straitstimes.com.sg/commentary/story/0,4386,189691,00.html (accessed dated May 18, 2003).

98 Levathes (note 97), p. 102.

99 *Ibid.*, p. 173 and p. 179.

100 See http://www.telegraph.co.uk/news/main.jhtml?xml=%22f2002%2fo3%2fo4%2fnexp04.xml (accessed March 4, 2002). In November 2002, his book, *1421: The Year China Discovered the World*, was published by Transworld Publishers/Bantam Press. See also space.com which publishes *Starry Night* software.

101 See Levathes (note 97), flyleaf and p. 20. A series of economic factors accounted for the dynasty to maintain shipyards for ocean-going vessels and a large coastal navy, such as the opening of the Grand Canal in 1415 and the severe inflation and paper money depreciation. One Chinese academic observed: "Tribute trade worked for the court as long as it kept its monopoly on trade and forced foreign countries to accept low prices and payment in paper currency." See *ibid.*, p. 177–178.

102 Deng Ruiping, *Chuanbe qinguan xingwei fa jichu lilun wenti yanjiu* (Beijing: Faluchubanshe, September 1999), p. 78.

103 The reasons were: First, the dynasty felt that there was order in the mainland; and second, foreign adventurists were willing to abide by the dynasty's rules and regulations. See Hu (note 35), p. 20.

104 In 1862, the Qing Dynasty bought several naval ships (Lay Osborn Fleet) but it did not succeed in creating a navy. In 1865, Changsheng was bought

from the United Kingdom (UK). See http://www.yaox.com/cwm/index.html. As early as 572 B.C., *zhoushi* (ship for fighting war at sea) appeared.

105   According to the Chinese Warships Museum in Taipei, Taiwan, ROC (http://www.yaox.com/cwm/index.html), the first Chinese-built naval ship, Tianji (later renamed as Huiji), was named by Zheng Guofan and it was commissioned in July 1868 by Shanghai's Jiangnan Shipyard. In November of the same year, it was captured by a British naval force. See http://www.china.tyfo.com/int/literature/history/1991109historytoday1.htm.

106   Qing and Hou (note 48), p. 1.

107   Zhang Houyi and Ming Lizhi, eds., *Zhongguosiyingqiyefazhanbaogao: 1999* (A Report on China's Development of Individual and Private Economy: 1999) (Beijing: Shehuikexuewenxianchubanshe, March 2000), pp. 254–255.

108   See http://www.udnnews.com/focusnews/taiwan-china/274558.htm (accessed January 16, 2000).

109   Levathes (note 97), p. 105.

110   http://www.chineseworld.co…h/today/17_0900.4/4tt(010524)25_tb.htm, dated May 22, 2001. In March 2004, Manh Thu Ha, a professor at Hanoi University of Technology, told me that the Vietnamese ancestors were from those three provinces.

111   Isaac Newton (January 1643–March 1727) predicted that in the year 2060 the world will be doomed. According to an astronomer in Hongkong, human beings have only one thousand more years of civilization. Natural resources will be used up someday. The human race can still enjoy a good life for the next 100 years. See *See Hua Weekly* (hereinafter SHW)(Kuching, Sarawak, Malaysia), July 17, 2004, p. 6.

112   See http://ads.cyberone.com.tw/hserver/SITE-CHINATIMES.TW/AREA=MAINLAND.CP/AAMSZ=336X28 (accessed February 7, 2004).

113   Central News Agency (hereinafter CNA)(Taipei), JM5F4303.CAP, dated May 13, 2004 and http://english.peopledaily.com.cn//200405/13/eng20040513_143224.html (accessed May 13, 2004).

CHAPTER 8

Slotting in the Data

There are two major steps in plugging the data into the various frameworks. First, we must determine which framework(s) are primary. Employing too many of them would simply not be wise. This is because the Chinese Communists do not want to burden themselves with unnecessary dialectical frameworks. In this study, the Rule of Law Politics Versus the Rule of Men Politics framework, with the Rule of Dialectical Politics as Number 5 constitutes the primary one. The Rule of Dialectical Politics has been played by the Chinese Communist political figures since October 1949, if not July 1921 when the Communists met for the very first time. It constitutes the mainstream line (*luxian*). Periodically, the CPC will say or practise something related to any other number or letter. Since Deng's southern inspection tour in early 1992, more and more Chinese people do not attach great importance to ideology, not to mention the Centralism Versus Democracy framework,[1] but the Rule of Dialectical Politics still applies at the central level, especially with the Political Bureau Central and the Standing Committee. When Jiang was talking about the Rule by Virtue, he actually wanted other people to be virtuous or to go to that Number. What was in his mind was the Rule by Virtue Politics Versus the Rule of Dialectical Politics model, thereby dropping the Rule of Men Politics and placing the Rule of Dialectical Politics as E. Needless to say, it is easier to say that than to accomplish. The party was also relying on the Rule of Law Politics and the Rule by Law Politics to check and balance those people who handle or associate with money. Those in the military also have to comply with this framework in addition to the primary framework for the armed forces, that is, Party Commands the Gun Versus the Gun Commands the Party and its variation.[2] Time is certainly not yet ripe for the CPC to practise the Rule by Virtue. Should one day the CPC officially abandon the Rule of Dialectical Politics or the party become an opposition party or disappear, it would no longer be necessary for us to apply a dialectical approach. But, would such a time come? If so, when?

Having entered into this primary framework or knowing that we have to position ourselves at 5, we are in a better position to assess where the PRC stands ideologically and politically in the framework of CHINA Versus china. A word must be added. First, the PRC, Prc, and prc[3] framework could also be set up. But, this framework is different from the CHINA, China, and china framework in that the former is exclusively for the period from October 1949 to the date that the PRC becomes history as any *Zhongguo* dynasties would. In other words, we can also set up other frameworks to describe and explain each *Zhongguo* dynasty, such as QING, Qing, and qing, which is just a part of the CHINA, China, and china framework. Second, when we discuss a certain event, phase, development, and so on, readers must keep in mind that they are discussed within a framework, even if this author did not mention the framework or a series of frameworks. Political figures who apply dialectics like to protect themselves from unnecessary criticism. For example, one business tycoon in the ROC on Taiwan, Gao Qingyuan, while meeting Wang Zhaoguo, invited the latter who is a high ranking CPC official to visit the Taiwan area. As a gesture of courtesy, Wang cheerfully accepted. But, on the next day, Xinhuashe (China News Agency) reported that no such invitation was accepted by Wang. In a word, the framework of Yes Versus No has been set up by Wang to protect himself. A third party like Gao, may well be confused by Wang's acceptance and non-acceptance of the invitation.

To the Chinese Communists, *guojia* (state or country), ideology, and politics (accompanied by military affairs, etc.), in that order, are the superstructures of the economic line(s).[4] The economic line is certainly related to ideology, and it is the primary ideology, whereas all the other ideological things are either secondary or not of too much importance. Jiang Zemin's Three Represents has also been a superstructure since May 2000.[5] Another way of saying the same thing is that economics, the lower structure, is the base/foundation, while state, ideology plus politics are the concentrated expression of economics.

Guojia is clear in our study. It refers to the PRC, since our main focus is after October 1949, unless it dialectically changes its national title. Ideology is reflected from the economic line. To shore up the line, other ideological frameworks have to be applied. The important framework to consider is the Communism Versus Capitalism. Deng once said he was a layman when it comes to (pure) economics. But, he acknowledged that he did say something about economics but it was entirely from the political perspectives.[6] So, after discussing the economic development of the PRC from October 1949 up to the present, we shall try to find out where a specific economic line, the PRC, and the way the CPC plays politics can be positioned in terms of the CHINA Versus china framework. By politics, we mean things, which are closely related to internal interactions between, for example, the party and the government, or between the mainland and Taiwan. Externally, it is related to diplomacy and, to some extent, military affairs. The time/space sequence component comes in "layers," with certain developments, trends, incidents, or events taking place first, to be followed by the next development, trend, incident, or event. They would not develop in a continuity, because the Chinese Communist mind constantly leaps or jumps from one framework to the next. There should be one primary development, trend, incident, or event at each time/space sequence. Unless the non-mainstream thought has the potential to upset the mainstream thought at any time/space sequence, we will not discuss it.

A. FOUR MAJOR ECONOMIC LINES AND OTHER SELECTED IDEOLOGICAL FRAMEWORKS

Ideology is important because it gives (at least a rough) direction as to where the (ruling) political party or the country is moving or heading. It guides political figures into the safe zone of a specific framework. Without ideology, most political figures will not follow what the party preaches. There would be no unity, not to mention solidarity. As a consequence, the party may not be able to wield power, influence, or have any clout. For this reason, after formally putting forward the 12 Major Relationships in September 1995 and making a propaganda of the Three Represents in May 2000, Jiang Zemin's theoreticians put forward the following catch phrase: Take the Whole Picture into Account/Consideration (*Xionghuai Quanju*), Together We Move in Accordance with Changing Times (*Yushijujin*). The first phrase in Chinese refers to the Communism Versus Capitalism framework, and the second, the mainstream economic line per se, depending on which two extremes the CPC has chosen.

It is necessary for us to first decide which economic lines have been taken by the CPC from October 1949 up to the present. The lines are obviously tied to ideology, primary and secondary. There are four major lines, and each constitutes the mainstream for the period under discussion:

Socialism, from October 1949 to the first half of 1957; Communism, from the second half of 1957 to November 1978; Socialism (with Chinese Characteristics), from December 1978 to January 1992; and Market Economy, symbolically from January 1992 or officially from September 1997 to the present. Needless to say, there has been a gradual shift from one line to the next. It is not abrupt, because the party has to announce it first and to make preparations for its implementation, to be followed by the government's implementation. Sometimes, other factors must be taken into account. For example, the State Council may make an announcement on a certain policy. But, due to objective or subjective circumstances, there is a delay or postponement in its execution. One of the finest examples is that of Deng's symbolic, southern inspection tour in early 1992. It was not until the 15th National Congress of the CPC that the party officially adopted the Market Economy line, although many PRC citizens, who were ideologically conscious, such as those in Shanghai Municipal City, immediately knew that line would be eventually taken. So, they started designing and eventually building many high-risers in the Pudong area, which became very modern by the turn of the 21st Century. Here, the framework of Content Versus Form must be used to describe and explain this phenomenon. Figure 9 depicts the four lines. 1937.09 refers to the second round of co-operation between the KMT and the CPC; 1939.05 refers to the time when Mao first mentioned something related to the New Democracy (*Xin Minzhuzhuyi*); 1940.01 refers to the time when Mao published his article, *On New Democracy*; 1945.10 refers to the signing of the an agreement between the KMT and the CPC on October 10, 1945; 1949.10 refers to the creation of the PRC; 1949.12 refers to the time when the ROC Government moved to Taiwan; 1956.08 refers to the time when Mao elaborated on the 10 Major Relationships (which are quite different from Jiang's 12 Major Relationships); 1976.09 refers to the time when Mao passed away; 1978.12 refers to the 3rd Plenum of the 11th National Congress of the CPC; and 1992.1.18 refers to the day when Deng embarked on his southern inspection trip.

After discussing each economic line, I will describe and explain where the PRC, can be positioned along the spectrum -CHINA, China, china. Of course, there could be other possibilities, such as Number 2, 3, and so on as well as Letters A, B, etc. Here, we have to add one caveat. In September 2000, an authoritative publication, *Zhongguogongchandangzhuzhishiziliao* (Source Materials of the Communist Party of China's Organizations) was published.

FIGURE 9

	COM				SOC			CAP		
	1	2	3	4	5	A	B	C	D	E
	Safe Zone					Danger Zone				
1937.09								✗		
1939.05								✗		
1940.01								✗		
1945.10								✗		
1949.10					✗					
1949.12					✗					
1956.08					✗					
1957.06					✗					
1957.07	✗									
1976.09	✗									
1978.11	✗									
1978.12					✗					
1992.01.17					✗					
1992.01.18								✗		
1992.09								✗		
1997.09 to the present								✗		

It regarded the period from October 1949 to May 1966 as the transitional period and socialism construction period. The GPCR's period was from May 1966 to October 1976. The period from October 1976 up to now is called the new period for developing socialist enterprises. Before the appearance of this publication, other publications had another way of dividing the periods after the creation of the PRC. For example, the period from October 1949 to August 1956 was regarded as the transitional period from New Democracy to Socialism and the period from October 1984 to August 1988 as the period of all-round reform and opening to the outside world.[7] In a word, there is a lack of consistency. In any case, we shall stick to our way of dividing the periods for the economic lines.

1. Taking the Socialism Line

The broad picture was that, when the PRC was created, mainland China was still in a mess. The reason that the Chinese PLA could easily sweep across many places was due to the fact that the then ruling party on the mainland, KMT, was corrupt and ineffective. To be more objective, the CPC was also good at propaganda. For example, one of its slogans was that poor people should become masters of their own destiny or be emancipated (*qiongren yao fanshen*). During this chaotic period, Socialism was seen as the new panacea for crime, unemployment, prostitution, famines, alcoholism, and the like, which were regarded as an integral component of the old, bourgeois society.

Of course, once it had taken hold of power, the CPC had to face reality. On the one hand, it admitted that there were 4.5 million members in the party at the end of 1949. Before July 1, 1950, there were more than five million members. But, two million new members' thoughts and actions were not pure plus the fact that some old members and cadres had become corrupt with the passage of time.[8] On the other hand, the CPC could right away wipe out all the capitalist companies, factories, and the like. But, it could not really do that. The PRC was economically weak at that time. In the late 1940s, there were about 100 big enterprises in mainland China. When the ROC Government was relocated to Taipei, Taiwan Province in December 1949, 20 such enterprises also moved to the biggest island of China.[9] The KMT also transported a lot of U.S. dollars, gold, and silver to the biggest island in China. In order to justify their transitional economic policy, Beijing leaders decided to allow the capitalists to have a grace period, that is, they could function on condition that their companies and factories accepted some cadres from the CPC. This is one example of blending Capitalism with Communism. Since the CPC was capable of sustaining its rule of the country, it was acceptable to do that for a period of time.

2. Leaping to the Communism Line

In November 1956, the Second Plenum of the 8th National Congress of the CPC was held. It was decided that from 1957, the party would start to rectify incorrect things, such as subjectivism, sectarianism/factionalism, etc. According to Deng and Ye Jianying, Mao's subjective intention was to thwart the restoration of capitalism in the mainland.[10] From May 1957 to July 1958, an anti-rightist campaign was carried out. In July 1957, Mao at a Qingdao conference said the CPC would crack down on the rightists within and outside the party. After the July and August Lushan conference in 1957, more than three million cadres and ordinary people including intellectuals (who can be positioned at C in the Communism Versus Capitalism framework) were branded as right-deviationist opportunists. And Mao from September 24 to 27 in the same year again urged class struggle. This meant weeding out whatever was capitalist. Guaranteeing the fulfilment of farm output quotas or the household responsibility system (*baochandaohu*) was deemed capitalist.[11] From September 20 to October 9, 1957, at the 3rd Plenum of the 8th National Congress of the CPC, it was decided that the primary contradiction was still the Proletariat Class Versus the Capitalist Class and that the majority of intellectuals belonged to the latter or were positioned at C or even E. As a result of this conference, the CPC embarked on moving further to the left extreme, to wit, the nascent stage of Communism or 1. According to official figures, more than 550,000 intellectuals or about 10 per cent of the total number of intellectuals were labelled as rightists. More than half of them lost their jobs in the public service.[12]

The Great Leap Forward, that is, leaping from Socialism to Communism, was one of the Three Red Flags, the other two being "Let a Hundred Flowers Bloom and Let a Hundred Schools of Thought Contend" and People's Commune. Mao personally pushed forward the Great Leap Forward movement from January to April in 1958 at Hangzhou, Nanning, Chengdu, Wuhan, Guangzhou, etc. In May of the same year, the Great Leap Forward officially spread across the country [13] until January 1961, when the Central Committee of the CPC, admitting that there had been artificial crop failures in the past few years, decided to curtail industrial production and to spend more time on resolving the problem of the increasingly lagging farm production.

From 1959 to 1962, there was famine across the mainland. The number of deaths increased alarmingly in the countryside, in many provinces. The situation was extremely grave by September 1960.[14] From January 11 to February 7, in 1962, 7,000 officials attended a Central conference of the CPC, trying to rectify the situation for having executed the Leap Forward policy. Within six months from this conference, the economic situation had gradually improved, meaning that the line had been shifted back to 3 or 4 from 1.

However, Mao did not give up his subconscious dream of converting the PRC into a Communist paradise within his lifetime. He launched the GPCR in May 1966. Earlier in May and June 1964, Mao mentioned the sensitive term, peaceful evolution, which had been enunciated by U.S. Secretary of State John F. Dulles in January 1953.[15] He was convinced that many representatives of capitalism had wormed their way into the party, government, the Chinese PLA, and the cultural sector.[16] In effect, he returned to 1, unlike Peng Zhen who wanted to limit the GPCR to academic and intellectual circles.[17] Because Mao had the power, practically no PRC political figure dared to be at 3, 4, or 5, with the exception of Deng, for example, who positioned himself at 5 throughout the period from October 1949 until his third return to the political arena in early 1977. However, he was powerless to reverse the trend until late 1978 at the 3rd Plenum of the 11th National Congress of the CPC. As a result, the PRC national economy during the GPCR suffered 500 billion Renminbi (RMB).[18]

3. Restoring the Socialism Line (with Distinct Chinese Characteristics)

The dialectical China did not go through the capitalist stage, even though there are some PRC academics who argue that it did. From the second half of the 16th century up to 1840, capitalism began to sprout in *Zhongguo*.[19] PRC textbooks always maintain that after the 1840 Opium War, *Zhongguo* as an independent feudal country had gradually became a semi-colonial and semi-feudal country. This meant that *Zhongguo* was positioned at C in the Socialism Versus Feudalism framework. Modern

Zhongguo's industry in 1920 only weighted 4.9 per cent of the gross product in industry and agriculture. In 1936, it was 10.8 per cent. And in 1949, the ratio was 17 per cent.[20] From a Marxist perspective, Great Britain began its capitalist revolution from 1640 to 1660. The United States had its turn from 1776 to 1783. And France started its capitalist revolution from 1789 to 1794.[21] Japan, on the other hand, began to shift leftward from feudalism to capitalism in 1868.

In April 1956, Mao, at an enlarged Central Committee meeting, spoke about the Major Ten Relationships. What he wanted to say was that not every Marxist-Leninist tenet could be applied to the mainland. As early as June 1938, Mao had already made a remark to that effect. In other words, from October 1949 up to April 1956, at least ideologically speaking, the situation was recasting the PRC to fit into the Marxist-Leninist framework. Following Mao's talk, the CPC tried to apply Marxism and Leninism in areas where it fitted the Chinese Communist situation on the mainland.

Deng certainly understood what Mao was saying and he supported it wholeheartedly. He, under Zhou Enlai, who became the Premier of the State Council (before September 1954, it was called the Central People's Government Administration Council [CPGAC]), was mainly in charge of handling economic affairs since August 1952 when he was promoted to become the Vice-Premier. But, he did not have the power to implement Socialism (with Chinese Characteristics). So, when Mao gradually shifted the economic line to Communism from the second half of 1957, Deng could not stop Mao. Mao in July 1959 at the Lushan Conference deliberately relegated Peng Dehuai to the danger zone, saying the latter was 30 kilometers from Capitalism or E. Because Deng believed in materialistic dialectics, he thought that mainland China should first stress production. In other words, based on what one had, then one could talk about state, ideology, politics, etc. To him, primary ideological purity could not be achieved when mainland China was poor and destitute (*yiqiongerbai*). But, Mao's wishful thinking, that of bringing the mainland to the Communism stage as early as possible, overwhelmed Deng. For this reason, Deng also became a target of criticism during the GPCR.

So, after his return to the political limelight, Deng at the 3rd Plenum of the 11th National Congress of the CPC stressed the following: Oppose Left ideology in the economic field (that is, stressing Communism in the

Communism Versus Capitalism framework) and Right ideology in the political field (that is adopting Western style political system in the One Party People's Democratic Dictatorship (as opposed to the expression of Proletarian Dictatorship in the September 1954 Constitution) Versus Multi-party Political System). He added the following words to Socialism: with Chinese Characteristics. Readers should bear in mind that Deng still held Marxism, Leninism, and Mao Zedong Thought at heart. His logic was simply that he could not abandon all of them. Otherwise, the dialectical frameworks would be shattered and the CPC would easily lose its legitimacy to rule the mainland and, consequently, the PRC would not last. However, Deng dropped Mao's *Jieji Douzheng Shi Gang, Qiyu Doushi Mu* (Class Struggle is the Key Link and Everything Else Hinges on It), because he is thinking of the Socialism (with Chinese Characteristics) Versus Capitalism framework and because he knows that, once the Chinese people became wealthy and powerful, there would be no capitalist class and the country would be run by the majority, to wit, proletariats or people, who are to be positioned at 1 in the Communism Versus Capitalism framework.

To facilitate changing the economic line, the CPC right after the arrest of the "Gang of Four" in October 1976 took over *People's Daily* (*Renmin Ribao*). A thorough investigation under Chi Haotian's instructions went on from October 1976 to April 1978,[22] so as to get rid of those workers who were still blindly adhering to Mao's dictums. This is important because, as a propaganda machine, the *People's Daily* and other newspapers could inform the people that the PRC would return to 5 in the Communism Versus Capitalism framework.

On the eve of the 3rd Plenum of the 11th National Congress of the CPC, there were only 140,000 individual enterprises (*getigongshangye*).[23] In July 1979, the PRC Government published its first legislation on joint ventures between the PRC and foreign companies. Under the new regulations, foreign companies would be permitted to invest in the mainland and repatriate part of their profits. In December 1982, the 5th Session of the 5th NPC for the first time legalized individual economy (*getijingji*). (In March 1999, the 2nd Session of the 9th NPC exercising its third amendment of the PRC Constitution, *inter alia*, provided "common development under a plurality of systems of ownership," the status of the private owned economy from a "complement to the socialist system of public ownership" to "an important component of the socialist market economy," and "the rule of law" as the highest priority of the mainland.)

In July 1979, the Central Committee of the CPC and the State Council agreed, in principle, that Guangdong and Fujian Provinces could set up zones where goods would be processed for export (*chukou jiagong qu*). In August 1980, the 15th Session of the 5th NPC confirmed Guangdong's Shenzhen, Zhuhai, and Shantou Special Economic Zones. In December 1980, Fujian's Xiamen was confirmed by the State Council. Such zones enjoy preferential treatment granted by the Central Government in Beijing. Several years later, more cities were opened to the outside world. Needless to say, duchy economy (*zhuhou jingji*) also surfaced in some places of the mainland, such as Guangzhou, which is associated with regionalism.

In 1987, from October 25 to November 1, the CPC held its 13th National Congress. One of the main things on the agenda was to confirm the "One Center, Two Basic Points." One Center refers to Economic Construction. It is the Roof/Housetop or Eaves. It incorporates the two basic points. The first point is called Four Insistences, such as adhering to Marxism, Leninism, and Mao Zedong Thought. It is fundamental, so it is positioned on the left extreme. To the CPC, anything positioned on the left extreme would triumph at time/space sequence (n), which could be 1,000 years later. While the second point, Opening to the Outside World might look good on the surface, the CPC, knew that it would bring many negative aspects of Capitalism into the mainland, so it was placed on the right extreme. This easy-to-remember framework is important, so as to remind the political figures what to conform to, that is, they have to know how to reconcile the Four Insistences and Opening to the Outside World at each time/space sequence by conducting anti-corruption campaigns. For example, if too many political figures were on the right extreme, the CPC would periodically conduct campaigns to urge them to come back to the safe zone. If not, they would be punished, remoulded, or re-educated.

Needless to say, even by applying dialectics, things may not subjectively flow in the way it is intended to. For example, in the year of 1988, there was rampant inflation due to problems in 1986 and 1987: 9.5 per cent in January; 11.2 per cent in February; 11.6 per cent in March; 12.6 per cent in April; 14.6 per cent in May; 16.5 per cent in June; 19.3 per cent in July; 23.2 per cent in August; 25.4 per cent in September; 26.1 per cent in October; 26.0 per cent in November; and

26.7 per cent in December.[24] It was not until August 1988 at Beidaihe that a price reform was implemented. It was not properly carried out with the result that people rushed to buy things across the country.[25] Seeing this, some people began to doubt the Socialism (with Chinese Characteristics) Versus Capitalism framework, thinking it might well bring about the collapse of the PRC. However, by the mid-1990s, inflation was under control. In the last one year or so, the mainland has again tried to counter inflation.

4. Gambling on the Market Economy Line

The Communist countries in Eastern Europe had collapsed one after another, following the tearing down of the Berlin Wall in late 1989. The Soviet Union also imploded in December 1991. Deng made a symbolic move which he had contemplated for a long time but hesitated to carry it out. He wanted to adopt the Market Economy Line, which is C in the Communism Versus Capitalism framework but 5 in the redefined Socialism (with Chinese Characteristics) Versus Capitalism framework. It was a gamble. Had it failed, it would certainly have spelt the end of the CPC and the PRC, because forces in the West were relying on the Capitalism Versus Communism framework, if we interpret it dialectically. But, if the line could revive the mainland's economy and other things, it would be regarded as a new lease of life for the CPC as well as the PRC.

Deng wanted to take this line but hesitated. He thought that the peasants who constituted the majority—or the subject—in the mainland population must first be taken care of. So, agriculture came first in his Four Modernization program. He also knew that it was an elephantine task to accomplish. Yet, the collapse of the Communist countries compelled him to take a drastic and unprecedented line. So, in January and February 1992, Deng visited places like Wuchang, Shenzhen, Zhuhai, and Shanghai. One of the most significant remarks which he made was his regret that he had not included Shanghai Municipal City, earlier, as one of the special economic zones. Deng's move was important, but as he was merely a Party member, there was a lapse of five years before it was officially endorsed by the CPC at the 15th National Congress in September 1997. The CPC still wanted to legalize what it said and did and the endorsement had not been made earlier because the CPC wanted to demonstrate that it was in control; time was also required to prepare for its acceptance by and support from the majority of the political figures.

By showing the latter that it was in control, the Party would thereby increase its own prestige as well the confidence of the former in the Party.

Normatively speaking, Deng believed that Socialism (with Chinese Characteristics) would ultimately replace Capitalism. This process would take 100 years, starting from the creation of the PRC. Eventually, Communism would replace Socialism (with Chinese Characteristics), however long it might take. But, in order to make the PRC prosperous, it was necessary to adopt the Market Economy, since market economy was not the monopoly of Capitalism. Deng argued that Socialism (with Chinese Characteristics) could also avail itself of the market economy. Jiang, speaking at the Central Party School in June 1992, said the term *Shehuizhuyishichangjingji* (Market Economy of Socialism) should be used.[26]

Most analysts in the West perceive that the PRC is taking the capitalist road. This is not the really the case, at least, in ideological terms. It would apply the Rule of Law Politics Versus Rule of Men Politics to check those who handled and managed money, as mentioned earlier. At best, only some political figures have gone to E. The CPC has always kept its distance from E, namely, Capitalism. The CPC can rationalize what it has been doing. The Third Plenum of the 11th National Congress of the CPC brought the line back to the middle of Communism Versus Capitalism. The 12th National Congress made it clear that the PRC was still in the nascent stage of Socialism. The 13th National Congress adopted the Socialism (with Chinese Characteristics) Versus Capitalism framework. The 14th National Congress said Socialism (with Chinese Characteristics) was the subject. The 15th National Congress further moved to the middle, that is, it adopted the Market Economy line. And the 16th Congress symbolized the end of economic reform and the beginning of political reform. By taking this middle line, the CPC is demonstrating that it is still keeping a distance from E, namely, Capitalism.

However, in some places of the mainland, some provincial local governments have encouraged their people to practise Capitalism. Zhejiang Province is one of the examples. How does the CPC rationalize this? Simply by electing Market Economy as Number 1, while maintaining Capitalism at E. Arranged in this way, it can further move closer to E by moving to Number 5, which should have a new label or concept. Besides, the government can argue that the land still belongs to the state and thus the Chinese PLA and those who work in state-owned enterprises belong to the public sector (and are accordingly being positioned at 1 in the Socialism [with Chinese Characteristics] Versus

Capitalism framework). Statistically speaking, up to the end of June 2001, the armed forces, worker and peasants accounted for 63.8 per cent of the total population on the mainland.[27] These are not capitalists. They have no means of production. So, on the whole, the PRC is still socialist, with distinct Chinese Characteristics. That is to say, so long as the spectrum ranging from Socialism (with Chinese Characteristics) to Market Economy represents 50.1 per cent (the rest being 49.9 per cent for the Letter spectrum), the balance is still tilting in favour of Number 1, which stands for Socialism (with Chinese Characteristics).

The road towards the initial stage of the Market Economy line was long. The All-China Federation of Industry and Commerce, a front of the Chinese People's Political Consultative Conference (CPPCC), was created in October 1953. But, during the GPCR, its activities were suspended. (In November 1994, Jiang stressed its non-governmental [*minjian*] character). In January 1979, Deng talked to several important figures in industry and commerce, such as Rong Yiren who was the richest person in September 1956 with a total private asset of RMB 65 million out of RMB 2.2 billion in the national total, and he said the PRC should not repeat the August 1958 mistake. He was referring to the decision of the Central Committee of the CPC to set up the first People's Commune at Beidaihe.[28] Deng also quoted Mao's saying that a section of the population might be permitted to be well-to-do.[29] This helped to alleviate the anxiety experienced by a section of those involved in industry and commerce as a result of the volatile policy changes and political campaigns arising from the application of the Rule of Dialectical Politics. When examining any dialectical framework, one observes that it is not consistently adhered to. This leads one to conclude that politics in the mainland is volatile since most CPC members do not adhere to the Centralism Versus Democracy framework. If politics were in command, then most people would definitely not obey law, and the Rule of Law or even the Rule by Law would not be possible, as a consequence.

We can provide some additional statistics.[30] In August 1956, when the New Democracy ended, the PRC practised a system of public and private enterprise. In effect, it was adopting the framework of the Publicly-owned Economy Versus Non-publicly-owned Economy [*feigongyouzhi*] (or Private or Individual and Private Economy [*getisiyingjingji*]). There were 160,000 private enterprises at that time with a value of RMB 3.3 billion, which is equivalent to today's RMB 33 billion. The number employed by private enterprises (*siyingqiye*) was 2.5 million. It was not until December 1982 that the 5th Session of the 5th NPC legalized individual economy. In the year 2000, individual and private enterprises increased to 1.76 million, employing 20.11 million workers. The total amount of assets was RMB 133.077 million. In September 2001, the PRC's Ministry of Foreign Trade and Economic Co-operation (MFTEC) made public that there were over eight million private small and medium enterprises in the mainland, amounting to 99 per cent of all the public and private enterprises.[31] Today, less than 2 per cent of the mainland people possess more than half of the individual and private economy financial assets and their production is about one-third of the total. The trend is towards national economic privatization (*guominjingjiminyinghua*). By the end of the 20th century, Guangdong, Jiangsu, Shangdong, Zhejiang, Henan, and Hebei Provinces plus Shanghai's individual and private economy had registered the highest levels of growth. At the end of 1978, the ratio of non-public-owned economy represented 1 per cent of the gross national product (GNP). By the end of 1998, it represented 24 per cent.[32] In the year 2000, the Gross Domestic Product (GDP) of the PRC reached RMB 8,940.4 billion, which is 56 times the figure in October 1949.[33] In July 2001, a high-ranking PRC official mentioned that, in five years' time, there would be 200 million Chinese people belonging to the middle-class. He added that, in developed countries, about 80 per cent of the people are in the same class.[34]

Jiang Zemin, the then General-Secretary of the CPC, had been very ideological. His successors will be the same. This shows that Jiang was executing the CPC's dialectical grand strategy under Deng and he wanted to maintain the CPC's status as the ruling party. In September 1995, Jiang at the 5th Plenum of the 14th National Congress of the CPC asked for a correct handling of what he called the 12 Major Relationships, as mentioned earlier. It was necessary, because the CPC would eventually be taking on something new, that is, the middle road in the Socialism (with Chinese Characteristics) Versus Capitalism. After officially putting forward the Three Represents, he reminded the people especially members of the CPC to embrace the framework of Communism Versus Capitalism and to move together as objective circumstances permit with the option of coming back to Number 5 someday, which could be generations later. In other words, what the CPC was doing should be understood in the context of the original framework, to wit, that of Communism Versus Capitalism, and the framework should not be abandoned. The new jargon, as mentioned before, indicated that the party represented the interests of advanced social productive forces, advanced culture, and the majority of the Chinese people. In other words, by taking the Market Economy line, the CPC is representing more people, including the intellectuals, the majority of whom had been labelled by the party as rightists or positioned by the party in the danger zone or C of the Communism Versus Capitalism framework in the 1950s. In a speech marking the 80th anniversary of the founding of the CPC, Jiang invited those in the individual and private sector to remain in and to join the party. At the 16th National Congress of the party, the Three Represents was included in the CPC Constitution. This is a logical move, to be sure. Those who voiced their opposition to this latest move, by positioning themselves in the safe zone of the Communism Versus Capitalism framework, were worried that Capitalism would again be revived in the mainland.

As a party member at the central level, what Jiang was doing should be affirmed. In February 2000, Jiang Zemin visited Guangdong Province, saying something about the Three Represents. Later in May 2000, while inspecting Jiangsu and Zhejiang Provinces, his remarks on the Three Represents became official and began to receive extensive media coverage in mainland China. He himself spoke about it to the party schools members in the following month.

The Three Represents was necessary, because the economic line of Market Economy represents a mid-way between Socialism and Capitalism-the Chinese version since September 1997, given that it is in between Socialism (with Chinese Characteristics) and Capitalism and within the safe zone. Certainly, this is something unprecedented, because, the CPC may well be the first Communist party in human history which is ruling a half-capitalist state. Karl Marx certainly did not say anything about this. (Countries like Vietnam, North Korea, and Cuba may also have to tag along by coming up with a similar jargon like the Three Represents.) To be sure, a Communist party would abolish private property when the Communism stage arrives or at the mature stage of socialism, broadly defined, because there are plenty of things for (all) workers and labourers who constitute the majority. But, a socialist or socialist-oriented party would still respect the private property system. And capitalism encourages personal wealth with the major portion of wealth being held in the hands of capitalists who are in the minority.

By advancing the Three Represents and by welcoming those in the individual and private sector to join the CPC, the party has, as a matter of fact, brought the mainland to the KMT days or January 1940 when Mao published his article, which was entitled *Xin Minzhuzhuyi Lun* (On the New Democracy Revolution), which is another way of referring to the Neo-Three Principles of the People (*Sanminzhuyi*, TPP). In short, it is appropriate for us to say that the CPC has been ideologically TPP-nized since September 1997, because the KMT in the mainland days and in TW days had never quashed the small and medium enterprises.

In sum, economic reform undertaken since the late 1970s had almost been completed by November 2002. At the end of 2002, the mainland exports and imports amounted, for the first time, to US$620 billion. In March 2004, the PRC accumulated for the first time a foreign exchange reserve of US$403.3 billion. The party will seriously embark on political reform from the 16th National Congress. The process may take decades to complete.

B. POSITIONING THE LINES

At this juncture, it is appropriate for this author to position each line in terms of CHINA Versus china. It is not necessary for us to position the secondary ideological frameworks. They are supplements or have the functions of supporting the primary lines. On the whole, the first line could be positioned at China. It is quite rational, because it still emphasized production. If the time/space sequence is long enough, China could gradually move to 5 and even 4. Because time was lost, that is, the PRC wasted production from the second half of 1957 to early 1992, Deng said it would take some one hundred years for the mainland to be developed. Had there been no waste of time, Deng would not have to mention 100 years. Needless to say, the PRC would require more time for the whole of the mainland to reach the level of development of the United States.

Taking the Communism line when the time was not yet ripe was certainly a disaster. Mao had the good intention of advancing the PRC to a developed status. So, in January 1958, Mao said the PRC could and should catch up with Britain within 15 years. But, he neglected the materialistic aspect of dialectics. He was ideological or even metaphysical. Thus, the line during this period of time pushed back China to the danger zone. In the early 1960s, it could be positioned at D or E. At the end of the GPCR, the PRC was almost like china. To those who do not understand dialectics, the PRC during the GPCR would be erroneously positioned at 1, 2, or 3 in the CHINA, China, and china framework. So, John K. Fairbank, writing in *Foreign Affairs*, mistakenly said the GPCR was a good thing for the mainland.

As to the Socialism (with Chinese Characteristics) line, it put the PRC back to the position of 5, at least psychologically in the first place. However, the June 1989 massacre relegated the mainland to china. There were many deaths and many people were hurt, angry, and frustrated. There was uncertainty. Jiang was deeply aware of this and he was also considering his position. So, he moved cautiously and conservatively. Sometimes, he even positioned himself at 3 in the Communism Versus Capitalism framework. Deng, of course, was not happy and he was thinking of pulling Jiang down and replacing him with someone else who would adopt the Socialism (with Chinese Characteristics) Versus Capitalism framework. But, Deng did not undertake this course of action because, conceivably, he might have thought that it would not be long before he met with Marx.

The January 1992 inspection tour by Deng was decisive. And the Market Economy line was finally adopted at the 15th National Congress of the CPC. This gave rise to the hope that the CPC might, again, make normative moves to the left, that is, from 5 to 4, from 4 to 3, etc., when the time came by, enlarging or going back to the framework as chosen by Mao. At that point the PRC might become CHINA, provided that the CPC can sustain its ruling power status.

ENDNOTES

1   At the 14th National Congress, the CPC revised the wording of what is Centralism Versus Democracy. It is more relaxed in terms of the party's control of economy. See *CT*, October 22, 1992, p. 10. This framework is also applicable to national institutions.

     See *Zhonggongshiwudawenjianxuexijianghua* (note 24, ch. 7), p. 122.

2   See my article, "The Dialectical Relationship of the Chinese Communist Party and the PLA," *Defense Analysis* (hereinafter DA)(UK), Vol. 16, No. 2 (August 2000), pp. 203–218.

3   Gordon G. Chang, who argued in *The Coming Collapse of China*, said the PRC is like a paper dragon. If it collapsed, it would be prc. Chang has worked in the mainland for some 20 years. See Patrick E. Tyler, "The Coming Collapse of China: Reckoning with a Paper Dragon," *NYT*, September 10, 2001, NYTimes.com. In January 2002, it was reported that starting 2006 the Japanese population will decline until 2050.

4   Lucian W. Pye noted the economy-polity relationship, that is, the economy providing the foundations for polity. See his article, "Asia Studies and the Discipline," *PS*, Vol. XXXIV, No. 4 (December 2001), p. 806.

5   Zhonggongzhongyangzhuzhibuketizhu (note 93, ch. 7), p. 2.

6   Committee on Zhongguomianxiangershiyishijideluoganzhanluewenti (hereinafter The Committee), *Zhongguomianxiangershiyishijideluogan-zhanluewenti* (Some Strategic Problems Faced by China in the 21st Century)(Beijing: Zhonggongzhongyangdangxiaochubanshe, May 2000), pp. 3–4. Indeed, there are many dialectical terms or jargon which cannot be understood by economists in the West. For example, in February 1988, the PRC began to negotiate its accession to the World Trade Organization (WTO). Many member economies cannot understand what was meant by "planned commodity economy." See *Qiaobao* (hereinafter QB)(New Jersey), November 9–15, 2001, p. A4. There are also analysts looking at the WTO in terms of dialectics. See Meng Yi, ed., *Shimaodamendakaile* (The Door of the World Trade Organization Has Been Finally Opened) (Beijing: Zhongguoduiwaifanyichubanshe, December 1999), p. 391.

7   See, for example, Li Ruoli, *Zhongguogongchandangquanjilu*, 1921 A.D.–1997 A.D. (Chronicle of Communist Chinese Party, 1921 A.D.–1997 A.D.)(Inner Mongolia: Neimonggolrenminchubanshe, January 1998).

8   Zhonggongzhongyangzhuzhibu *et. al.*, *Zhongguogongchandang-zhuzhishiziliao* (Source Materials for the Communist Party of China's Organizations), Vol. 5 (Beijing: Zhonggongdangshichubanshe, September 2000), p. 4.

9   *Ibid.*, p. 424.

10   Guo Tieqiang, *Taigangzhonggongdangshi* (Taiwan and Hongkong's Writings on the Chinese Communist History)(Foshan City: Guangdongrenmin-chubanshe, June 2000), pp. 457 and 459.

11   Zhonggongzhongyangzhuzhibu *et. al.* (note 8), pp. 23–24.

12   *Ibid.*, p. 19.

13   *Ibid.*, p. 34.

14   *Ibid.*, p. 117.

15   Guo (note 10), p. 460.

16   *Ibid.*, p. 458.

17   *China* (note 30, ch. 7), p. 163.

18   Guo (note 10), p. 427.

19   Chen (note 32, ch. 7), p. 69.

20   Cited in Guojiajiaoweigaoxiaoshehuikexuefazhanyanjiuzhongxinzuzhi (note 44, ch. 7), p. 54.

21   *Ibid.*, pp. 5–31.

22   Zhonggongzhongyangzhuzhibu *et. al.*, *Zhongguogongchandang-zhuzhishiziliao* (Source Materials of the Communist Party of China's Organizations), Vol. 7 (the first volume)(Beijing: Zhonggongdangshichubanshe, September 2000), p. 254. In January 1967, Shanghai newspapers such as *Wenhuibao* (WHB) and *Jiefangribao* (JFRB) were controlled by the "Gang of Four." Thereafter,

29 provincial, municipal, and autonomous region's party and government institutions were taken over by the gang. See Liu *et. al.* (note 32, ch. 7), p. 353.

23 Tian Jiyun, "Understanding and Treating the Role of the Individual and Private Economy Properly" in Zhang and Ming (note 107, ch. 7), p. 6.

24 Cheng Zhiping, ed., *Wujiawushinian* (The Price of Chinese Commodities Over the Last 50 Years)(Beijing: Zhongguowujiachubanshe, August 1998), p. 543.

25 Zhang and Ming (note 107, ch. 7), p. 21.

26 Zhou Hong *et. al.*, *Zhongguoershishijidashiiji* (Important Events of China in the 20th Century)(Shandong: Shandongrenminchubanshe, March 2000), pp. 904–905. In 1979 (and later in 1983), Deng meeting with foreign guests said, "Why can't a socialist country have a market economy?" Later, the mainland created four Special Economic Zones (SEZ).

27 *LHZB*, July 1, 2001, p. 18. They receive less than 5 per cent of the PRC Government's total budget.

28 No author, "The Representative Figures of No-public [sic] Owned Economy is the Important Object of the United Front in New Era" in Zhang and Ming (note 107, ch. 7), p. 11.

29 Leng Rong, *Deng Xiaoping Lilung Yu Dangdai Zhongguo Jiben Wenti* (Deng Xiaoping Theory and Contemporary China's Fundamental Problems)(Beijing: Faluchubanshe, January 2000), p. 31.

30 See *Zhenli De Zhuiqiu* (hereinafter ZLDZQ)(Beijing), No. 131 (May 2001), pp. 2 and 17. See also Zhang and Ming (note 107, ch. 7).

31 CNA, September 26, 2001 at 22:51 pm. In April 2002, it was reported that by the end of 2001, private small and medium enterprises numbered 2.02 million.

32 *UDN*, June 30, 2001, p. 13.

33 *Jiefangjunbao* (hereinafter JFJB)(Beijing), July 12, 2001, p. 1.

34 See http://www.mingpaonews.com/20010721/cfb1hr.htm (accessed July 21, 2001).

CHAPTER 9

The State

We shall now discuss the state or country, that is, the PRC, which is associated with other things like national title, national anthem, national flag, national emblem, etc. Is the PRC CHINA, China, or china? We should consider all other possibilities. Before reaching the stage of being CHINA, it is possible that the PRC might have already disappeared, just like any *Zhongguo* Dynasties, only to find its revival several thousand years from now, thanks to Chinese political figures who might believe in Marxism and thereby revive the PRC 1,000 years from now.

It has been said that, should an asteroid hit Earth, there would be a tidal wave (*tsunami*) and countries like the United States may disappear. If it were possible for America to become history, so too might a dialectical China. But, our framework can afford to describe and explain that phenomenon, because it anticipates future developments whether positive, negative, or somewhere in between, as any framework takes the opposite into context or consideration. As a related question, can we set up PRC (as 1), Prc (as 5), and prc (as E)? Certainly, this is possible, as mentioned earlier. But, qualifications must be made, as mentioned before. For example, there should be another way of writing the conventional PRC. Otherwise, readers might become confused between the conventional writing—PRC—with that of PRC in the dialectical framework. In any case, the conventional PRC is, most likely, just a drop in the 10,000-year recorded history of *Zhongguo*/the dialectical China.[1] This means that, even if the conventional PRC were to reach the stage of the PRC in the dialectical framework of PRC (as 1), Prc (as 5) and prc (as E), it does not necessarily mean that the conventional PRC will remain there, because there is always a possibility of the conventional PRC's becoming china one day or becoming extinct. Again, this possibility should never be ruled out, dialectically speaking. For this reason, our sub-title for Part II has a question mark, as mentioned earlier.

Prior to the creation of the PRC, Chinese Communists and other non-Chinese Communists were discussing what national title to use. In

June 1949, Mao mentioned the *Zhonghuarenminminzhugongheguo* (The Chinese People's Democratic Republic), which was also used by other Communists.[2] After extended discussion, Mao decided on the PRC. He also said the short version of the PRC was the ROC. This was necessitated by the fact that he saw an overlapping of Dr. Sun Yat-sen's TPP and the CPC's New Democracy. In this connection, the CPC never opposed Sun. For example, in October 1965, the first meeting to discuss how to celebrate the 100th anniversary of Sun's birthday was held and chaired by the PRC Chairman Liu Shaoqi. Needless to say, Mao still had Communism in mind. The Chinese characters *renmin* can be symbolically reflected from Communism. *Renmin* or the superstructure means a lot of people or proletariats, to be more precise, and the CPC will still represent them at that stage. To the CPC, capitalist countries are controlled by capitalists who are small in number. Another reason is that the ROC had not ceased to exist. Thus, Mao had to set up a dialectical framework, that is, PRC Versus ROC, with the ultimate intention of eliminating the ROC at time/space sequence (n).

In February 1967, Mao mentioned the national title of *Zhonghuarenmingongshe* (Chinese People's Commune). He wanted to move the mainland to the Communist stage within his life time, and, therefore, he considered using this as a national title. It was, however, short-lived.

In late 1970, Mao, in an interview with Edgar Snow, lamented that he had made a mistake in October 1949 by adopting the national title of the PRC. Why did he say that? Well, it was a tactical lament. Having made that remark, he returned to the PRC at the next time/space sequence. There could be other reasons. Mao might have felt that, by that time, he was wielding absolute power in the mainland. That is to say, he was at the zenith of his political career and prestige, for good or bad. What he should achieve next was the political reunification of China. In other words, he wanted to be a second Qing Shihuang or Emperor Qing. So, Mao mentioned the ROC, thinking that if he had not changed the national title, he would have been the most powerful in *both* mainland China and Taiwan.

On March 23, 1996, the day of the first direct presidential election in Chinese history in the ROC on Taiwan, it was reported that Deng did think about using the new national title of the *Zhonghuagongheguo* (ROC).[3] The English translation for this title is the same as the one created by

Dr. Sun Yat-sen in January 1912, ROC.[4] In this connection, from November 1933 to January 1934, a Revolutionary Government of the ROC (*Zhonghuagongheguogeminzhenfu*) existed in Fuzhou City, Fujian Province, which was basically anti-Chiang Kai-shek and anti-Imperial Japan, and the Chinese Communists at that time were also critical of it, labelling it as "anti-revolutionary" for forging ties with foreign powers. But, for the sake of distinguishing between Sun's ROC and Deng's *ROC*, Deng's version should be put in italics.

Why did Deng think about the change? This is because he believed that the economic line would not affect changes in a state, ideology, and politics. In other words, he had brought the PRC back from Communism (or 1) to Socialism (with Chinese Characteristics) (or Number 5) at the Third Plenum of the 11th National Congress of the CPC. Many, if not most, CPC members knew that he would eventually move the mainland further towards Capitalism. The change was unavoidable and inevitable. Indeed, at the 14th National Congress of the party, he had adopted the Socialism (with Chinese Characteristics) Versus Capitalism framework. The former had been redefined as Number 1, Market Economy as 5, with Capitalism, remaining the same, that is, E. His successor Jiang Zemin further moved to the middle by maintaining Deng's middle of road strategy, that is, Market Economy, in this latest dialectical framework at the 15th National Congress of the CPC. In a word, the PRC had moved back to January 1940. Because since September 1997, the economic line had been officially shifted to emphasizing Market Economy, it was all right for the CPC to change the national title of mainland China and, for that matter, encouraged Taiwan to do the same. This then is the course of the CPC's action.

To be certain, Socialism (with Chinese Characteristics) reflects the PRC. The superstructure of the Market Economy, on the other hand, is the ROC. Because 1 and 5 are in the safe zone, both PRC and ROC can be accepted, at least ideologically. But, since the CPC still wants to remain as the ruling party on the mainland, it has politically chosen not to totally identify itself with the ROC (i.e., 100 per cent). And since the Chinese reunification issue has not yet been resolved, a change in the national title may facilitate that. So, the CPC is willing to go to 3 and, at the same time, it is asking the KMT and other ruling political parties to move to 3 as well. If Taipei agrees to do that, both sides of the Taiwan Strait will have a new national title at least until the mid-21st century. But, normatively speaking, since 3 will inevitably move on to 2, and, finally, to 1, what the CPC is doing is merely carrying out a dialectical tactic for the eventual absorbtion of the Taiwan area at time/space sequence (n), if Taipei does not know about it, unless Taipei should succeed in overthrowing Beijing at time/space sequence (n) by applying another framework, such as the ROC Versus PRC, thereby bringing about a multi-party system as the dynamic, operational concept. In any case, the March 1996 election in the Taiwan area was a historic, direct presidential election. The March 2000 election in the Taiwan area brought about a peaceful transformation of the KMT from a ruling party to an opposition party. The March 2004 election symbolized the separation of the party from the state. And the March 2008 election could again mean a change of the ruling party status for the Democratic Progressive Party (DPP). In a word, there is a lot of pressure on the CPC to follow suit.

Nevertheless, Deng dropped the *ROC*. This is because his advisor Wu Xueqian told him that the English translation for the *ROC* is the same as the ROC. Apparently, Deng did not have time to think of a new one. So, Deng's successors including Jiang simply used China right after the 15th National Congress of the CPC. Wang Daohan is the political figure who in November 1997 told General Xu Linong and others of the New Party from the Taiwan area. However, with the change in the regime in Taiwan since May 2000, it has been increasingly difficult for Taiwan to negotiate with the mainland on having a new national title for a politically reunified China. The DPP has been trying to freeze the acceptance of the One China principle. In December 1992, the then ruling party, KMT, agreed to have "One China, but Respective Interpretations" with the CPC. The latter prefers the term the 1992 consensus. This is because the CPC does not want a third party to non-dialectically recognize the existence of the ROC. By this, is meant that, in international law, there is no such thing as a partial recognition of a state. But, according to the Rule of Dialectical Politics, partial acceptance of a state is possible and normal. In any case, for the next several decades, Taiwan should be able to use its existing title, so long as Taipei accepts the "One China" principle or, at least, the 1992 consensus. To be sure, the DPP regime since May 2000 has only briefly accepted the consensus, and the closest concepts advanced by the DPP are "One Chinese (*yige zhonghua*)," which reflects the spirit, and the "Hong Kong Talk.".

A caveat should be noted. Because the relationship between the mainland and Taiwan since September 1997 has been turned into People's Contradictions (*renmin neibu maodun*) from Contradiction between the

Enemy and Ourselves (*diwo maodun*), at least from the CPC's perspective, if Taipei did not change the national title, it could still be safe. The latter contradiction is zero-sum. To repeat, the Market Economy reflects the ROC or 5, while Socialism (with Chinese Characteristics) reflects the PRC at 1. This means that if Taipei refuses to change its national title, Beijing can only use democratic methods to persuade Taipei to think of a mutually acceptable new national title by agreeing to move for example, to Number 3. In other words, it cannot use force, unless Taipei leaves the safe zone of the Socialism (with Chinese Characteristics) Versus Capitalism framework. When Wang Daohan mentioned China, he was thinking of Number 3. Needless to say, the CPC will not voluntarily tell its counterpart in Taiwan what primary framework it is relying on. However, Beijing can change its national title to something else first by moving itself from Number 1 to Number 3, so as to show sincerity. (Ideologically speaking, it can even travel to 5, i.e., to use the ROC as the title.) Later, if the ROC feels comfortable, it can position itself at Number 3 as well, meaning political reunification of the dialectical China. Some ROC academics like Li Nianzu argue that, even though the ROC Government had moved to Taiwan and carried out constitutional amendments, the ROC inherent territory (*guyoujiangyu*) as enshrined in its December 1947 constitution would not have changed a whit. It is the PRC, which left the ROC, not vice versa.[5] While Beijing claims Taiwan as part of the PRC or *Zhongguo*, other countries like the United States have domestic laws or some treaties (as opposed to agreements) protecting Taiwan and even Hongkong and Macao.

Speaking of the arrangement in the framework, Beijing can even move to 5 in the Socialism (with Chinese Characteristics) Versus Capitalism. By doing that, this author means that the PRC can become the ROC. On record, the PRC does not include Outer Mongolia. It does not possess Taiwan. It can only claim Taiwan as part of the PRC. However, the ROC equates to the mainland plus (at least politically) Outer Mongolia, Taiwan, Hongkong, and Macao.

In any case, if we take the whole picture into consideration, from the PRC's perspective, and provided that it were confident enough, the possibility exists for a politically reunified dialectical China to return to Number 1 in the Socialism (with Chinese Characteristics) Versus Capitalism framework, perhaps decades later. In any case, there could be a change in the national title of the PRC.

"One Country, Two Systems," which was first publicly announced in September 1982 when the then British iron lady, Prime Minister Margaret Thatcher, visited Beijing, should be understood in terms of the Communism Versus Capitalism framework. In this framework, it was positioned at 5. This meant that once Deng had consolidated his power in the late 1970s, he intended to eventually apply the Socialism (with Chinese Characteristics) Versus Capitalism framework and travel to the middle road, that is, the Market Economy. Because he was determined, he thought that it was all right to reveal his "One Country, Two Systems" formula to Thatcher. But, the CPC was flexible enough to adopt the "One Country, Three Systems" because this is reflected in the Market Economy line in the Socialism (with Chinese Characteristics) Versus Capitalism. In a word, if we apply the Communism Versus Capitalism framework, 1 means "One Country, One System;"[6] 5 means "One Country, Two Systems," C means "One Country, Three Systems," and E means "One Country, Multi-systems." Similarly, if we speak of political parties, 1 would be One-Party-People's Democratic (or Proletarian)-Dictatorship System, which according to one scholar was first put forward by Dr. Sun Yat-sen; 5, Multi-party Cooperation System; C, Systems of Socialist Democracy (or roughly Multi-party Competition System); and E, Multi-party System. But, for the present, because the ratio is still tilting in favor of Socialism (with Chinese Characteristics), if we talk about it in the context of economic statistics, the CPC will only occasionally mention the "One Country, Three Systems." For this reason, Qian Qichen, the then Vice-Premier of the State Council, was not willing to volunteer saying the "One Country, Three Systems" is now in force. He only said yes when a reporter asked him whether what he said in June 2000 was "One Country, Three Systems." Does this mean that the CPC is disobeying Deng's "One Country, Two Systems"? No. In any case, both 1 and 5 are acceptable or tolerated in the Socialism (with Chinese Characteristics) Versus Capitalism framework, due to the fact that they are in the safe zone. Indeed, in July 2001, the very first party-to-party consultative negotiations were conducted between the New Party[7] in Taiwan and the CPC. A high-ranking PRC official, Wang Zaixi, said, in substance, there is no difference between "One Country, Two Systems" and "One Country, Three Systems."[8] To the CPC, it is *chabuduo* (not much difference). Indeed, dialectically speaking.

When we talk about the state, we can discuss a related topic, that is, the boundary of the PRC. This is because sovereignty, jurisdiction, etc., are involved, which were invented by the Europeans. Since October 1949, there have been some changes. Beijing gave up some land, firmed up some land boundaries, and struggled to retain or to recover some land. Outer Mongolia (OM) is one of the finest examples in the first category. The PRC needed the Soviet Union's support from the very beginning. So, before finalizing the 30-year Treaty of Friendship, Alliance, and Mutual Assistance between the PRC and the Soviet Union in February 1950, the former reluctantly signed a secret, supplement agreement regarding several parts of China, such as Xinjiang Autonomous Region, over which no other foreign countries could wield any influence.[9]

Under the U.S. threat, the Chinese Communists could not say to the Soviets that they wanted to get back OM. If the United States was clear that it would not support the ROC, the PRC could have chosen the option of not recognizing the independence of OM, as the ROC argued that since diplomatic relations between the ROC and the Soviet Union had been broken off, the ROC did not have to recognize OM's independence. There are other examples to support the ROC's argument. After nine weeks of negotiation in Moscow, in February 1950, both Beijing and Moscow declared the Soviet Union's August 1945 Treaty of Friendship and Alliance with the ROC null and void. The George H. Bush, Jr. administration also said it would not recognize the May 1972 Treaty on the Limitation of Anti-ballistic Missile Systems because it was a treaty signed with the Soviet Union which was demised in December 1991. Until recently, the ROC in Taiwan had chosen to politically regard OM as part of the ROC.[10]

Yan Jiaqi urged Jiang Zemin not to give up some Chinese territories at the latter's meeting with Vladimir V. Putin in July 2001.[11] When the PRC signed the 30-year Treaty, two subsidiary agreements, and one secret agreement in February 1950, the PRC's border problems with the Soviet Union were put aside. The latter, since the signing of the unequal treaties with the Qing Dynasty in the 1850s, had occupied more than 1.4 million square kilometers of Chinese territory. In October 1992, the PRC and Russia signed an agreement on topographical mapping of the border between the PRC, Russia, and three other newly created countries, namely, Kazakhstan, Kyrgyzstan, and Tajikistan. In December 1999, the PRC and Russia signed documents regarding their borders. Apparently, to this day, the mainland has not yet publicized the content of these documents, plus the October 2004 agreement on Heixiazi Island.

There are other direct and indirect border problems. Before the collapse of the Soviet Union, the PRC had 12 sovereign neighbors. After that, there were 15 states. The three new states were formerly part of the Soviet Union. We shall only mention the major ones to show that the PRC, at the macro-level, may not be always positioned at 5 in the CHINA Versus china framework, despite the existence of the Five Principles of Peaceful Coexistence which can be traced back to Mao's June 1949 statement on establishing diplomatic relations with other countries and which witnessed its first appearance in an agreement reached between the PRC and India in June 1954.[12] In other words, depending on the case at a specific time/space sequence, the PRC, at the tactical level, may be applying any one of the following frameworks: Friendly Relations Versus Not Friendly Relations, Strong Versus Weak, Reasonable Versus Unreasonable, Nice Versus Tough, Generous Versus Non-generous, and so on. To be sure, this author's model enables one to parse even a symbol like * to be * Versus Non-* or Non-* Versus *. In any case, Beijing chose to gradually side with the Third World from the second half of 1957, which is usually considered poor and backward but which makes up the overwhelming majority of the world's nation-states in the Third World Versus First World framework.[13] To the CPC, the Third World will ultimately triumph, given time, even Huntington included African civilization as a possible force which may clash with seven other civilizations.

The first test came in June 1950, when the Democratic People's Republic of Korea (DPRK) invaded the Republic of Korea (ROK). Mao was worried that the American imperialists might take the opportunity to move their troops into the mainland.[14] He did not want to escalate the crisis in which the PRC might be burned. So, instead of sending Chinese PLA troops (as 1), he dispatched the Chinese People's Volunteers Forces (*Zhiyuanjun* [CPVF]) who belonged to the Northeast Frontier Forces (*Dongbeibianfangjun* [NFF]) (as 5).[15] If he were to employ proxies or mercenaries, the latter would be considered E. We can provide some more descriptions and explanations.

In August 1945, Joseph V. Stalin approved Harry S. Truman's General Order Number One, providing for the "temporary" division of Korea at the 38th Parallel of latitude into Soviet and United States temporary zones of military occupation. In August 1948, the ROK was formally created. In September 1948, the DPRK was established. But, in February 1948, (North) Korean People's Army (KPA) was formally activated. In June 1949, last American occupation troops left the ROK. In January 1950, U.S. Secretary of State Dean Acheson, in a speech before the National Press Club in Washington, D.C., omitted South Korea from the United States' Asian defense perimeter. In other words, the ROK should rely upon its own resources until the UN could mobilize its forces to help the country to defend itself against an aggressor. From January to March 1950, General Douglas MacArthur's Intelligence Section evaluated reports of impending invasion of the ROK from the North (including one that pinpointed the month of June 1950).[16] From March 30 to April 25, 1950, Kim was in the Soviet Union, urging Soviet leaders to assist the North Korean military attack.[17] On May 13, 1950, Kim visited Beijing and, two days later, he succeeded in asking Beijing leaders to help his country. War broke out in June 1950. Three days later, Seoul fell to advancing North Korean troops. On August 15, 1950, the North Korean government was moved from Pyongyang to Seoul in South Korea. On September 26, Seoul was recaptured. (But, on January 4, 1951, Seoul fell to the North Koreans [along with the CPVF] for the second time. It was not reoccupied by the UN troops until March 14, 1951.)

It was Kim Il Sung, who on October 1, 1950, asked a high-ranking official to present his personal letter to Mao, hoping the latter might dispatch the Chinese PLA to Korea. It was also he who fired the first shot on the invading troops.[18] To some analysts, the Korean War, involving more than three million troops from both sides, along with the World War II and Vietnam War, over the past one and a half centuries was among the most catastrophic with far-reaching implications.[19] In July 1950, the UN Security Council, and in the absence of the Soviet Union delegates , voted to appoint MacArthur as UN commander in Korea. In October 1950, the CPVF,[20] made up of 425,482 troops, launched their First Phase offensive against the U.S.-led 17-country forces. This was the very first anti-invasion war crossing the Yalu River under the slogan of *Kang Mei Yuan Chao, Bao Jia Wei Guo* (Resist U.S. Aggression and Aid Korea, Protect Our Homes and Defend Our Motherland) in the history of Chinese Communist Party, according to *Jiefangjun Bao* (Liberation Army Daily).[21] On January 4, 1951, the CPVF took over Seoul. But, to avoid being lured into an ambush, the CPVF stopped the battle on January 8.[22]

Mao's strategy and tactics in this war for the right cause or righteous (*zhengyi*) war were: You fight your own way, I fight with my way (*ni da ni de; wo da wo de*). In other words, the United States could use its atomic weapons, while the PRC would use its grenades. But, Beijing would seize on the weakness of its enemy and ultimately defeat it.[23] This is precisely dialectical. But, Beijing had to take half of its heavy industries in Northeast China into serious consideration. If the United States were to take over the entire Korean Peninsula, mainland China would be under heavy American threat.[24] However, in July 1951, the first meeting for a cease-fire or truce began. In November 1951, a provisional agreement was reached at Panmunjom, an abandoned village, on the line of military demarcation and the Demilitarized Zone. In August 1952, North Korean leader Kim Il Sung conceded in a speech at Pyongyang that the Korean War had reached a stalemate. He said he would accept an armistice under which the "Americans are not the winners and the Koreans the losers."[25] In July 1953, an armistice or truce was finally signed or reached between North Korea, the PRC, and the United States. In May 1953, Dulles asked the Indian Prime Minister, Jawaharlal Nehru, to inform Mao that the American President Dwight D. Eisenhower had decided to resort to "tactical use of atomic bombs," if truce negotiations failed in Korea.[26] Later, Dulles gave a second warning via Burmese Prime Minister U Nu that Washington "meant business."[27] In any case, the war ended in a stalemate, which is 5 in the Win Versus Lose framework.

In August 1950, two months after the outbreak of the Korean War, the Chinese PLA moved into Xizang. This is like fighting two fronts. Because some elements in the international community do not recognize the fact that Xizang is part of China, they termed what the Chinese PLA did as an invasion, which ended in March 1951. Needless to say, the international image of the PRC was tarnished somewhat by the foreign mass media. But, in March 1951, a Tibetan delegation led by the pro-PRC Panchen Lama concluded negotiations in Beijing and two months later signed a 17-point agreement on behalf of the local government of Tibet. Beijing's image was also somewhat improved in April 1954 when the PRC and India signed an agreement regulating trade and travel between the latter and "the Xizang region of China."

On the surface, it appeared that there was peace and tranquillity. But, in March 1959, there were demonstrations against the PRC in Xizang. On March 25, the Xizang Cabinet declared *de jure* independence from the PRC and demanded that the PRC withdraw from Xizang. But, on the same day, the Chinese PLA troops occupied Lhasa after heavy fighting. India sided with the pro-independence refugees and allowed them to go to India on an individual basis. From October 1987 to March 1989, there were several large-scale riots (*saoluan*) in Xizang. From March 1989 to April 1990, martial law was in force. On record, the U.S. Central Intelligence Agency (CIA) was also involved. From 1958 to 1962, it trained 170 Tibetan armed personnel and spies, and most of them were sent back to Xizang after training in the Colorado State. As can be seen, the issue cannot be solved easily, when both the houses of U.S. Congress had passed resolutions, for example, in December 1987, saying that Xizang did not belong to China or mentioning that there had been an effort by the Han Chinese to sinicize Xizang.[28]

Elsewhere, in July 1956, Burma charged that several thousand Chinese PLA troops had occupied a large area in northeastern Burma. Burmese officials said there had been sporadic fighting between both sides, but the threat was not regarded as very serious and negotiations were underway for removal of the troops.[29] In November of the same year, both countries issued a joint statement saying that each side would withdraw from designated areas.[30] On October 1, 1960, both countries signed a border treaty, which overcame difficulties and resolved their disputes.

In September 1959, New Delhi said the Chinese PLA had violated its northern border and Indian troops had been dispatched to two Himalayan mountain passes to guard roads from Xizang (Tibet) to Sikkim and India. A day later, India said the PRC had accused the former of "aggression."[31] Later in October, following a series of minor incidents, the most serious fighting broke out between the Chinese PLA and the Indian troops at the Kongka Pass, a remote section of Kashmir.[32] In April 1960, Indian Prime Minister Jawaharlal Nehru and Zhou issued a joint statement after a week of talks in New Delhi on the border dispute between the two sides. The two leaders admitted that the talks "did not result in resolving differences that had arisen," but they agreed "to avoid friction and clashes in the border areas."[33]

The Sino-Indian dispute continued to May 1962. India protested to the mainland that proposed negotiations between the PRC and Pakistan over the Kashmir border formed a part of the PRC's "aggressive designs" against Indian territory. Beijing replied that New Delhi was pursuing a policy of "out-and-out great power chauvinism."[34] On October 10, 1962, serious fighting broke out between the Chinese PLA and the Indian troops near the Indian outpost of Dhola Strip, which was on the

Chinese side of the McMahon Line but which was claimed by New Delhi as its northeastern frontier. The Chinese PLA said what it did was self-defense (*ziweihuanji* or *ziweifanji*).[35] Ten days later, Sino-Indian tension erupted into war as the Chinese PLA opened an offensive that drove Indian forces back in the northeast and also in the Ladakh section of Kashimir. The fighting lasted until October 27, and the Indian troops did poorly.[36] On October 29, 1960, Nehru made a direct appeal to the United States for arms and military equipment. On November 10, the State Department announced that the arms airlifted to India had been completed. On November 21, the PRC announced a unilateral cease-fire and withdrawal to begin at midnight of the same day: "Chinese frontier guards will withdraw to positions 20 kilometers (12.5 miles) behind the lines of actual control which existed between China and India on November 7, 1959." What had been taken to be a Chinese PLA invasion was merely a punitive expedition.[37] On November 28, 1965, the two countries had exchanged protest notes, each charging the other with border violations amounting to "aggression."[38] In February 1968, *People's Daily* published an article by "Commentator"—indicating high-level approval—condemning Soviet Premier Aleksei Kosygin's recent visit to India, charging that he had "completely taken over Khruschchev's policy of supporting India against China, and has gone even further."[39]

Relations remained strained. But, in February 1979, Indian Foreign Minister A. B. Vajpayee arrived in Beijing. Meeting with Deng, he said the border dispute was still the primary obstacle to good relations between the two countries.[40] Indeed, Beijing protested in December 1986 when a piece of land occupied by India became a state.[41] It was not until many years later that relations between the two countries normalized. In December 1992, PRC Premier Li Peng visited India. In September 1993, Indian Prime Minister Shri P. V. Narasimha Rao visited the mainland and he signed the *Agreement on the Maintenance of Peace and Tranquility Along the Line of Actual Control* (AMPTALAC) in the India-China Border areas. This was followed by the first ever visit to an Indian naval port, Bombay, of a Chinese PLA training ship, Zhenghe. What Beijing wanted to signal was that it was at 1, which stands for Peace, while the opposite of it was War.

The PRC airspace had been often violated by some foreign powers. In May 1960, Beijing charged that American U-2 jets had made at least three flights over the Chinese mainland.[42] In April 1962, Beijing tallied U.S. intrusions: "During the past 15 months of the Kennedy administration the record of United States intrusion into China's territorial waters and airspace is 52 warships on 40 occasions and 64 sorties by the United States aircraft."[43]

A more recent incident took place in April 2001. Earlier in May 1999, the PRC embassy in Belgrade, Federal Republic of Yugoslavia (FRY) was (mistakenly?) damaged by five U.S. ballistic missiles. It also showed that the PRC was still weak. On the first day of that month, an American Navy EP-3 spy plane, which is about the size of a Boeing 737 and which was gathering electronic intelligence related to the planned small, underground nuclear test in Lop Nur, Xinjiang, was forced to make an emergency landing in Lingshui Air Base of mainland China's Hainan Province,[44] after a mid-air collision with one of the Chinese PLA F-8 fighter jets at the time of incident.

On April 11, the United States Ambassador to Beijing, Joseph W. Prueher, in an official letter stated that he was very sorry about the accident. The 24 American crew members were allowed to return home on April 12. Six days later, both sides started the first round of negotiations on returning the plane. But, nothing came out of it. From May 2 to May 4, 2001, American civilian technicians inspected the damaged EP-3 and they said the plane can still fly home. On May 10, a PRC official said the crisis between the two sides had been resolved.[45] On May 28, Beijing announced that the plane would be dismantled and permitted to leave the PRC. In July, the plane was sent back to the United States.

The incident took place about 104 kilometers off Hainan Island.[46] The U.S. side insisted that its plane was flying on international airspace. However, the PRC in June 1998 promulgated "the PRC Law on the Exclusive Economic Zone (EEZ) and the Continental Shelf," extending up to 200 nautical miles (n.m.) from the baselines of the territorial sea.

In any case, the United States resumed its routine reconnaissance and surveillance flights off mainland Chinese coast and EEZ on May 7, 2001. But, is the airspace above EEZ international?[47] The answer to this question is yes, if we are only talking about the 1982 United Nations Convention on the Law of the Sea (UNCLOS). Article 58 guarantees freedom of overflight or innocent passage over the EEZ.

But, EEZ is a *sui generis* zone, which in the words of a U.S. navy commander, Stephen A. Rose, is "a sorely troubled frontier." Once a foreign plane conducts reconnaissance and surveillance, the flight is called into (serious) question, because it is not giving "due regard" for the rights and duties of the coastal state.[48] If the coastal state is strong enough, it may challenge this kind of activity. Here, national jurisdiction certainly can come in. (See Articles 55–75.)

Besides, a word must be said about the Chinese (broken) U-shaped line in the SCS.[49] The line was first drawn in December 1947 by an official of the ROC Government. The ROC Constitution also states that it has the right to take back lost territory as time is ripe. The PRC inherited this line in October 1949.

Mark J. Valencia of the East-West Center in Hawaii regarded the line as an "extreme jurisdictional claim." Another academic in Taipei once said the line and the Chinese EEZ are contradictory.

If the line is extreme, Valencia should also criticize the Philippines Kalayaan zone, which is also provocative to the ROC, Vietnam, Brunei, and Malaysia. Moreover, the line and the EEZ are not contradictory, because the Chinese wanted double insurance. If the line cannot protect Chinese interests, then the EEZ should, and vice versa. In this world, it is not just the 1982 UNCLOS, which cannot solve all maritime problems and issues. There are other international laws, including customary law, at work. So, in May 1995, the U.S. State Department stated that it would rely on the UNCLOS and other international laws to handle maritime affairs in the SCS, especially with regard to the Nansha Island Group. If so, why not the Chinese side?

Noting that the Chinese maintain a U-shaped line in the SCS, Chris Carleton, a British official at the Hydrographic Office, Law of the Sea Division, said "[t]he only airspace that is national is above Internal Waters and the Territorial Sea." To be sure, as Valencia said, the Chinese are "asserting sovereignty over virtually the entire" SCS as "historic waters." Indeed, some Chinese academics and experts regard its historic waters as a "Chinese lake," something akin to internal waters, just as some people regard the Indian Ocean as an "Indian lake." Interestingly, there is one Western analyst who perceives that the SCS will remain the "American lake." In any case, Washington should pay due respect to the rights and duties of the Chinese claim and should modify its navy's Freedom of Navigation Program to some extent, so as to reduce mutual tension.

As pointed out by Valencia, Beijing banned planes at certain heights from October 1979 to February 1980 over four "danger" zones south and east of Hainan Island; and the United States navy may test any provocative claim which it feels violates international laws governing freedom of navigation.

Power means might. Might can be translated into right. When there is right, there is wrong. So, if Washington says the airspace over the EEZ is international, it can rally support from some sympathizers.

In any case, the ultimate question is: Does Beijing want to initiate a war? The answer is no. First, at the time of the incident, there were two Chinese fighters trying to intercept the American plane. One of them, after seeing the collision, requested for permission to shoot down the American plane. But, his request was denied by the Chinese PLA air control center.[50]

Second, Jiang Zemin, the then President of the PRC, still went to visit six countries in Latin America. If Beijing wanted to fight back by military means, he would have stayed home. As pointed out by Choon-ho Park, the judge at the International Tribunal for the Law of the Sea at Hamburg, Germany, in his email to me, the incident is "more a political issue than a legal one." In any case, the whole episode ended in July 2001. In September 2001, after the terrorist attacks of the United States, the then PRC Foreign Minister Tang Jiaxuan said, although there are U.S.-PRC differences, "[t]here are no insurmountable barriers between us."[51] Indeed, in the same month, both countries after two days of talk in Guam entered into the *Military Maritime Consultative Agreement* (MMCA).

Returning to April 1960, Zhou left Katmandu, Nepal after signing a treaty with Nepalese Premier B. P. Koirala. A joint statement issued after Zhou's departure announced ratification of the treaty, which settled Nepalese-Tibetan border disputes. Zhou told the Nepalese Parliament that the agreement was a step toward "peaceful coexistence between countries of different social systems."[52] In a word, the treaty helped to preserve the PRC's image as China. It did not bully a small country and relations remained friendly. The distance between them is certainly almost non-existent.

In May 1960, the PRC and Mongolian People's Republic (MPR) signed a *Treaty of Friendship and Mutual Assistance* in Ulan Bator, which shares a 2,500-mile border with China and a 1,700-mile border with the then Soviet Union, tended to lean towards the Soviet Union in the Sino-Soviet dispute. In December 1962, the PRC and Outer Mongolia's Premiers signed an agreement in Beijing delineating their 2,500-mile border. The agreement was extremely favorable to Outer Mongolia.[53] Again, the image of the PRC as China has been preserved. Many foreign observers used to argue that the PRC would use force to take back this neighboring country to the north but it did not. Actually, it was Beijing which was disturbed when Moscow and Ulan Bator in January 1966 signed a *Treaty of Friendship, Cooperation, and Mutual Aid* for a period of 20 or 30 years, and would be more so if neither had expressed the intention of abrogating it at the end of the 19th year. Article 5 stated in part that "[t]he Parties will extend mutual aid in ensuring the defense capacity of both countries in conformity with the tasks of constant strengthening of the defense might of the socialist commonwealth.... The Parties ... will jointly undertake all the necessary measures, including military ones, aimed at ensuring the security ... of both countries."[54] So far, no major battle or war has taken place in that part of the world. In May 1990, a top Mongolian leader visited Beijing for the first time since December 1962, and was received by the then PRC President Yang Shangkun.

In May 1961, Cambodia signed a Treaty of Friendship and Non-aggression with the PRC. This move also helped other neighbouring countries to perceive the mainland positively. In April 1970, the PRC condemned the United States when its troops along with those from the Republic of Vietnam (ROV or South Vietnam) moved into that kingdom. (In an agreement with Laos in August 1968, the Chinese PLA went to that landlocked country to pave roads. More than 110,000 engineers, artillery units, logistic troops, etc., were involved, and they returned to the mainland in May 1978 after completing their mission.)

In July 1961, Beijing and Pyongyang signed a treaty of Friendship, Cooperation, and Mutual Assistance, which represented a PRC diplomatic coup, tying North Korea closer to the mainland and drawing the same away from the Soviet Union.[55] To this day, North Korea is closer to the mainland than to Russia, on the whole.

In December 1962, the PRC and Pakistan announced "complete agreement in principle in regard to the alignment of the common border of the China-Xinjiang contiguous area, the defense of which is the responsibility of Pakistan." The treaty constituted Chinese Communist recognition of Pakistan's control over the Kashmir, which was still being disputed between Pakistan and India.[56] In March 1963, the PRC and Pakistan signed an agreement defining the 300-mile boundary between the mainland's Xinjiang and the section of Kashmir controlled by Pakistan but claimed by India. Needless to say, India protested the agreement.[57] The dispute is still not resolved to this day.

In September 1963, the Soviet Union charged the PRC for border violations, that is, the PRC had been "systematically" violating the Sino-Soviet border since 1960. It said that 5,000 violations were reported in 1962 and that "there have even been attempts in the most flagrant manner to appropriate sections of Soviet territory."[58] Not to be outdone, Beijing accused Moscow in September 1964 of having created "constant border incidents" in the Ili area of Xinjiang.[59] It was around this time that the Soviet Union began its military build-up along the Sino-Soviet border. From October 1964 to March 1969, there were as many as 4,189 conflicts along the Sino-Soviet border, culminating in the March 1969 bloodshed at Zhenbao Island (Damansky), Hulin County, Heilongjiang Province, in the Wusuli (Ussuri) River, and the August 1969 armed clash in Xinjiang.[60] According to the PRC source, it was the Soviets who fired the first shot at Zhenbao Island.[61]

On August 21, 1968, the Soviet Union and four other East European countries troops moved into another Communist country, Czechoslovakia. Later on September 26, the Soviet party organ *Pravda* advanced a new, ideological argument to justify its move, saying the world socialist community had a right to intervene when socialism came under attack in a fraternal socialist country.[62] Following a Prague radio announcement not to resist, there was little fighting. The occupation put an end to the "Prague Spring," a period during which the Czech Communist Party First Secretary Alexander Dubcek had been liberalizing life in Czechslovakia and leading the country away from its ties to the Soviet Union. Moscow's forceful intervention in another Communist country further raised fears in Beijing, and is often credited as one of the major factors which led the Chinese Communist leaders to respond favorably to U.S. initiatives for rapprochement. On August 23, *Renmin Ribao* published the first strongly worded negative reaction of the PRC to the Warsaw Pact's invasion of Czechoslovakia. The author of that article was "Commentator," indicating high level approval. On September 16, Beijing charged that the Soviets had violated its northeastern borders 29 times between August 9 and August 29 and 119 times during 1967. *Izvestia* on November 9 denied the charges.[63]

In March 1969, following a series of minor incidents, serious fightings flared up on the Sino-Soviet border as the CPLA forces, in self-defense, attacked a Soviet company making a routine patrol of the disputed Zhenbao Island. In all, there were more than 400 skirmishes along the border in the year 1969. Beijing was not happy with the development. So, in March 1969, it was reported in Moscow that the mainland had halted all Soviet shipments across its territory to North Vietnam.[64] In May 1969, the PLA and Soviet troops clashed in the Bakhty region of Kazakhstan. In June 1969, they fought at Dazheng north of Yumin in the Barluk mountains (northwestern Xinjiang). In July, the troops clashed on Pacha (Goldinsky) Island in the Heilongjiang (Amur River). In October of the same year, Mao issued a directive, saying "dig tunnels deep, store grain everywhere, and never seek hegemony."

In May 1969, in an unprecedented public policy statement, Beijing stated that "the status quo of the boundary should be maintained and conflicts averted." It also mentioned that the Soviet Union had thought about using nuclear weapons, if serious fighting were to break out on the border.[65] In March 1973, Xinhuashe reported that the PRC and the Soviet Union had failed to reach an accord on navigation in rivers along their common boundary.[66] In February 1976, Xinhuashe reported a border clash between the Chinese PLA and Soviet troops in northwest Xinjinag. In February 1978, the Soviet Union sent a private message to Beijing suggesting that the two countries issue a joint statement to the effect that their mutual relations would be based on peaceful coexistence. This peaceful overture was rejected by Beijing on March 9. In their reply, the PRC again demanded withdrawal of Soviet troops from the MPR and, for the first time, Soviet withdrawal from the entire length of the Sino-Soviet border.[67] In March, Soviet President Leonid I. Brezhnev, accompanied by Defense Minister Dmitir F. Ustinov, began an unusual 13-day tour of Siberia and the Sino-Soviet border. Later in May, some 30 Soviet border guards crossed the Wusuli River and penetrated about 2.5 miles into Chinese territory. Beijing promptly filed a note of protest.[68] In any case, not until February 1989, did the two countries normalize their relations, as Deng said, upon the visit of the Soviet foreign minister,[69] to be followed by that of the Soviet leader M. Gorbachev in May 1989. In April 1990, PRC Premier Li Peng returned the visit, marking the first time since Zhou Enlai's visit in November 1964, a few weeks after Khrushchev's ouster. In May 1991, a border agreement on the eastern part was signed. In September 1994, in a joint statement, it was stated, *inter alia*, that both sides would not first use nuclear weapons against each other. At the same time, a document regarding Sino-Russian border in the western part was signed. Later in April 1996, relations became warmer when Russian President Boris Yeltsin visited

Beijing and both sides announced the establishment of a "Comprehensive Strategic Relationship." In July 2001, both sides in Moscow signed a friendship and cooperation treaty, the first landmark treaty in some 50 years. Because it is for the next 20 years, their distance has been narrowed down a great deal.

Turning to Vietnam, in July 1954, two Vietnamese states were formed along the 17th parallel, following the defeat of France at Dienbienphu, Vietnam in May 1954. The two Vietnams began to fight against each other. Earlier in March 1954, military advisors of the Chinese PLA assisted the Viet Minh Army in their Dienbienphu battle in North Vietnam, which is near the Vietnam-Laos border. In August 1964, the Gulf of Tokin crisis developed, when the U.S. destroyer *Maddox* was attacked by three North Vietnamese boats in international waters about 30 miles off the coast of North Vietnam. In March 1965, Richard M. Nixon said the Vietnam War was not one between the North and the South Vietnams but was in fact a war between the United States and the PRC. "A United States defeat in Vietnam," said Nixon, "means a [Chinese] Communist victory."[70] Washington began to gradually increase the number of its troops in South Vietnam since then. In April 1965, the PRC agreed to allow the Soviet Union to send supplies to North Vietnam by rail instead of by sea, to avoid encounters with the U.S. 7th Fleet. In June 1965 up to 1968, the Chinese PLA, under an agreement with North Vietnam, dispatched its artillery, engineering, railroad, and logistic troops who did not wear military uniform, so as to fight against the American imperialists. The number of military personnel involved numbered more than 320,000, some of whom were killed. In July 1970, the troops were sent home gradually. The amount of assistance totalled more than US$20 billion.[71] From July 1972 to August 1973, the Chinese PLA also dispatched its mine-sweeping ships to northern Vietnam. In January 1973, representatives of the United States, North Vietnam, South Vietnam, and the Viet Cong signed a peace agreement in Paris, calling for a ceasefire in Vietnam. Beijing was in favor of this move.

However, there was some friction between Beijing and Moscow. In May 1966, the PRC Ministry of Foreign Affairs said "China has never hampered the transit of Soviet aid materials to North Vietnam." Beijing insisted that "[a]ll military aid materials which Vietnam asked for and which the Soviet Union had delivered to China had been transported to Vietnam by China with priority, at high speed and free of charge."[72] In

April 1966, B-52 heavy jet bombers staged bombings on North Vietnam for the very first time.

Later in January 1974, the PRC and the ROV began a two-day war over possession of the uninhabited Xisha (Paracel) Island Group, claimed by both countries. The former succeeded in taking back all the islands held by the latter, sinking one South Vietnamese escort ship and damaged three destroyers and it stated that it was the South Vietnamese Navy fleet HQ4, HQ5, HQ16, and HQ10 which faithfully obeyed the orders from their commanders and fired the first shot, which was later confirmed by a junior naval officer working at the Naval Headquarters of Riverine Mobile Operations in Cat-lai, South Vietnam.[73] No other countries intervened.[74] But, the South Vietnamese moved to occupy some islands in the Nansha (Spratly) Island Group.

In September 1978, Hanoi's official army newspaper charged that Beijing had sent troops to the border area between the two countries.[75] Deng visited the United States in late January and early February 1979. While in the United States, Deng told reporters that Vietnam's massive armed aggression against Cambodia had "the full backing of the Soviet Union." Vietnam also had been provoking the Chinese along their border. "But as to actions to take, we will have to wait and see. I can only say two things: one, that for us Chinese, we mean what we say, and second, we Chinese do not act rashly."[76] On February 7, 1979, on his three-day visit to Japan, Deng told the Japanese Premier that Vietnam must be punished for its action against Cambodia. On the same day, Hanoi said that the Vietnamese had agreed with the Chinese in 1957–1958 to maintain the border agreements established in treaties of 1887 and 1895 but that the Chinese Communists had violated the border and provoked incidents increasingly since 1974.[77] On February 17, the Chinese PLA in Yunnan and Guangxi Province/Autonomous Region began a punitive attack[78] of Vietnam's Quang Ninh Province with its infantry, artillery, and armoured forces. Its justification was that the Vietnamese armed forces had encroached on Chinese territory and attacked Chinese frontier guards and inhabitants.[79] On March 5, 1979, after capturing the Vietnamese provincial capital of Lang Son, the Chinese PLA stated that it would commence the withdrawal of troops.[80] On March 16, PRC Foreign Minister Huang Hua announced that Chinese PLA, "after attaining their set goals," had completed their withdrawal from Vietnam that day. Huang went on to claim that the Chinese had captured more than 20 cities, towns, and strategic points.[81] On April 18, peace talks began between Beijing and Hanoi. In May 1979, Beijing said that 20,000 Chinese PLA soldiers had been killed or wounded in the recent attack of Vietnam and that the Vietnamese had suffered 50,000 casualties.[82] In May and June 1981, April 1984, January 1987, and October 1987, battles were also engaged between the Chinese PLA and the Vietnamese troops on land or in the air. Another one which had caught the international media's attention had to do with the clash between Beijing and Hanoi in March 1988 in Chigua Jiao (Gac Ma Reef), a small insular or geographic feature, in the Nansha Island Group. And, in February 1992, in a less publicized incident, the mainland Chinese and Vietnamese clashed again after the Chinese PLA landed on Da Ba Dau/Whitsun Reef in the Jiuzhang Huanjiao, which is near the Vietnamese-occupied island of Ranqing Shazhou (Sin Cowe East Cay/Sin Ton Dong) and Jinhong Dao (Sin Cowe Island/Sin Tonh). The issue has not yet been resolved. In September 1990, SRV leader Vo Nguyen Giap visited Beijing to attend the opening ceremony of the Asian Games. He is the highest ranking official to visit China since both sides' relations became sour in the late 1970s. In October 1993, a Sino-Vietnamese border agreement was signed in Hanoi, thereby further reducing their distance. In August 1999, the last mine in the Jingxi County, Guangxi Autonomous Region along the Sino-Vietnamese border was cleared. It has taken seven years to clear all the mines.[83] And in December 2000, an Agreement on Fishery Cooperation in the Beibu Gulf between the Government of the PRC and the Government of the SRV was finally signed.

In December 1979, the Soviet Union troops entered into Afghanistan, which shares a 57-mile border with the PRC. Beijing regarded the Soviet invasion as "a threat to China's security" and said it "cannot but arouse the grave concern of the Chinese people."[84] The Soviet explanation was that Afghanistan had made such a request for military assistance to put down a rebellion armed and led by the CIA in the United States as well as by the UK and the PRC agents.[85]

ENDNOTES

1   In summer 2001, a few Taiwan archaeologists in Mazu Island discovered some relics of the Yue people dating back to 6,000 years. In March 2004, it was reported that a 7,400-year-old plaited bamboo mat or bamboo article had been found in the Gaomiao cultural relic site in the outlying Yanli Village of Hongjiang City in the western part of Hunan Province.

2   *CT*, February 19, 1997, p. 9.

3   *UDN*, March 23, 1996, p. 1.

4   After the creation of the Hong League Fund Raising Bureau in July 1911, gold coin bonds issued by it bear the name of Sun Wen (or Sun Yat-sen) on it and were imprinted with the English words "The Chung Hwa [Chinese] Republic." See Ngai-ha Ng Lun and others, eds., *Historical Traces of Sun Yat-sen's Activities in Hong Kong, Macao, and Overseas* (Hongkong: United College, the Chinese University of Hong King, no date), p. 152. In Volume Two of *The Complete Works of Dr. Sun Yat-sen* (Taipei) on page 352, Sun explained why he had chosen the ROC rather than the Chinese Republic. It was because he had discovered the real meaning of *Min* (the people or the public). It is more than representative government. It included the right to initiate, to abrogate, as well as to recall. In short, it endorsed a new spirit.

5   *UDN*, December 25, 2000, p. 15. Another academic, Xu Zongli, said the bicoastal relationship is such that one country still refers to the ROC and that mainland China has a special domestic relationship with the ROC. See *ibid.*

6   To Chiang Ching-kuo, it is called "One Country, One Good System (*liangzhi*)," which was put forward on April 16, 1987. See *Central Daily News* (hereinafter CDN)(Taipei) on that day.

7   In December 2001, the party only won one seat in the Legislative *Yuan* (branch) and one county magistrate position.

8   *CT*, July 12, 2001, p. 11 and *UDN*, July 12, 2001, p. 13.

9   Quxin, "The China Policies of the United States and the Soviet Union in the Early Part of the Post-War Era and the Historical Status of China's 'One-sided' Diplomatic Strategy Toward the Soviet Union" in Joseph Y. S. Cheng, ed., *China's Diplomacy Entering the 21st Century* (Hongkong: Cosmos Books, 2001), p. 28.

10   In an official map released by the ROC's Ministry of Interior (MOI), OM is still regarded as part of the ROC. See *CT*, June 4, 1998, p. 4.

11   *UDN*, July 9, 2001, p. 14. See also Yao Chi-ching, "Research on Treaties of Unequality and International Law," paper presented to the Conference on the History of the Republic of China, held in Taipei, Taiwan, ROC, from August 23–28, 1981, 22 pages, and a critique by Hu Zhiwei's article, "Treaties with Imperial Russia: China Suffered," in *World Journal* (hereinafter WJ)(New York), August 2, 2001, p. C13.

12   The principles are: 1) respect for each other's sovereignty and territorial integrity; 2) mutual non-aggression; 3) non-interference in each other's internal affairs; 4) quality and mutual benefit; and 5) peaceful coexistence.

13   Deng in April 1974 gave a speech at the UN General Assembly on the Theory of the Three Worlds. See *Beijing Review* (hereinafter BR)(Beijing), supplement to No. 15 (April 12, 1974), p. i–v.

14   Zhou Enlai protested against the spread of germs in the airspace of Northeast China from February 29 to March 5, 1952. He said the United

States started using the germs in Korea from January 28, 1952. See Liu *et. al.* (note 32, ch. 7), pp. 50–51, 54, 58, and 64.

15   In mid-January 1954, the UN received 14,209 Chinese and 7,582 North Korean prisoners. In late January 1954, 347 pro-PRC Chinese including 21 Americans were handed over to the mainland and North Korean authorities. In the Association of Fourteen Thousand Freedom Fighters placed an advertisement in the January 30, 1979 issue of the *NYT*, urging the U.S. support of the ROC. In 1950, at the request of Ho Chi Minh, the CPLA dispatched its military advisors to North Vietnam. See Liu *et. al.* (note 32, ch. 7), p. 89. The term used by the PRC was *Zhongguozhiyuanbudui* (Chinese Support Troops). See *ibid.*, p. 332.

16   Stanley Sandler, *The Korean War: No Victor, No Vanquished* (London: UCL Press, 1999), p. 316. In April 1951, Lt.-Gen. Matthew B. Ridgway replaced MacArthur, and the former delivered a speech, No Substitute for Victory/ Old Soldiers Never Die. In May 1952, General Mark Clark succeeds General Ridgway as UN Commander.

17   Details given by Lee Kwon Ho, my student, dated May 16, 2001. See also the Soviet confidential documents, as reported in http://www.udn.com/ News/World/WOR1/1470083.shtml (accessed July 27, 2003).

18   *CT*, November 19, 2000, p. 13 and http://star2001.net/liberty/3-30f.htm, dated March 30, 2001.

19   *JFJB*, October 25, 2000, Military Technology Weekly.

20   Mao did not want to have a war between the PRC and the United States. That is why the troops were called the CPVF. Washington also did not want to escalate the war. See *ibid.*, October 16, 2000, p. 7. General George C. Marshall told a joint session of the Senate Foreign Relations and Armed Services Committees that there are four reasons why the United States had not intervened directly: "In view of the general world situation, our own military weakness, the global reaction to this situation, and my own knowledge out of that brief contact with China we could not afford to commit this Government to such a procedure." See *China* (note 30, ch. 7), p. 95.

21   *JFJB*, October 25, 2000, Military Technology Weekly. In March 1958, the PVF announced that it would go back to the mainland before the end of October 1958. See *JFJB*, October 16, 2000, p. 9.

22   Liu Yuanxun, *Zhongguojunduiduiwaizuozhanzhongdashilu* (Important Records on Chinese Military's War Outside of China)(Tibet: Xizangrenminchubanshe, May 2000), p. 359.

23   *JFJB*, October 25, 2000, Military Technology Weekly.

24   *Ibid.*, October 16, 2000, p. 7 and October 25, 2000, Military Technology Weekly.

25   Cited in *China* (note 30, ch. 7), p. 98.

26   *Ibid.*, p. 108.

27   *Ibid.*

28   But, Beijing said just before October 1949 there were only about one million Tibetans. By the end of 1987, there were a little over two million

people living there. Only about 3.5 per cent of the population are Chinese. See *Ta Kung Pao* (hereinafter TKP)(Hongkong), December 28, 1987, p. 2.

29   *China* (note 30, ch. 7), p. 109.

30   Liu *et. al.* (note 32, ch. 7), p. 157.

31   China (note 30, ch. 7), p. 120.

32   *Ibid.*, p. 121.

33   *Ibid.*, p. 123.

34   *Ibid.*, p. 130.

35   *Zhongguoguoqingbaogao* (Report on China's National Conditions)(Shenyang: Liaoningrenminchubanshe, December 1990), p. 1101. In September 1959, Zhou Enlai in a letter to his Indian counterpart said the PRC did not recognize the McMahon Line and, in order to maintain peace and tranquillity, the CPLA has never crossed this line. See Liu *et. al.* (note 32, ch. 7), p. 218.

36   *China* (note 30, ch. 7), p. 132.

37   *Ibid.*, p. 133.

38   *Ibid.*, p. 157.

39   *Ibid.*, p. 178.

40   *Ibid.*, p. 246.

41   Liu *et. al.* (note 32, ch. 7), p. 749.

42   *China* (note 30, ch. 7), p. 123.

43   *Ibid.*, p. 130.

44   In February 1970, a pilotless, American spy aircraft alighted on Hainan Island.

45   *CT*, May 12, 2001, p. 11.

46   Before April 1969, American reconnaissance aircraft could fly as close as 20 miles from the mainland coast.

47   When the PRC can routinely conduct spy flights over the United States EEZ, would Washington still argue that the airspace over EEZ is international? It is doubtful.

48   James C. Hsiung, "Chinese Haven't Gotten the 'Sorry' They Want," *NYT*, April 14, 2001, op-ed.

49   See my article, "The Chinese (Broken) U-shaped Line in the South China Sea: Points, Lines, and Zones," *Journal of Contemporary Southeast Asia* (Singapore), Vol. 25, No. 3 (2003), pp. 405–430.

50   *LHZB*, April 10, 2001, p. 36.

51   Cited in www.taiwansecurity.org/Reu/2001/Reuters-092101.htm.

52   *China* (note 30, ch. 7), p. 123.

53   *Ibid.*, p. 134.

54   *Current Digest of the Soviet Press* (hereinafter CDSP)(U.S.), Vol. XVIII, No. 3 (February 9, 1966), p. 7. Reportedly, they concluded a secret protocol,

which authorized the Soviet Union to station its troops freely in the MPR. See Thomas M. Gottlieb, *Chinese Foreign Policy Factionalism and the Origins of the Strategic Triangle*, R-1902-NA (Santa Monica, CA: Rand Corporation, November 1977), p. 34.

55   *China* (note 30, ch. 7), p. 127.

56   *Ibid.*, p. 134.

57   *Ibid.*, pp. 134–135.

58   *Ibid.*, p. 137.

59   *Ibid.*, p. 145.

60   Guo (note 10, ch. 8), pp. 441–442.

61   Liu *et. al.* (note 32, ch. 7), p. 381.

62   *China* (note 30, ch. 7), p. 181.

63   *Ibid.*, p. 181.

64   *Ibid.*, p. 184.

65   *Ibid.*, p. 185.

66   *Ibid.*, p. 209.

67   *Ibid.*, p. 236.

68   *Ibid.*, p. 237.

69   Zhou *et. al.* (note 26, ch. 8), pp. 881 and 883.

70   Cited in *ibid.*, p. 151.

71   Liu *et. al.* (note 32, ch. 7), p. 332.

72   Cited in *China* (note 30, ch. 7), p. 163.

73   *Zhongguorenminjiefangjunjungguanshouce* (note 58, ch. 7), p. 487. For this version, see http://www.vietquoc.com/hoangsa.htm (accessed January 1998). According to the same author, In March 1988, the SRV "troops could not return any fire while the Chinese troops defeated them...."

74   The 7th Fleet only provided intelligence, including false information. See *ibid.* and *China* (note 30, ch. 7), p. 212.

75   *China* (note 30, ch. 7), p. 240. The PRC said the SRV from August to December 1978 occupied more than 100 places of Guangxi Autonomous Region. See Zhou *et. al.* (note 26, ch. 8), p. 67.

76   *China* (note 30, ch. 7), p. 245.

77   *Ibid.*, p. 246.

78   Another wording is *ziweifanjizhan* (self-defense counter-attack). See Zhou *et. al.* (note 26, ch. 8), p. 67. Peng Dehuai also said in October 1958 that what the CPLA did to Jinmen was a punitive act. See Liu *et. al.* (note 32, ch. 7), p. 200. The PRC also regarded the October 1962 war with India as self-defense counter-attack.

79   *China* (note 30, ch. 7), p. 351.

80   *Ibid.*, p. 247.

81   *Ibid.*, p. 248.

82   *Ibid.*, p. 249.

83   Zhou *et. al.*(note 26, ch. 8), pp. 958 and 971. From July 1972 to August 1973, the CPLA navy also sweeped sea mines off North Vietnam.
84   *China* (note 30, ch. 7), p. 259.
85   *Ibid.*, p. 260.

CHAPTER 10

Politics: PRC's Position in Terms of the CHINA Versus china Framework

This section also represents a discussion at the macro-level. When Beijing leaders took the Socialism line, they were positioning themselves at 5 or A. This is because the CPC was starting from scratch. It did not have experience in running a government, in governing the society, etc. But, its success in seizing state power did help China get rid of most of the unequal treaties. This meant the return of sovereignty, independence, pride, etc. to the Chinese people. When the PRC was facing the Soviet Union, it can be said to have positioned itself at 5 or A, because Beijing had to treat Moscow as the Big Brother. Thus, it had sometimes to comply with and be submissive towards the latter. When Mao gradually shifted the line to Communism, he was actually stressing ideological purity at an inappropriate time. Many, if not most, Chinese people followed him, however, at the expense of production. Thus, the PRC could be regarded as china when the GPCR was at its zenith. Its image was tarnished, as most Bicoastal China observers found out what the Red Guards had done to the state. In a word, it had achieved the opposite effect. Mao thought he could bring the PRC to the CHINA stage within his lifetime. Yet, he failed miserably. The result was to position china at or D or E along the Letter spectrum. Deng was pragmatic. He knew that to move the PRC to the position of CHINA, mainland China had to stress production. He also knew that he would meet with opposition from some political figures in the mainland, fearful that Capitalism would dominate the PRC. So, Deng came up with One Centre, Two Basic Points. In doing so, he wanted all the people especially the political figures to keep a distance from E, something considered negative and very negative by Mao. The mainland was moving in the normative direction of becoming CHINA after Deng's 1992 inspection tour. Needless to say, it will take a long time for the mainland to achieve the status of being CHINA, because it is not just an economic matter. Besides, becoming an official member of the WTO in November 2001 meant that the mainland would have to give up something in exchange for something else. As long as the SOEs are not able to compete in the international market, mainland China will be on the defensive for a long period of time. Certainly, politics may interfere and the military likewise.

Having discussed the lines and along with it other secondary ideological frameworks, we are in a position to talk about internal (as opposed to domestic, in view of the "One China" principle or the 1992 consensus and the existence of the ROC on Taiwan) political affairs and external political affairs which mainly involve military affairs, etc. We shall conduct our discussion in terms of the four basic periods, namely, taking the Socialism line, leaping to the Communism line, restoring the Socialism with Chinese Characteristics line, and gambling on the Market Economy line.

TAKING THE SOCIALISM LINE

A1. Internal—The Mainland

The CPC adopts the Centralism Versus Democracy framework before and after the establishment of the PRC. To begin with, Centralism is 1 and Democracy, E. Democracy is not a bad thing, if it is observed and practised before reaching a final decision or consensus by the party, because CPC members can freely voice their opinions in the first place. Once a decision or a consensus has been made, one has to travel back to the safe zone, preferably to position oneself at 1. If every, or most, members, adhere or comply with this rule of the game, the CPC can present itself to the non-party members or other political parties as a force, if not an armada.

Earlier on, the CPC relied on another framework, that of Politics Versus Economics. Another way of saying the same thing is Let Politics Take Command Versus Let Economics Take Command. (The framework could be reversed, that is, it can become Economics Versus Politics.) Given the chaotic situation after seizing power, the party had emphasized politics, i.e., 1, 2, and 3, most of the time. One has also to bear in mind the following facts. When the mainland changed its colour from blue (representing the KMT) to red (representing the CPC), there were more than two million political bandits, more than 600,000 people with special missions and spies, more than 600,000 reactionaries and counter-revolutionaries of the KMT.[1] In the southwestern part of the mainland, there were more than one million bandits. From January to October 1950, there were 818 times of counter-revolutionary violence. From spring to the fall of 1950, more than 40,000 cadres had been killed by them. So, from December 1950, the CPC started to crack down on those counter-revolutionary activists. A year later, the overall situation had begun to calm down.

Until the CPC felt that it was in control of the situation, it would not move itself to 5 in the Politics Versus Economics framework. The Public (*gong*) Versus Private (*si*) was another major framework used. What it did, on the whole, was quite successful. By the end of 1952, industrial and agricultural production had reached the highest point in history.[2] From 1953 to 1956, the market was prosperous and prices, stable.[3] Drastic land reform was being carried out.[4] In June 1927, the KMT published a figure, saying the rich peasants and the small, medium, and big land-owners constituted 14.4 per cent of the total population and that they possessed 81 per cent of the land. By 1950, according to a CPC calculation, before the land reform, rich peasants and land-owners constituted 9.41 per cent of the total population and they possessed 51.92 per cent of the land. To remind readers, some of them were liquidated and executed. In connection with the land reform, June 1950, the Agrarian Reform Law was passed in connection with the land reform. The reform ended in spring 1953. Generally speaking, most mainland residents who were poor supported this move. The CPC's legitimacy and support were strengthened as a result.

We can provide other information regarding Beijing and Shanghai.[5] When the Chinese PLA troops entered into Beijing, which was called Beiping, on January 31, 1949, there was already hyperinflation. For example, one bag of flour on August 19, 1948, the first day of issuing its new currency, cost 10 gold Yuan notes/certificates. By the time Beijing was encircled by the Chinese PLA in December 1948, the same bag cost more than 400. After World War II and up to the end of 1948, Beijing's price was more than eight million times the original price.[6]

From April 1949 to early 1950, some capitalists took advantage of economic instability by raising prices of important items like grains and gauze four times. To put down hyper-inflation, state-owned enterprises managed to get hold of those items in large quantities and sold them at a cheaper price in the market, thereby solving the price-hike.[7]

The CPC's policy was to benefit workers, students, teachers, and urban poor people first.[8] They can exchange up to 500 gold Yuan. For each 3 gold Yuan, they can get one Renminbi. Others, could exchange 10 gold Yuan for one Renminbi. In March 1949, the People's Bank of Beiping City and two other banks began operations.

Another important city deserves some discussion. In Shanghai, on December 31, 1948, the wholesale price index (1937 = 1) hit 21,568,000. This meant that it took more than that much Yuan to buy what had cost one Yuan in 1937. (On December 31, 1946, the index was 1,143,000.)[9]

In May 1949, Shanghai Municipal City was liberated.[10] There was the question of how to handle the capitalists.[11] The policy was buying-out or redemption. People in the northwest and southwest would make orders of many light industry goods. Publicly-owned department stores would try to control resources for making these goods. But, the Shanghai capitalists were opposed to such control. Inflation hit the city and many goods could not be sold. The next vicious cycle was that the capitalists had to lay off workers, because they had no money to pay their wages. In the winter of 1954, the State Council began to talk about turning private enterprises into semi-public (*gongsi*) ones, which is 5 in the Public Versus Private framework. Two months later, action was taken in that direction. By January 1956, the private business sector including Beijing, Shanghai, Tianjin, Nanjing, Guangzhou, and Wuhan had basically become semi-public.[12] The move was initiatied in Beijing followed by Shanghai and Tianjin. Furthermore, after the anti-rightist campaign which started in May 1957 and ended in July 1958,[13] all semi-public enterprises also became state-owned, and the first People's Commune was organized in August 1958.

On matters related to political parties, the framework of One-Party-People's-Democratic-(or Proletarian)-Dictatorship Versus Multi-party System, among others, was adopted. The CPC was the ruling party but it was cooperating with other political parties. So, the CPC chose 5 or the Multi-party Cooperation System. This arrangement mirrored the Communism Versus Capitalism framework. In other words, when Communism arrived, the One-Party-People's-Democratic-(or Proletarian)-Dictatorship would be implemented. To the party, this was necessary, because it was not possible to weed out political parties which were close to Capitalism. At least on the surface, the CPC had delivered its promise. Take the NPC as an example. In September 1954, it held its first meeting. There were 668 members who belonged to the CPC, whereas the non-Communist membership was 558. While the NPC Chairman of the Standing Committee was a CPC member, the CPC allowed 8 non-CPC members out of 13 Vice-Chairmen to be the Vice-Chairmen, constituting 61.5 per cent.[14]

During the first period, there were non-mainstream challenges. In February 1957, Mao delivered a four-hour speech to a closed session of the Supreme State Conference entitled "On the Correct Handling of Contradictions Among the People." Mao issued an unprecedented call for criticism of his regime: "As a scientific truth, Marxism fears no criticism." Thus, Mao added, counter-revolutionary ideas should not be met with "coercive measures" but with "discussion, criticism, and reasoning." Mao's slogan, which appeared for the first time in May 1956 for the new movement, was "Let a Hundred Flowers Bloom and Let a Hundred Schools of Thought Contend." Later in June, Mao's speech was published but criticism of PRC life and politics increased.[15] The struggle between the mainstream and non-mainstream ended in that the PRC Minister of Security Luo Reiqing said, 100,000 intellectuals had been purged between June 1955 and October 1957 for criticizing the government.[16]

A2. Internal—Bicoastal Chinese or Cross-Strait

In December 1949, the ROC Executive *Yuan* (branch) was moved to Taipei. Only then, can we say that the ROC was politically divided. Taiwan was certainly vulnerable up to the outbreak of the Korean War and it could, like South Korea, "be gobbled up to be added to the rest of Red Asia." And a State Department memorandum dated December 23, 1949 said Taiwan held "no special military significance."[17] However, because North Korea made the first move to attack the South, the unfavourable tide to Taipei was suddenly reversed in June 1950.

On March 1, 1950, Chiang Kai-shek reclaimed his presidency.[18] The Chinese Won't Attack Chinese Versus Chinese Would Attack Chinese framework resurfaced[19] in January 1952 for the first time since October 1949 when the ROC forces attempted to take back Dongshan Dao, Fujian Province, which is a strategic island. In July 1953, a division of the ROC forces tried to recover the same Island again. But,

3,379 officers and soldiers were killed by the Chinese PLA.[20] (In June and July 2004, the PRC Armed Forces conducted a military exercise codenamed Liberation No. 1.) Later in September 1954 the Chinese PLA shelled the ROC-held island of Jinmen, and the latter returned fire. This framework first appeared after Imperial Japan's occupation of northeast China in September 1931.[21] The shelling was followed by a development not to the PRC's liking. In December 1954, Dulles signed a mutual defense treaty with his counterpart in the ROC, and Washington unilaterally drew the middle line in the Taiwan Strait. The treaty required the United States and the ROC to:

1. Maintain and develop "jointly by self-help and mutual aid" their individual and collective capacity to resist armed attack and Communist subversion directed against them "from without";
2. Cooperate in economic development;
3. Consult on implementation of the treaty; and
4. Act to meet an armed attack "in the West Pacific area directed against the territories" of either the United States or the ROC , including Taiwan, Penghu (Pescadores Islands), and "such other territories as may be determined by mutual agreement."

This was a blow to the PRC, after the creation of Southeast Asian Treaty Organization (SEATO) in September 1954 which is an "Asiatic Monroe Doctrine." In effect, the United States tried to contain the PRC. We can use the following framework to illustrate their positions: PRC Versus the United States, with the ROC at E. To the relief of Beijing, the December 1954 treaty did not cover ROC-held islands along the southeast coast of the mainland.

The PRC's morale was heightened in February 1955 when the ROC Government decided to withdraw from Dachen Islands, part of the Zhejiang Province. This meant that all the coastal islands except Jinmen and Mazu were recovered by the Chinese PLA. In January 1955, the Chinese PLA conducted the largest air raids of the civil war against those islands. In the same month, it seized Yijiang Island, which is eight miles north of the Dachen Islands. However, to get even, the ROC's ships and warplanes in February 1955 struck against PRC convoys en route to the Communist-held Daishan Islands.

At the international level, both sides of the Taiwan Strait continued to compete for legitimacy and representation. As mentioned by Lee Teng-hui in October 1993, Chiang Kai-shek never said anything about the One China principle.[22] But, there is a distinction. Chiang only says ROC, because he was confident and he believed that only his Government represented the whole of China. In other words, the One China principle representing the Roof/Housetop or Eaves is Beijing's choice of words.[23] In any case, the framework PRC Versus ROC or, for that matter, ROC Versus PRC, can describe their struggle at the international level. In October 1958, a joint communiqué between Taipei and Washington for the time did not mention the slogan-recovery of the mainland.

B. External

During this first period, according to a PRC academic, the relationship between the PRC and the Soviet Union was equal and mutually beneficial, although Mao's policy was leaning to one side, towards the latter[24] in the Soviet Union Versus the United States framework. But, this is not entirely true. The American Secretary of State Dean Acheson on February 15, 1950 commented that he felt the Sino-Soviet Treaty of February 1950 was detrimental to the mainland since the Soviet Union would attempt to convert the mainland into a Soviet satellite.[25] In May 1950, U.S. President Harry S. Truman accused the Soviet Union of being "heartless and indifferent" toward mainland China's famine, for once the Chinese Communists had "sent to the Soviet Union food which is desperately needed by the Chinese people."[26]

When the PRC was formally created on October 1, 1949, Zhou in his speech repeated Mao's three principles concerning recognition of the PRC on "the basis of the principles of equality, mutual benefit, and mutual respect for territorial integrity and sovereignty."[27] A boost for the PRC came in December 1949 when the British Cabinet decided to recognize the Chinese Communist regime in January 1950. Beijing accepted British recognition three days later. But, both countries did not exchange ambassadors until March 1972, as the United Kingdom had insisted on maintaining the consulate in Kaohsiung City, southern Taiwan which had been in operation since the Qing Dynasty. So, the appropriate framework for their relationships could be Maintaining Good Diplomatic Relations Versus Maintaining Bad Diplomatic Relations, and Beijing was willing to choose 5, until early 1972.

The seizure of the U.S. consulate in Beijing on January 14, 1950 led Acheson to say that Beijing did not want American recognition.[28]

The above-mentioned framework can also be applied here. It goes without saying, that Washington wanted to position itself at 5 but Beijing selected E, because it had to side with Moscow, the Big Brother. This led to other violent incidents, arising from the Soviet Union's failure in its attempt, at the Security Council, to propose the admission of the PRC to the UN during its voting on January 13, 1950 when the Soviet delegate Yakov A. Malik walked out of the Security Council for the second time. What occurred the following day definitely positioned the PRC at E.

In April 1955, a conference participated by 340 delegates from 29 Asian and African countries convened in Bandung, Indonesia. Zhou gave a speech, and it indicated a major change in the PRC foreign policy by choosing a middle road by courting countries in Asia and Africa.

On August 1, 1955, the PRC ambassador to Poland, Wang Bingnan, began talks with the American ambassador to Czechoslovakia, U. Alexis Johnson, in Geneva, Switzerland. This first meeting represented an upgrading of the talks from the consular to the ambassadorial level. So, the framework of Ambassadorial Level Versus non-Ambassadorial Level can be applied, with Consular level as 5. To show goodwill, the PRC on the same day announced the release of 11 American fliers who had been imprisoned as spies in the mainland. Should their relations become sour, this would mean that one or both of them would move sideways to the right.

In February 1956, Soviet Communist Party First Secretary Nikita S. Khrushchev gave two speeches which sent shock waves through Communist parties in the world.[29] In the first speech, the Soviet leader said war with "capitalist imperialism" was no longer inevitable. In other words, each Communist party should try to find a "peaceful" road to power. In the second speech, Khrushchev denounced the late Stalin. Of the two speeches, the message that the PRC received was that it cannot expect to rely a great deal on the Soviet Union in foreign affairs and it has lost the protection of the Soviet nuclear umbrella. The Chinese Communists dated the origins of their split with the Soviets from these speeches.

In May 1957, the British Government announced that it would not apply the same restrictions on trade with the PRC as those applied on trade with the Soviet bloc. This is like a breach in the dike. The U.S. Department of State was "most disappointed" by the British move and said the United States contemplated no change in its total embargo on trade with the mainland.[30] What the U.K. had done was to position itself to 4 or 3 from 5 in the Maintaining Good Diplomatic Relations Versus Maintaining Bad Diplomatic Relations framework. In a word, Beijing's standing in the international community had quite improved.

LEAPING TO THE COMMUNISM LINE

A1. Internal—The Mainland

In October 1958, Moscow scrapped more than 600 contracts with Beijing, although in February 1959, Beijing and Moscow had signed a trade pact, the latter of which was slated to export industrial equipment to the mainland. As a result, 250 enterprises could not function or were functioning only at half-capacity.[31] This dealt a severe blow to the mainland. In June 1959, the Soviet Union secretly told the PRC that it was abrogating its October 1957 agreement which promised to help the PRC to develop its nuclear arsenal and to offer the same a sample of atomic bomb. (In August 1957, the Soviet Union conducted its first successful test of an Intercontinental Ballistic Missile [ICBM]. Two months later, Moscow launched the first "artificial earth satellite," dubbed Sputnik. In November 1957, Dulles conceded that the Untied States would be able to catch up.[32]) In July 1960, 1,390 experts of the Soviet Union working in the mainland decided to return home, leaving the 156 major construction projects unfinished and discontinuing the supplies, resulting in serious economic losses.

In April 1960, the CPC theoretical journal, *Hongqi* (Red Flag), published the first public indication of the Sino-Soviet split.[33] Entitled "Long Live Leninism," the article sought to demonstrate the theoretical legitimacy of Chinese Communism and Mao, and the deviation and heresy of the Soviet Union. Without naming Khrushchev, the article labelled him a "revisionist," a reference to his attempt to work in harmony with the West. The split certainly helped the Chinese Communists to construct the Third World Versus First World framework. The latter World refers to the United States and the Soviet Union. The *Hongqi* article concluded that there was no "peaceful road to socialism," and stated that a nuclear war would be followed by "a civilization thousands of times higher than the capitalist system." Certainly the Not Extreme Versus Extreme framework can describe and explain the last sentence. In any case, it was not until the period from September 1963 to July 1964 that *Remin Ribao* and *Hongqi* detailed the origin and development of the Sino-Soviet split.

Due to perceived worsening of the situation, during this period, many coastal factories and industries in the mainland were moved to the Third Line (*sanxian*), resulting in a great loss of more than US$100 billion, according to one figure.[34] *Yuanqidashang* (sap in mainland China's vitality or vigor) is an accurate description of the PRC at the time. The PRC's economic development was further retarded.

Unfortunately, politics was still in command. Mao standing at 1 in the Communism Versus Capitalism and the Politics Versus Economics frameworks, initiated and launched the GPCR.[35] He thought that, by accomplishing this in ideological terms, the PRC might be brought to the Communism stage. His followers and supporters attempted to eliminate all "capitalist vestiges" such as giving material incentives or overtime payments for increased production. The Chinese people, male and female alike, were transformed into "blue ants" clad in dull, blue clothing. During this period, there was indiscriminate killing; countless dead bodies could be seen floating down rivers; and there was wanton destruction of ancient cultural relics like temples. The first phase occurred between May 1966 to April 1969, when the CPC held its 9th National Congress. Mao erroneously said there were capitalists in the CPC. Peng Zhen, Lo Ruiqing, Lu Dingyi, and Yang Shangkun were criticized at the CPC's enlarged Political Bureau meeting held in May 1966. On June 2, 1966, the first big character poster was published in *Renmin Ribao*. On August 1, Mao's first big character poster was circulated at the CPC meeting, naming Liu Shaoqi as the person who should be responsible for taking the capitalist road. From August 1 to 12, Liu and Deng were criticized, and the GPCR began on a full-scale. From August 18 to November 26, 1966, Mao received the Red Guards eight times. In December 1966, Peng Dehuai who was sent to the Third Line to work was kidnapped by the Red Guards upon the instruction of Jiang Qing and others in Sichuan Province as well as imprisoned and struggled against in a Beijing jail.[36] By January 1967, many organizations had ceased to or could no longer function. On January 6, 1967, Shanghai had a "January Storm (*feng bao*)," and its *Wenhuibao* and *Jiefangribao* were taken over by those such as Wang Hongwen who supported the GPCR.

The Chinese PLA was ordered by Mao to conduct "Three Supports and Two Militaries (*Sanzhiliangjun*)," that is, the military forces must support industry (that is, workers), agriculture (namely peasants), and the broad masses of the Left and it must engage in military control (at chaotic places and vital units like the public security offices, courts, and banks) and conduct political and military training. From January 1967 to August 1972, some 2.8 million officers and soldiers participated in this movement. Deng of course did not like this, because the PRC armed forces might interfere in politics again in the future and the party might not be able to control the guns. For the record, even before the GPCR, Lin Biao, who was the Defense Minister, fully understood Mao's logic. He, in order to gain favour with Mao, emphasized 1 in the Politics Versus Military framework.[37] He suspended many military training exercises and closed many military academies. And the *Sanzhiliangjun* movement lasted until August 1972. Earlier in February 1967, in the so-called "February Counter-Current" (*Eryue Niliu*), some elder revolutionaries challenged Lin, Jiang Qing, and others, saying the latter's actions had brought chaos and instability to the country. In April 1967, Liu was branded China's Khrushchev. In July 1967, there were armed struggles, fomented by Jiang Qing, at Nanning, Shanghai, Nanjing, etc. At Wuhan in the same month, there were demonstrations involving more than 100,000 people including members of the Chinese PLA. In summer 1967, for two months, armed personnel in power together with poor peasants at the 36 People's Communes of Dao County, Hunan Province killed 4,500 landlords and rich people as well as their relatives including old people and babies.[38] By July 1968, Lin and Jiang Qing had become more powerful within the Chinese PLA and the CPC. In April 1969, the CPC held its 9th National Congress, and Lin was written into the party Constitution as Mao's "closest comrade-in-arms" and his successor. In November 1969, Liu Shaoqi passed away at Zhengzhou, and his death affected some 28,000 people for having been related to him. Earlier in October 1968, the 12th Plenum of the 8th Central Committee of the CPC met in Beijing. The meeting announced that Liu, the foremost revisionist in the CPC had been removed from all his posts in the state and the party. Liu was expelled from the CPC forever.

In December 1965, Luo Ruiqing, who was then the Secretary-General of the Central Military Commission (CMC) of the Chinese PLA, was labelled by Mao, *inter alia*, as someone who was against giving first priority to politics. Why was this so? Well, the CPC had also applied the framework of Politics Versus Military, as mentioned earlier. The Chinese

PLA had adopted a middle road, that is, Number 5, which stands for political-military. In other words, politics and military were equally important but the emphasis was still on politics, so as to enable the party to command the guns or the armed forces. But, because the economic line had been shifted to Number 1 which stood for Communism, there was no need for the military. This is because, with the advent of Communism, countries would disappear. When countries do not exist, there is no need for military forces. So, logically, the PRC should emphasize only politics. Lin, as early as September 1959, was doing that already by putting politics in command. In November 1964, in order to further please Mao, Lin at a military work meeting, again stressed the importance of politics. By December 1965, military training was suppressed. In February 1969, 82 military academies and schools were closed down.

A countless number of people were sent from urban areas to the countryside or the "front line of agricultural production" where conditions were most arduous, so as to learn from the masses. In December 1968, Mao personally approved the "down to the countryside (*Xiafang*)" policy. According to some analysts, Mao was actually thinking of removing the Red Guards from the cities so as to allow the military to restore order.[39] Actually, Mao wanted, for example, intellectuals to learn from the peasants, so that their writings would not be purely idealistic or out of touch with reality.

The second phase of the GPCR was from the end of the 9th National Congress of the CPC up to August 1973. In February 1971, Lin and others took measures to stage an armed coup, according to the official version. In March 1971, Lin drafted a plan to conduct an armed coup entitled "571 Project Minutes" (*Wuqiyi Gongcheng Jiyao*). *Wuqiyi* is the homophonic of "armed uprising." In September 1971, Lin fled the mainland, after his plan to assassinate Mao had been foiled.[40] He and others died in a plane crash in Wenduerkai, Outer Mongolia. In March 1973, Deng was proposed by Mao and Zhou and the CPC later endorsed his return to political life and resumption of his position as the Vice-Premier of the State Council.

The CPC's 10th National Congress was held in August 1973. The period dating from the end of the congress up to October 1976, was regarded as the GPCR's third phase. In October 1974, Mao proposed for Deng to become the First Vice-Premier of the State Council. In

January 1975, Deng was appointed the Vice-Chairman of the CPC. In the second half of 1975, Mao's illness became grave. In January 1976, Zhou passed away. In 1976, trains could not move as scheduled at Zhengzhou, a very important junction; this affected 12 provinces. Other railroad bureaus like Lanzhou and Taiyuan faced similar traffic jams.[41] Before and after Mao's death in September 1976, supporters of the "Gang of Four" had armed the Shanghai militia in August. On September 11, Wang Hongwen attempted to take over the central leadership at Zhongnanhai. On October 8, some "Gang of Four" supporters, after hearing that Jiang Qing and three others had been arrested, mobilized and deployed 33,500 militia. But, they failed in their plot to revolt.

The GPCR resembled and recalled earlier Ming and Qing Dynasties. In the last few years of the Ming, the prohibition of both coastal and overseas trade was reimposed. For periods of varying lengths between 1661 and 1683, the population of the coastal strip from Zhejiang and Guangdong Provinces was forcibly removed inland, and most settlements—villages, market towns, and cities—were razed to the ground under the scorched-earth policy of the Qing. "In 1717, Chinese were forbidden once again to go privately overseas, and in 1757 the fate of the whole Southeast Coast region was sealed for nearly a century by the designation of Guangzhou as the sole legal port for foreign trade."[42] Jiang Qing at one point also advocated that the entire navy be scrapped. She said the PRC only needed four of them, so as to enable Mao to cruise and inspect the coastal area of China.[43]

In April 1975, Chiang Kai-shek died. That he died before Mao symbolized the end of the Mao Versus Chiang framework. And in September 1976, Mao also passed away. Soon after, the "Gang of Four" were ousted in the October 6, 1976 coup. Some supporters of the "Gang of Four" tried to make a come-back, for example, in December 1976 in Baoding, which is a city 100 miles south of Beijing.[44]

A gradual change began to take place. Hua Guofeng, who had been hand-picked by Mao to succeed him, gradually became a figurehead. In February 1977, the CPC theoretical journal, *Hongqi*, expressed its approval of selective private production, largely in the fields of agriculture and handicrafts. Such private production had been in disrepute since the onset of the GPCR.[45] In any case, with politics in command, by 1978, *gongyouzhijingji* (public ownership) constituted 99 per cent. Non-*gongyouzhijingji* had only 1 per cent. As to the first, second, and third *chanye* (industries), it was 28.4 per cent, 48.6 per cent, and 23 per cent respectively.[46]

A2. Internal—Bicoastal Chinese or Cross-Strait

In August 1958, the second Taiwan Strait crisis erupted. From that day to September 21, 1958, the ROC had 3,000 civilian and 1,000 military casualties in Jinmen alone. On September 4, 1958, the PRC proclaimed extension of its territorial waters to within 12-miles of its coasts, thus including Jinmen, Mazu, etc. The United States immediately said it would only recognize the traditional three-nautical mile (n.m.) territorial sea limit. On September 14, the ROC naval ships accomplished their first successful convoy to the beleaguered island of Jinmen, marking a shift in military advantage away from Beijing.[47] The United States was clearly on the ROC's side. For example, the Pentagon announced that American pilots were authorized to follow a "hot pursuit" policy against any Chinese PLA plane which might attack them, including following the plane over the PRC-held territory.[48] On October 6, the PRC's Defence Minister, Peng Dehuai, announced over the radio a one-week cease-fire in the Taiwan Strait area. He also said the crisis was an internal matter, that is, it was not a matter between the PRC and the United States.[49] On October 25, the PRC announced that there would be no bombardment of Jinmen airfield, wharf, or beach landing areas on "even dates" of the month (so the offshore islands could get adequate supplies), but that "exception will be taken if there should be escorts" by foreign powers.[50]

In May 1962, the ROC planned to conduct a counter-attack of the mainland. Chiang Kai-shek ordered more than 40 groups (*gu*) of Anti-Communist Salvation fighters (*fangongjiuguoyongshi*) to be air-dropped and sea-ferried to the mainland coastal area.[51] From October to December 1962, nine groups of the ROC guerrillas had raided the coastal area of the mainland but all of them were exterminated.[52] Chiang did have some kind of American support, at least psychologically. In February 1961, the United States began to monitor the PRC's nuclear weapons development program. Two months later, a report mentioned what to do with the PRC: containing the mainland, infiltrate and sabotage the mainland's nuclear weapons development program, help the ROC to conduct a counter-attack of the mainland, and conduct a surgical strike of the mainland's nuclear facilities and bases.[53] In a word, the struggle between which framework would prevail continued: PRC Versus ROC or ROC Versus PRC?

In January 1966, a small Chinese PLA landing craft defected to Mazu, a remote island under ROC jurisdiction. The three defectors after killing the captain were taken to Taiwan on board an unarmed hydroplane. But, the plane was shot down by six Chinese PLA fighters, after receiving an order from Zhou Enlai.[54]

B. External

In June 1957, Dulles said "diplomatic recognition gives the recognized regime valuable rights and privileges, and, in the world of today, recognition by the United States gives the recipient much added prestige and influence at home and abroad."[55] In January 1964, France established diplomatic relations with the PRC. This was a further boost to the latter's legitimacy, because the former had been a Western power. The U.S. State Department called the French action "an unfortunate step, particularly at a time when the Chinese Communists are actively promoting aggression and subversion in Southeast Asia and elsewhere."[56] In January 1969, Nixon became the U.S. President. It meant that relations between the PRC and the United States would be gradually improved at the expense of diplomatic ties between the ROC and the United States. In April 1969, for example, the Secretary of State William P. Rogers said a Communist China exists on the mainland, and it is a fact of life.[57] In July 1969, Nixon put forward his doctrine, that is, the United States would no longer contain mainland China since the Korean War. In February 1971, in his second annual State of the World Report to the U.S. Congress, Nixon for the first time used the formal name adopted by the Beijing Government since October 1949.

Pressure from the Soviet Union began to mount gradually. In spring and summer, Mao refused Khrushchev's suggestion of creating a joint submarine fleet. Mao asked his Soviet counterpart to make the guiding principle (*fangzhen*) clear: Would the Chinese PLA Navy be in charge of everything? Was it a joint effort? And if it were not the latter, would Moscow refuse to render help?[58]

Other internal developments made the PRC more vulnerable. So, the PRC in May 1969 decided to end its self-imposed isolation by naming Geng Biao as ambassador to Albania. This move implied that Beijing could equally improve relations with Washington. Efforts were also made to reduce tension between the two Communist giants. For example, in August 1969, the two sides signed a protocol "recording agreement by the two sides to carry out certain measures during the 1969 navigational season to improve the shipping" on various rivers along the border.[59] In March 1971, Sino-Soviet polemics resumed after a nine-month pause.

Washington and Moscow certainly began to worry about Beijing's ability to go nuclear. In October 1964, the PRC successfully tested its first nuclear device and said it "will never … under any circumstances be the first to use nuclear weapons."[60] In December of the same year, the United States announced that a U.S. submarine carrying nuclear missiles was on station off the coast of the mainland. But, to Beijing, this was an act of "nuclear blackmail."[61] In June 1967, two years and eight months after its first detonation of an atomic bomb, the RPC tested its first hydrogen bomb. It had taken the United States seven years and the Soviet Union four years to accomplish the same feat.[62]

Beijing continued its effort in exporting its brand of Communism to other countries, spending some US$50 billion in the 1960s and 1970s. In January 1965, Burundi broke off diplomatic ties with the PRC for the reason that the Chinese Communists were training Congolese rebels in Burundi.[63] In February 1965, Niger's President, Hamani Diori, charged that the PRC had plotted and financed an unsuccessful revolt in the fall of 1964 against his government. In January 1969, a radio program began broadcasting in the Malay, Thai, Chinese, and English languages.[64] The radio station was located in Yiyang City, Hunan Province, rather than Yunnan Province, as mistakenly thought by the CIA. It is close to Changsha City, which is a gathering place for Communists from Southeast Asia and a place for transferring goods and services to those foreign countries. It lasted until early 1980s.

By October 1967, at the height of the GPCR, the PRC had managed to pick quarrels with 32 countries, many of which had broken off or downgraded diplomatic ties with the PRC.[65]

In April 1970, the PRC launched its first satellite. This helped to enhance the PRC's image as an important actor in the Asia-Pacific region. In September 1971, the Chinese PLA had its first nuclear submarine. (In passing, it should be noted that, in October 1982, the Chinese PLA had launched its first carrier rocket from an underwater conventional submarine. In September 1988, a submerged nuclear submarine made by the PRC launched its first carrier rocket off Zhejiang Province.)

In October 1970, Canada, after negotiating with the PRC since February 1969, recognized the latter. The statement said that "the Chinese Government reaffirms that Taiwan is an inalienable part of the territory of the PRC. The Canadian Government takes note of this position of the Chinese Government."[66] In a word, the handling of the Taiwan problem in this wording had become a model for many other countries.

In October 1971, the PRC was finally admitted into the UN as well as the Security Council. Beijing did not expect this to take place until a few years later. PRC media propagandised this entry as a victory of Mao Zedong Thought. However, the PRC suffered from a diplomatic setback, when India in December 1971, fortified by Soviet military aid and a new 20-year Treaty of Peace, Friendship, and Cooperation, signed in August 1971, attacked East Pakistan in support of the Bangladesh rebels who had been defeated by Pakistan in April. The Pakistan defeat was also a defeat for the PRC, which had supported Pakistan, in the first of the Sino-Soviet "proxy wars."[67]

There was another major development. In January 1972, the Soviet Foreign Minister, Andrei A. Gromyko, while in Tokyo, issued a statement, concerning the upcoming visit by Nixon to Beijing: "The Soviet Union desires that other countries have friendly relations with China," but on the condition that these relations did not "affect adversely the safety and interest of the Soviet Union."[68] Moscow was fearful of collusion between Beijing and Washington. In the framework of Moscow Versus Washington, the former positions itself at 1, while the latter, E. PRC was certainly at A or B. At a time when Tokyo was making arrangements to have diplomatic ties with Beijing, Washington officials in September 1972 were saying that the Soviets were adding their mechanized divisions along the Sino-Soviet border, which constituted one-third of the Soviet army.[69]

The PRC's prestige was further boosted when Nixon arrived on the mainland for a seven-day visit in February 1972. That Nixon had to go to the PRC, that is, Mao did not have to visit the United States in person, simply shows that it is the United States which needs the PRC to deter the Soviet Union and not the other way around. The visit also ended hostility between the two countries.

In March 1972, the UK and the PRC agreed to exchange ambassadors. In the joint communiqué, Britain said it was "acknowledging the position of the Chinese Government that Taiwan is a province of the PRC," thereby ending its insistence that the status of Taiwan was "undetermined."[70]

In January 1973, representatives of the United States, South Vietnam, and the Viet Cong signed a peace agreement in Paris. Although the agreement called for a ceasefire in Vietnam, it did not end the fighting in Laos nor Cambodia. The PRC welcomed the agreement very favourably, stating that it "will have a positive influence on reducing tension in Asia and the world."[71] As a matter of fact, the American military presence in Vietnam had been the greatest source of tension between the PRC and the United States. In March 1973, the United States withdrew its remaining 2,500 troops from South Vietnam, thus officially ending American military presence in that country.

In February 1973, a ceasefire agreement was signed regarding Laos in which foreign military personnel must withdraw from that country. Beijing's *Renmin Ribao* praised the ceasefire and called upon the Untied States also to scrupulously carry out and observe the July 1962 Geneva Agreement guaranteeing the country's neutrality and independence.[72]

In February 1973, the PRC and the United States announced that liaison offices in each other's capitals would be established, which they did less than three months later. This was a big blow to the ROC. But, a twist came when in February 1974, Nixon appointed a career foreign service officer as the new ambassador to the ROC, so as to increase the United States' bargaining chips and to pacify resistance in the Congress, led by Senator Barry M. Goldwater and others. Some analysts thought that Nixon would leave the position vacant in view of the momentum of closer ties between the PRC and United State.[73]

In June 1973, the United States withdrew a six-man marine unit from the American liaison office in Beijing. The PRC was sensitive about this, because the marines were "the only recognizable foreign military unit in China."[74] If the withdrawal became true, the framework of There are No More Foreign Military Troops in China Versus There are Foreign Troops in China could be abandoned or, at least frozen. The PRC was pleased when in October 1973, the U.S. Congress repealed the January 1955 Formosa Resolution, which had given the President the power to intervene in the Taiwan Strait in order to defend Taiwan.

In April 1975, Cambodia, which was renamed "the State of Democratic Kampuchea" in January 1976, was seized by the insurgent

Communist-led Khmer Rouge. In the same month, Saigon also fell. In August 1975, the Communist-led Pathet Lao (the State of Laos) took over Laos. Since these countries belonged to the PRC's sphere of influence, these developments represented a victory for the PRC at the international level.

As soon as Indochina became Communist, contradiction between Beijing and Hanoi began to surface. In November 1975, *Renmin Ribao* published an article that spelled out in full Chinese claims to the four island groups in the SCS. By doing this, the PRC is saying that its sovereignty over the island groups had been challenged by, for example, the newly reunified Vietnam. Prior to April 1975, Hanoi used to say it recognized the Chinese possession of those island groups.

Beijing's prestige began to plummet, when, in July 1978, PRC Vice-Premier, Li Xiannian, for the very first time, told a visiting Mitsui delegation from Japan in Beijing that the mainland was willing to accept foreign funds to finance its modernization programs.[75] Before that Beijing would not approach any capitalist country for financial assistance. Tokyo was certainly willing to lend a helping hand, because the two capitals were on good terms, as can be seen in August 1978, when the PRC and Japan signed the Treaty of Peace and Friendship after three years of intermittent negotiations,[76] thereby terminating the April 1952 Treaty of Peace between the ROC and Japan.[77] To the Chinese, this could be interpreted as Japan's second surrender.

RESTORING THE SOCIALISM WITH CHINESE CHARACTERISTICS LINE

A1. Internal—The Mainland

In late 1978, Deng consolidated his power. The CPC gradually became less ideological and more pragmatic.[78] Under Deng, it began to remove those who still stuck to 1. At the same time, more party members began to realize that ideology alone cannot help to modernize the PRC. It must be first accompanied by production. So, on August 10, 1980, Deng, for the first time, said there should be separation between the CPC and the government. His logic was simple, opportunity to do business could be lost, if the party were to take too long to make a decision.

In June 1981, Hua Guofeng was relieved of his duty as the Chairman of the Central Committee of the CPC and the Chairman of the CMC. Hu Yaobang took over the Central Committee's chairmanship, and Deng, the CMC chairmanship. By the end of 1982, the PRC had been rehabilitated and revised the verdicts of about three million cadres and more than 470,000 people's CPC memberships were restored.[79] This meant that they had chosen 5 in the Communism Versus Capitalism framework.

In September 1982, the 12th National Congress of the CPC was held. Deng in the opening speech said the PRC should adopt the Socialism with Chinese Characteristics, mainly exercising the planned economy, while making market regulation subsidiary (*jihuajingji wei zhu, shichangtiaojie wei fu*).

The Congress also proposed to spend three years to complete the task of consolidating the CPC organization. In October 1983, at the 2nd Plenum, a committee headed by Hu Yaobang was set up. In winter 1983, the campaign began. By the end of May 1987, the CPC basically summarized what it had done. 5,449 members were found to have participated in the GPCR.[80] 43,074 members had committed grave mistakes. 33,896 people were ousted from the CPC. 90,069 applications to join the party were not approved. 145,456 people were asked to postpone their intention to submit their application forms. And 184,071 members were disciplined.

In late 1986 and early 1987, several cities in southern China encountered chaos.[81] Many problems surfaced after the opening of China to the outside world. This was certainly eventually mirrored in the June 1989 tragedy in Tiananmen Square, Beijing.[82] In May 989, martial law was declared in certain parts of Beijing, which lasted until January 1990. In February 1990, the CPC's Organization Committee admitted that the Centralism Versus Democracy framework had not been sufficiently properly implemented within the party.[83]

A2. Internal—Bicoastal Chinese or Cross-Strait

The ascendancy of Deng helped to improve relations between Beijing and Taipei. Deng and Chiang Ching-kuo were classmates in the Fall of 1925 when they attended Zhongshan University in Moscow. They knew each other's dialectical, ideological games. For this reason, Deng in January 1980 said Chinese reunification and two other goals could be achieved within the decade of 1980. In February 1985, Xinhuashe reported that the Chinese People's Revolutionary Military Museum would show the KMT troops' effort during the eight-year war against Japan. In October 1991, the Standing Committee of the CPC gathered for a rally to commemorate the 80th anniversary of the 1911 Xinhai Revolution. But, it is very doubtful whether Chiang and his subordinates were truly familiar with Deng's Socialism with Chinese Characteristics Versus Communism framework. In effect, this new framework could transform the zero-sum game, which should be understood in the context of Communism Versus Capitalism into a non-zero-sum game, which should be understood in the context of Socialism with Chinese Characteristics Versus Capitalism framework. In other words, Socialism with Chinese Characteristics is 5 in the Communism Versus Capitalism framework but it became 1 in the Socialism with Chinese Characteristics Versus Capitalism framework. As noted earlier, the new framework brought the PRC back to January 1940, that is, the ROC era in the mainland days.[84]

The *Taiwan Relations Act* (TRA), which was passed by the U.S. Congress in April 1979, is an abridgement of Chinese sovereignty. The same can be said with regard to the acts between the United States and Hongkong and Macao. The August 17, 1982 Communiqué between the PRC and the United States said the latter would gradually reduce the sale of arms to the ROC. But, to this day, Washington has not done that, because, in December 1995, the Senate had amended the military clause in the TRA saying it took precedence over the 1982 Communiqué.[85]

In October 1991, the State Council said it would not allow the DPP of the Taiwan Province to create a Republic of Taiwan (ROT). In March 2000, the then PRC Premier Zhu Rongji said Beijing was willing to make concessions to Taipei, when he was informed that the DPP might win the presidential election in Taiwan. The struggle became more complex upon Chen Shui-bian's victory, because he advocated Taiwan's independence. In December 2001, the DPP also became the biggest party in the Legislative *Yuan* for the first time. In September 2003, Chen called for the making of a new constitution. But, after getting re-elected in March 2004, he said he would re-engineer it in 2006.

B. External

The United States established diplomatic ties with the PRC on January 1, 1979. On the same day, the American State Department formally notified the ROC that, under Article X of their 1954 Mutual Defence

Treaty, the United States was abrogating the treaty, effective January 1, 1980.[86] This was a triumph for the PRC. But, the PRC proclaimed in September 1982 that it would not form an alliance with any superpower, such as the United States, the Soviet Union, and Japan. In addition, it should be noted that the game of getting rid of the ROC in the PRC Versus ROC framework had not yet ended, because the United States has yet to see a free and democratic system emerging in mainland China.

Since late 1989, one East European country after another had begun to collapse. In December 1991, it was the Soviet Union's turn. When the Communist camp under the leadership of Moscow imploded, many political observers in the West were asking whether the PRC would follow suit. When Beijing was able to survive,[87] the same observers began to put forward another argument, that is, would mainland China pose a threat to many countries. This kind of observation in the Untied States and the UK began in April 1992.[88] Some Japanese academics and experts, as early as May 1990, also wrote about the same thing, so as to hamper the PRC's attempt to develop friendly relations with other countries.

There were many instances where the PRC had encountered foreign interference. Yinhe (Milky Way), a PRC merchant vessel, is one case in point. In July 1993, it was suspected by the United States of shipping materials for making chemical weapons to Iran. The vessel was monitored en route from August 1 by the American navy, which relied on the U.S. domestic law to sanction the Chinese vessel.[89] The United States and Saudi Arabia conducted some checks on the containers. So, from late August to early September 1993, the United States and Saudi Arabia, spent 12 days checking 782 questionable containers on that vessel and found nothing. According to international law, a ship is part of a country's territory. As a result of this incident, the vessel lost US$12.93 million. From this incident, it is accurate to say that the PRC was perceived as being still weak, because it could not do much to deter the intervention of foreign powers.

Another incident occurred on October 27, 1994, when a PRC nuclear submarine was patrolling the Huang Sea. It was monitored by two American naval anti-submarine planes. Three days later, the submarine was stalked and harassed by Kitty Hawk, a U.S. aircraft carrier. Only with Chinese PLA fighters' protection, did the American planes fly away.

GAMBLING ON THE MARKET ECONOMY LINE

A1. Internal—The Mainland

Hu Sheng, a CPC theoretician, mentioned that modernization is industrialization which is accompanied by changes in economics, politics, and culture. He added that from the late 1800s to early 1900s, modernization should be understood in terms of capitalization.[90] In the early 20th century, capitalists invested US$1.5 billion in *Zhongguo*. Before the eight-year war of resistance against Imperial Japan, they had invested US$4.3 billion.[91]

Jiang in his 15th National Congress of the CPC political report made it clear that the mainland "needs a long-lasting peaceful international environment for its development." The mainland requires a lot of foreign investment. At the same time, free markets have begun to flourish. The number of street hawkers has grown. And cooperatives (which are really small businesses for profit) are thriving. By the end of 1999, there were still 1.4 million people living under the poverty line, with peasants, for example, earning RMB 1,255 per year.[92] However, by the end of 2003, the mainland's GNP per capita was a little over US$1,000 for the first time and ahead of schedule.

Hong Kong re-embraced the PRC in July 1997. The *United States-Hong Kong Policy Act* of 1992, which was passed in January 1992, established the domestic framework in the United States for treating the Hong Kong Special Administrative Region (SAR) as a distinct entity under Chinese sovereignty. Hong Kong is important to the United States.[93] Over 1,100 resident American firms employ an estimated number of 250,000 Hong Kong workers (or 10 per cent of the work force). Furthermore, in late 1999, the regularity of port calls and aircraft visits by the U.S. Navy began to return to previous levels (50–70 ships and 100 planes per year).[94] The U.S. Navy together with the Chinese PLA Hong Kong Garrison participate in the annual Hong Kong's Search and Rescue Exercise. Nevertheless, it infringes upon Chinese sovereignty.

Macao was returned to the PRC in December 1999. The *United States-Macao Policy Act* of 2000 was signed by American President Bill Clinton in December 2000 and released in January 2001. This domestic act of the United States acknowledges the special status of the Macao SAR and establishes a clear legal framework for recognizing Macao's commercial, social, cultural, legal, and economic autonomy under the "One Country, Two Systems" formula.

In September 2001, Macao held its first direct and indirect election after becoming a SAR. Democratic candidates like Ng Kuok Cheong who led the Association for a Democratic New Macau (ANMD) secured about 21 per cent of the total valid votes. The Chief Executive Edmund Ho said the result showed that the principles of "One Country, Two Systems," "Macao People Ruling Macao," and high autonomy for the SAR had been realized. But, because Macao is tiny, Ng was not allowed to form a political party; hence usage of the word Association. In this connection, his association has been labelled as a subversive group by Beijing.[95]

A2. Internal—Bicoastal Chinese or Cross-Strait

In November 1993, the then ROC President Lee said the principle of One China is the ROC had not changed and it would not change.[96] In July 1999, the then ROC President Lee put forward the "special state-to-state relationship" policy. Beijing leaders understood what that policy meant but were angry that Lee had done so, because it showed that Taiwan did not want to be reunified with the mainland, at least for a period of time. However, due to pressure from the United States, the policy was shelved after three weeks. The PRC officials also acknowledged the special kind of relationship between the mainland and Taiwan. For example, in January 2001, referring to the three links, the then PRC State Council Vice Premier, Qian Qichen, used the term special domestic links, while the then PRC Minister of Communications, Hong Shanxiang, used the term "domestic routes under special management". One former native Taiwanese official, Chen Kuimiao, said the "continental personality" of mainland China seemed stronger, while the "maritime personality" might describe Taiwan's. The former personality is idealistic, and the latter, more pragmatic.[97] Hoping to gain from the PRC's formal entry into the WTO, up to the third quarter of 2000, Taiwan businessmen had invested some 3,500 billion New Taiwan Dollars in the mainland.[98] In his national address on December 31, 2000, Chen said "economy first, politics later." In March 2001, former Premier of the ROC, Vincent W. Siew, created the Cross-strait Common Market Foundation (CCMF), which is modelled after the European Union (EU). The foundation would provide a forum for experts from both sides of the Taiwan Strait and the international community to explore the feasibility of a Taiwan-mainland free-trade area and common market. In May 2001, Siew met Qian in Beijing, though he was coolly received by the latter. Later in October 2001, the DPP Government dropped the "No Haste, Be Patient/Go Slow, Be Patient" policy under the Lee Teng-hui regime which was put forward in September/October 1996. It advocated an "Active Opening, Effective Management" policy instead, with the rescue of Taiwan's economy in mind. Just before the end of 2002, Xinhuashe reported that, for the first time, the mainland had become Taiwan's foremost export market, with the latter enjoying US$180 billion over the years. In 2003 alone, Taiwan earned some US$40 billion from the mainland. And, in the first five months of 2004, Taiwan enjoyed a surplus of around 11.56 billion in terms of exports and imports from the mainland, and, for the first time, the accumulative surplus in May 2004 exceeded US$10 billion.

B. External

One of the weaknesses of the PRC, from the American perspective, is the human rights violations of the mainland leaders. With an aim to compelling the PRC to improve its human rights record, the United States in April 2001, in its tenth attempt, to win censure of PRC human rights policies, such as not giving its citizens a fair trial and freedom of association and assembly, at the UN Human Rights Commission (UNHRC). But, its attempt in Geneva was "foiled once again," according to Xinhuashe.[99] Beijing fought back by accusing Washington of being hypocritical, citing racial violence in Cincinnati City, Ohio in April. The abuse of Iraqi troops by U.S. troops between August 2003 and early 2004 was another pertinent example. In January and February 1947, a number of committees including the UNHRC which had drafted the Universal Declaration of Human Rights conducted their first meetings. In May 2001, the United States was abandoned for the first time and at the same time the Republic of Sudan (ROS) which had been accused of an array of violations during its civil war, including slavery, was voted in.[100] Since November 1991, the State Council of the PRC have been fighting back by publishing its white papers on human rights, saying, for example, that the PRC had signed documents relating to human rights, for example, in October 1997 and October 1998.[101] There has been a marked improvement in its respect for human rights.

Militarily, 15–25 per cent of the Chinese PLA have been reorganized into elite troops, so-called rapid-response or rapid-reaction units or fist forces. The PRC armed forces have also acquired SU-27s and SU-30s, Sovremennyi destroyers, and Kilo-class submarines. But, according to Avery Goldstein, the Chinese PLA "will not turn the waters of East Asia into a Chinese lake, but it will create a situation in which the U.S. can no longer expect easily to dominate in limited conventional military engagements."[102]

The PRC's relations with Russia have been considered as good. A high-ranking Russian foreign ministry official, in a July 1994 interview, said, in its recent military build-up (*jianjun*) guidelines, Russia had stated that, should it be attacked, it would first use its nuclear weapons.[103] Before the collapse of the Soviet Union, Moscow's policy was to resort to nuclear weapons under any circumstances. In this connection, the foreign ministries of the PRC and Russia, in a joint communiqué, stated that the countries would not use nuclear weapons against each other. To further cement their friendship, in July 2001, they signed an accord to build a 2,400-km pipeline, which was to be completed as early as 2005 and which can ship 20 million metric tons (147 million barrels) a year to northeastern PRC like Heilongjiang Province.

The PRC has been perceived as a "bad boy" for abetting rogue states-now officially designated by the United States as "states of concern"-such as Pakistan, Iran, Iraq, and North Korea, to develop arms of mass lethal destruction, including chemical and biological weapons. But, in November 2000, the PRC Foreign Ministry stated that mainland China "has no intention to assist, in any way, any country in the development of ballistic missiles that can be used to deliver nuclear weapons."[104] As a result of issuing this statement, the PRC can acquire multi-billion-dollar satellite and other high-technology deals from the United States. There are military figures in the United States who do not want to make the PRC another "Soviet bear" threatening the United States.[105]

There are examples where the PRC has been perceived by foreign powers as being expansionist. In late 1999, debates began in the Republic of Kiribati, regarding a satellite base built by the PRC, which can monitor American tests of its missile defence system in the Marshal Islands.[106] As another example, in August 2000, it was reported that an oilfield in the ROS in north-eastern Africa had begun its operation three years ago. According to an internal document of Sudan, many Chinese PLA troops and prisoners under the guise of guards were sent to Sudan to protect the oilfield.[107]

ENDNOTES

1   Guo (note 10, ch. 8), pp. 406–407. According to the CPLA's report on July 31, 1950, from July 1, 1946 to June 30, 1950, it killed 8.07 million KMT troops. From July 1, 1949 to June 30, 1950, it had killed 2.37 million KMT troops. See also Liu *et. al.* (note 32, ch. 7), p. 87.

2   Zhonggongzhongyangzhuzibu *et. al.* (note 22, ch. 8), p. 1. According to the October 5, 1951 issue of *Renminribao* (RMRB), the PRC enjoyed a surplus of foreign exchange in trade and commerce with foreign countries in the first two years of its creation.

3   Zhonggongzhongyangzhuzibu *et. al* (note 22, ch. 8), p. 1.

4   Guo (note 10, ch. 8), pp. 402–406.

5   See, for example, Cheng (note 24, ch. 8). In February 1952, the CPC cracked down on a group of capitalists in Chongqing City who tried to profit from the SOEs, See Liu *et. al.* (note 32, ch. 7), p. 50. The CPC also thinks that, besides Shanghai, Nanjing and Wuhan are important. So, in spring 1953, a study was made about those three cities' economy. See Liu *et. al.* (note 32, ch. 7), p. 73.

6   Zhao (note 52, ch. 7), pp. 12 and 17.

7   *China* (note 30, ch. 7), p. 114.

8   *Ibid.*, p. 146.

9   *Ibid.*, p. 85.

10   The ROC airforce twice in January and February 1950 dropped bombs on Shanghai.

11   Xu Dixin, *Qinlizhongdalishishijianshilu* (The Record on Personal Involvement in Major Events)(Beijing: Dangjianduwuchubanshe and Zhongguowenlianchubanshe, March 2000), pp. 478–495.

12   Zhonggongzhongyangzhuzhibu *et. al.* (note 32, ch. 7), p. 413 and Liu *et. al.* (note 32, ch. 7), p. 139.

13   Liao Gailong, *et. al.*, *Dangdaizhongguozhengzhidashidian*, *1949–1990* (Changcun City: Jilinwenshichubanshe, July 1991), pp. 588–589.

14   Guo (note 10, ch. 8), pp. 399–400. A caveat must be added. In November 1933, Cai Tingkai and other KMT generals in Fuzhou City, Fujian Province, created the *Zhonghuagongheguorenmingeminzhengfu* (The People's Revolutionary Government of the *ROC*). The Government lasted until January 1934 and it was anti-Chiang Kai-shek and anti-Imperial Japanese. In April 1962, at the Third Session Cai became the Vice-chairman of the Second National People's Congress. In other words, it was a united front tactic.

15   *China* (note 30, ch. 7), pp. 109 and 111.

16   *Ibid.*, p. 112.

17   Cited in *China* (note 30, ch. 7), p. 88. In February 1986, in order to deter the Soviet Union, the United States regarded 16 straits as choke points, such as the Straits of Malacca. But, the Taiwan Strait was not included.

18   After that Sun Lijen was approached by the Americans at least twice. Sun in 1950 wanted to overthrow Chiang so as to save Taiwan from Chinese Communist rule. See http://www.chineseworld.com/publish/today/11_0900.4w/t/4wts(011029)02_t_tb.htm (accessed October 28, 2001).

19   In October 2001, Zhang Xueliang passed away. He, talking about the Xian Incident said the KMT under Chiang Kai-shek and the CPC should not fight each other since we were all Chinese. Zhang was for fighting against the Imperial Japanese. Chiang wanted to weed out the Chinese Communists first. But, Chiang later agreed not to encircle the Chinese Communists, and the former was willing to cooperate with the latter. See *WJ*, October 28, 2001, pp. A1 and A9.

20   Liu *et. al.* (note 32, ch. 7), p. 77. Xinhuashe reported that from October 1949 to June 1954, the CPLA killed 352,526 ROC officers and soldiers. See *ibid.*, p. 103. Taipei basically operated along the coastal areas of Jiangsu, Zhejiang, Fujian, and Guangdong Provinces.

21   It may well be Zhang Xueliang who first uttered these words. Later Chiang Kai-shek, after the Xian Incident, promised to stop fighting the Chinese Communists and would instead cooperate with them. See *Taipei Journal* (hereinafter TJ)(Taipei), November 23, 2001, p. 7.

22   *THWDN*, October 2, 1993, p. 1.

23   Dialectically, the two usages are not different. See the elaboration in the comments section of the fourth chapter.

24   Guo (note 10, ch. 8), p. 429.

25   *China* (note 30, ch. 7), p. 89.

26   *Ibid.*, p. 90.

27   Cited in *ibid.*, p. 86.

28   *Ibid.*, p. 89.

29   *Ibid.*, p. 109.

30   *Ibid.*, p. 112.

31   Guo (note 10, ch. 8), p. 441.

32   *China* (note 30, ch. 7), p. 114.

33   *Ibid.*, p. 122.

34   Chen Ping, "Bicoastal China's Interactions and Prospects in the Post-Cold War Era" in *Taiwan Experience and Development Strategy of Both Sides of the Strait*, edited by Xu Dianqing (Beijing: Zhonguojingjichubanshe, February 1996), pp. 32–35.

35   See Zhonggongzhongyangzhuzhibu *et. al.* (note 22, ch. 8), *Zhongguogongchandangzhuzhishiziliao*, Vol. 6 (Source Materials for the Communist Party of China's Organization) (Beijing: Zhonggongdangshi-chubanshe, September 2000), pp. 1–16.

36   Liu *et. al.* (note 32, ch. 7), p. 352.

37   The January 1966 issue of *Hongqi*'s editorial said politics is the supreme commander and spirit. The opposite of this is *geren mingli* (Personal Fame and Gain). See Liu *et. al.* (note 32, ch. 7), p. 336. For what Jiang Qing and others did to the judicial system, see Wang Renbo and Cheng Liaoyuan, *Fazhilun* (On Rule of Law), (Jinan, Shandong: Shandongrenminchubanshe, July 1998), pp. 309–318

38   See the July and August 2001 issues of *Open Magazine* (hereinafter OM)(Hongkong), especially p. 64 in the July 2001 issue.

39   *China* (note 30, ch. 7), p. 183.

40   There were counter-arguments. See, for example, Frederick C. Teiwes and Warren Sun, *The Tragedy of Lin Biao* (Honolulu, Hawaii: University of Hawaii Press, 1997).

41   Liu *et. al.* (note 32, ch. 7), p. 482. The pivotal railroad stations are: Beijing, Harbin, Shenyang, Tianjin, Shijiachuang, Zhengzhou, Jinan, Lanzhou, Wuhan, Nanjing, Zhuzhou, Liuzhou, Chengdu, etc.

42   Skinner (note 6), p. 278.

43   In April 1949, the CPLA Navy was created. In February 1953, Mao, for the first time, was on board *Changjiang*, a CPLA Navy vessel manufactured by the PRC from Wuhan to Nanjing. *Zhongguo* did not have protection at sea, as pointed out by Mao. When foreign powers cannot conduct "gunboat diplomacy, *Zhongguo* is safe. But, when they do, *Zhongguo* would be in trouble." See *JFJB*, April 9, 2001, p. 7.

44   *China* (note 30, ch. 7), p. 227.

45   *Ibid.*, p. 228.

46   The Committee (note 6, ch. 8), p. 17.

47   *China* (note 30, ch. 7), p. 117.

48   *Ibid.*, p. 117.

49   *Ibid.*, p. 118.

50   Cited in *ibid.*, p. 119.

51   Guo (note 10, ch. 8), p. 412. Citing an internal source, Liu Chengzong of the Political Warfare College in Taipei said, from 1962 to 1964, the ROC raided Fujian, Zhejiang, and Northern Jiangsu Provinces 131 times.

52   *China* (note 30, ch. 7), p. 134. In 1965, two Japanese and two South Koreans worked on a ROC spy ship. See Liu *et. al.* (note 32, ch. 7), p. 475.

53   *LHZB*, January 14, 2001, p. 30.

54   *WJ*, September 25, 2001, pp. A1 and A3.

55   Cited in *China* (note 30, ch. 7), p. 113.

56   Cited in *ibid.*, p. 140.

57   *Ibid.*, p. 185.

58   Guo (note 10, ch. 8), p. 243.

59   *China* (note 30, ch. 7), p. 186.

60   Cited in *ibid.*, p. 146.

61   *Ibid.*, p. 148.

62   *Ibid.*, p. 174.

63   *Ibid.*, p. 149.

64   *Yazhouzhoukan* (hereinafter YZZK)(Hongkong), June 26–July 2, 2001, pp. 46–49.

65   *China* (note 30, ch. 7), p. 176.

66   *Ibid.*, p. 194.

67   *Ibid.*, p. 202.

68   *Ibid.*, p. 203.

69   *Ibid.*, p. 206.

70   *Ibid.*, p. 204.

71   Cited in *ibid.*, p. 208.

72   *Ibid.*, pp. 131 and 208.

73   *Ibid.*, p. 213.

74   *Ibid.*, p. 214.

75   *Ibid.*, p. 238.

76   See *Beijing Review* (hereinafter BR)(Beijing), August 18, 1978, pp. 7–8.

77   See Document 24 in Winberg Chai and May-lee Chai, eds., *Chinese Mainland and Taiwan* (Dubuque, Iowa: Kendall/Hunt Publishing Company, 1996). According to a secret Japanese document, in September 1972, when Zhou Enlai and Japanese Prime Minister Kakuei Tanaka were discussing the draft treaty, the latter said, because Taipei chose not to ask for reparations from Tokyo, Beijing does not have the right to ask for reparations. Zhou replied this is a big insult. See *UDN*, June 24, 2001, p. 13 and *CT*, June 24, 2001, p. 11.

78   On October 11, 1978, Huang Xiang put the first big character poster on the democracy wall at Wangfujin Street in Beijing. He thought he would be arrested. But, later, he realized that Deng Xiaoping needed the posters to ward off his political enemies. See *UDN*, October 13, 1998, p. 13.

79   Zhongguozhongyangzhuzhibu *et. al.* (note 22, ch. 8), p. 7.

80   *Ibid.*, pp. 17–18.

81   Leng (note 29, ch. 8), p. 51.

82   According to James C. Hsiung, who witnessed what happened at Beijing Hotel on June 3rd and 4th, 1989, which "was very different from what the outside world saw on TV or was led to believe by the Western media." To Hsiung, he does not "believe that anyone really gave the orders to kill at Tiananmen," Muxudi, and Gongzhufen. "… the firing and killings (at least on my side of the long Changan Street) seemed to be a spontaneous act of retaliation [by the People's Liberation Army]. Not something by prior orders." His email to my former student, David T. K. Wei, dated April 25, 2001.

83   Charles E. Greer, ed., *China Facts & Figures Annual*, Vol. 14 (Florida: Academic International Press, 1991), p. 46.

84   In December 2000, I presented a research paper in Taipei, Taiwan, ROC. Afterwards, the ROC Central Government officials told me that what I

wrote was helpful to their understanding of the CPC's logic. One of the senior officials said in his 10 years serving the Mainland Affairs Council (MAC), he has never seen Figure 7 before. My immediate reaction was: What? That is, what had the Taiwan academics and experts been doing? In other words, a lot of money and time had been wasted.

85   *UDN*, December 16, 1995, p. 1.

86   See "The Question of Presidential Power to Terminate Treaties," *Congressional Digest* (hereinafter CD)(U.S.), June–July 1979, pp. 161–192, Jacob K. Javits, "Congress and Foreign Relations: The Taiwan Relations Act," *Foreign Affairs* (hereinafter FA), Vol. 60, No. 1 (Fall 1981), pp. 54–62, David J. Scheffer, "The Law of Treaty Termination as Applied to the United States De-recognition of the Republic of China," *Harvard International Law Journal* (hereinafter HILJ), Vol. 19, No. 3 (Fall 1978), pp. 931–1009, Ahmed Sheikh, "The United States and Taiwan After Derecognition: Consequences and Legal Remedies," *Washington and Lee Law* Review (hereinafter WLLR), Vol. XXXVII, No. 2 (Spring 1980), pp. 323–341, and Barry M. Goldwater, *China and the Abrogation of Treaties* (Washington, D.C.: The Heritage Foundation, 1978), 40 pages. For inside story by James Lilley on the August 1982 Communiqué and the six-point guarantee by the Ronald Reagan Administration before the issuance of the former, see http://www.chinatimes.com.tw/news/papers/online/china/c8931110.htm (accessed March 11, 2000).

87   In a study commissioned by the CIA, Gary Fuller, a geography professor at the University of Hawaii, studied potential Asian ethnic "fracture zones" and he did not think that there would be an ethnic break-up in mainland China. Because he did not support the CIA's view, he was sacked as the head of that US$245,000 project. See *ST*, November 20, 1998, p. 35.

88   *Executive Intelligence Review* (hereinafter EIR)(U.S.), Chinese ed., Vol. 6, No. 9 (September 30, 1995), p. 17. Institute for Strategic and International Studies (IISS) and Royal Institute of International Affairs (RIIA) were mentioned on p. 17. One article published in the *Renminribao* (RMRB) said such a vicious observation began in late 1992. See *UDN*, December 23, 1995, p. 10. One Chinese book said it was the United States in early 1992 which first put forward the "China threat." See Ling Haijian, *Zhonggongjunduixinjiangxing* (The Profile of Prominent Military Chiefs in China"(Hongkong: The Pacific Century Press, August 1999), p. 422. The cover page of the July 29 to August 4, 1995 issue of *The Economist* (UK), which is a mouthpiece of the Lazard Bank, the Rothschilds, and the City of London, was printed with the words "Containing China." The April 20, 1996 cover story of *The Economist* was entitled "Will China Disintegrate?" After the tearing down of the Berlin Wall in late 1989, a Japanese professor teaching in a Japanese military university began to write about the China threat.

89   Zhang (note 79, ch. 7), p. 140.

90   Hu (note 35, ch. 7), p. 9.

91   *Ibid.*, p. 16.

92   CNA, October 21, 2001 at 21:09 hr.

93   See, for example, Brett C. Lippencott, "America's Stake in Hong Kong," *Asian Studies Center Backgrounder*, No. 137 (October 2, 1995), 7 pages.

94   *United States Hong Kong Policy Act Report, as of April 1, 2000.*

95   http://www.chineseworld.com (accessed September 25, 2001).

96   *THWDN*, November 25, 1993, p. 1. On January 1, 1949, Mao mentioned the conspiracy by the KMT to use the Changjiang as the dividing line between the CPC and the KMT. At that time, the Soviet Union remained neutral and wanted to act as a mediator.

97   What he meant was that ideology does not have much market in Taiwan. See *UDN*, January 30, 2001, p. 15.

98   *UDN*, March 15, 2001, p. 2.

99   *ST*, April 20, 2001, p. A9. The United States and other countries introduced the draft resolution since 1989. With the exception of 1995, they were procedurally defeated.

100   *Ibid.*, May 5, 2001, p. 8. As a result, the U.S. Congress passed a motion, asking the American government not to pay US$244 million that the United States owed to the UN.

101   See *JFJB*, April 10, 2001, p. 2.

102   Avery Goldstein, "Second Thoughts About China's Military Power," *A Catalyst for Ideas*, Vol. 6, No. 4 (April 1998), 5 pp. In May 1990, MURAI Tomohide of the National Defense Academy in Yokosuka, Japan, wrote an article, which was entitled "On the Potential Threat of China." See Tian Yuan, *Ribenxinyinmou* (Japan's New Conspiracy)(Hongkong: Mirror Books, May 1997), p. 9.

103   *UDN*, July 17, 1994, p. 10.

104   *ST*, November 23, 2000, p. A4.

105   *LHZB*, December 16, 2000, p. 43.

106   *UDN*, October 27, 2000, p. 11. In late 2003, diplomatic ties were severed between the two countries.

107   *CT*, August 28, 2000, p. 14.

11

Comments and Major Observations

This chapter is divided into two parts. This author will first make some comments. Then, I shall put forward some observations.

COMMENTS

First, V. O. Key, Jr. in his presidential address to members of the American Political Science Association (APSA), reminded us that "[m]ethod without substance may be sterile, but substance without method is only fortuitously substantial."[1] The reason for applying a model or a theory is because we as human beings cannot remember what has been written from the first page to the last page, unless one is the author of the publication, be it a background brief, working paper, occasional paper, journal article, monograph, or book. In other words, we can only have an impression of what has been written; even the author after a period of time may forget everything that has been printed. If one can remember what the model looks like or what the theory is, the author can be said to have been successful in having presented the final product. More importantly, we want to know whether the model or theory can sustain the test of rapidly changing times. That is to say, if a model is well constructed, whether it can still describe and explain political phenomena one hundred or one thousand years from now. The same thing goes for a theory, which must anticipate the future political development, trend, etc. If successful, the model or theory can become a school and ultimately becoming a paradigm, overshadowing any model or theory, which is in fashion.

Because our framework of thought and action has the time/space sequence component, it can be elevated to the status of being a paradigm, which is enshrined in the German terms *Denkstil* (thought style) and *Denkkollektiv* (thought collective)[2] and which is not equivalent to universal knowledge or universal truths.[3] If enough people in the West collectively accept my model, a paradigm shift would have taken place, because, up to this day, most academics in the West do not apply a dialectical approach in studying Bicoastal China.

Second, George W. Tsai argues that knowing dialectics is a plus in understanding the politics of Chinese Communists.[4] But, he also believes that it is necessary for us to apply other non-dialectical approaches. While I am not against non-dialectical approaches, I would like to argue that he, like some others, may not fully understand my version of dialectics. Also, without first applying a dialectical approach, a student of Chinese (Communist) politics would not be able to capture the macro-level understanding of it. That is to say, the picture is incomplete. So, a two-legged approach is called for, preceded by the dialectical approach. When Chinese (Communist) political figures play dialectical games, they certainly have a series of frameworks in mind. They would try to navigate within the safe zone or spectrum of each dialectical model. It is doubtful that the Central Committee members of the CPC would use a non-dialectical, political language to communicate with each other. If a political bureau or central committee member applies game theory, then he or she would probably have to spend a lot of time to describe and explain to others what a Prisoner's dilemma is, for example. Realistically speaking, would the members want to waste their time over something which is foreign to them? Certainly not. Thus, when Lee Teng-hui put forward the special state-to-state policy in July 1999, the Chinese Communists understood what was meant by that jargon. By adding the word special, Taipei is simply saying that it is adopting a 1.5-China policy, which is neither One China nor Two Chinas but something in between the two extremes or Number 5. Because Mao and Deng once said that they were against 1.5 Chinas, Jiang and his successors have that kind of baggage to oppose 1.5 Chinas. Related to this is the "One China" principle. This principle, to Beijing, is the Roof/Housetop or Eaves framework. Lee Teng-hui said in October 1993 that Chiang Kai-shek had never mentioned the "One China" principle. Lee is somewhat misleading those who do not understand dialectics. When Chiang, mentioned the ROC, he regarded himself as the Roof/Housetop or Eaves. In other words, for him, the PRC simply did not exist, because he or his, Chiang's state or country alone was legal and legitimate, pure and simple.

So, a way out for the struggle between a purely dialectical study and a purely non-dialectical study is to have a chapter, which compares and contrasts the two different approaches, using the same sources. Perhaps, in this way, the readers can notice the differences, nuances, heuristic values, etc. Another way is to construct a new model, which accommodates both approaches. This is because, if as Chen Weixing jokingly argued, politics in mainland China is no longer dialectical after Deng's southern inspection tour, due to the collapse of ideology,[5] then how do we justify taking the dialectical approach from October 1949 to January 1992 and the non-dialectical approach from January 1992 onwards? Intuitively, methodological confusion already exists. It is still possible for us to apply dialectics in the study of the PRC's words and deeds at the macro-level after January 1992. It is always possible to convert something non-dialectical into something dialectical.

A few words may also be added. A country cannot do without a theorist. The same thing speaks for a political party. When there is a theorist, there is an ideology. When there is an ideology, there is a (series of) framework of thought and action. If the dialectical framework I presented is not the one in Chinese (Communist) political figures' mind, then, what is it? More importantly, how does a non-dialectical model look like?

Third, Philip C. C. Huang in one of his research papers published in *Modern China* mentioned the "paradigmatic crisis in Chinese studies." If Chinese (Communist) political figures were to discard the dialectical approach, would they be able to find another approach in time? If not, would there be chaos and confusion at least in meetings? In this connection, how much time would it need to find a new non-dialectical paradigm? To be certain, Chinese (Communist) political figures feel uncomfortable when they see the term political party,[6] (international) regime(s), state, empire, sovereignty, capitalism, etc., because they are foreign to the Chinese and, therefore, they do not apply to the Chinese (Communist) context. Yet, at the same time, the Chinese want to be modern. So, they have to adjust themselves by adopting such concepts. For example,[7] we say *Daqing Diguo*. The *closest* term in Chinese is the Qing Dynasty, not the Qing Empire. *Tianxia* is not empire.[8] But, to Western people, where there is empire, it should, at the end of the day, break up into nation-states. So, the Chinese people have always been caught in a dilemma.

Fourth, on June 26, 2001, Wang Gugnwu gave a talk on scholarship, social sciences, and China studies at the East Asian Institute (EAI), NUS. In the social sciences of the West, a model or a theory can only be either normative or empirical. In my framework of thought and action, it is both normative and empirical. The time/space sequence component reflects the empirical dimension, while the Numbers, Letters, etc. are normative. It is normative, because, at time/space sequence (n), things will end up in favour of the dialectical player who chooses the left extreme. To many historians, historicism holds that "events are determined or influenced by conditions and inherent processes beyond the control of human beings."[9] It is empirical, because, before time/space sequence (n), things change and shift, twist and turn, zig and zag, etc. For this reason, the CPC is not totally against behavioral studies, so long as the words and deeds do not exceed the major, important frameworks. Needless to say, it is afraid that methodological pluralism, once prevailing in mainland China, may shatter dialectics. *Minzhujizhongzhi* (Centralism Versus Democracy) is one framework adopted by the CPC. Should game theory, system theory, rational choice theory, and so on prevail, this Centralism and Democracy model would be called into serious question, and the CPC members cannot act in unison. In passing, it should be noted that democratic centralism—the way the phrase is usually translated by non-dialecticians—cannot capture the true, whole meaning of the framework. It only depicts part of the dialectical process.

Perhaps by giving another concrete example, readers will know better what I am going to say. Take the Communism Versus Capitalism framework as an example. Normatively speaking, Capitalism will move on to the Socialism stage and, ultimately, Socialism will be transformed into Communism, even the United States today is not totally capitalist. Empirically, life is not that simple. There are always progress, setbacks, consolidations, decay, etc. In October 1949, the Chinese Communists, started with Socialism. But, by September 1997, they had retreated to C in the same framework. Needless to say, they will come back to 5, at least after a few generations, as Jiang Zemin had hoped for when he delivered his political report at the 15th National Congress of the CPC.

The above discussion leads to the follow-up, which is related. Andrew C. Janos pointed out that paradigms could be either materialist or idealist.[10] Again, my model incorporates both aspects. Dialectically speaking, the following possibilities cannot be ruled out: materialistically idealist, idealistically materialist, and so on. For example, the ideal in the Communism Versus Capitalism model is that social movement flows from Primitive Communism to Feudalism, from Feudalism to Capitalism, from Capitalism to Socialism, and from Socialism to Communism. Of course, in reality, social movement walks back and forth between the two dots/points/extremes. In other words, at each phase, stage, etc., one could have at least somewhat different kinds of states, ideologies, politics, etc.

Fifth, this writing can be faulted for its lack of train of thought. In Western scholarship, one has to describe and explain the cause and effect in everything. In other words, what is that thing which leads to the next. However, in dialectical analysis, this could still be done, even if we know that a dialectician would leap from one framework to another framework. That is to say, we can construct a new framework to link the two totally separated dialectical models. An outsider who does not hold the key to the secret may find the dialectician illogical, unsystematic, and incoherent. In fact, most non-dialectical politicians are illogical, unsystematic, and incoherent in what they do and say. Usually their subordinates have to come forward to rationalize what they have said or did.

Sixth, the CPC speaks of program (*gangling*), line, guiding principle (*fangzhen*), policy, principle (*yuanze*), method (*fangfa*), and measure/step (*cuoshi*). One of the principles is Unite to be followed by Criticize and, then, Unite. In other words, when struggle exists within the party and contradictions must be resolved, the CPC relies on the principle. Actually, the framework is Unite Versus Criticize. In other words, the motion starts with 1. Then, one should go to E. Finally, one should come back to 1. However, it is very doubtful that game theory, system theory, rational choice theory, and so on can function like the Unite Versus Criticize model.

Seventh, dialectics is related to ideology. It gives hope to the dialectical player who thinks that he or she can be the ultimate winner at time/space sequence (n). This boosts the psychological confidence of the dialectician. Needless to say, the end result may not turn out to be what was expected. Even so, the dialectical player can still rationalize the end result by using another framework to describe and explain what had happened. Ideology is certainly related to politics. It shapes politics and affects decision-making, and vice versa. And *guojia* (state), ideology, and politics are the superstructures of a mainstream economic line. Because there is an ingredient of ideology, detractors of dialectics do not appreciate it. They may question the way one might predict that the dialectical player can emerge as winner. But, because a dialectical player makes a crab-like move, if things do not move forward, that is, moving toward the left extreme, it can move backward or toward the right extreme. This reflects life, and, therefore, the detractors should not totally reject dialectics, especially when he or she sees that it makes contribution to the work.

Eighth, so long as there is ideology, there should be a framework of thought and action. Nationalism could be an ideology. Yet, if one does not have a model in his or her study of nationalism, isn't something wrong? The CPC, in May 2000, officially publicized the Three Represents. And, at the 16th National Congress of the CPC, Jiang again urged his party members to keep "pace with the times" meaning that all the theory and work of the CPC "must conform to the times, follow the law of development and display great creativity." In other words, party members must take a broad vision of the overall situation (*xionghuai quanju*), that is, to bear in mind the whole framework, Communism Versus Capitalism, which has to do with mainstream economic lines and proceed accordingly with the changing of circumstances (*yushi jujin*). Hu Jintao also, on numerous occasions, has said the party must develop new theories and engage in new practices, so as to meet new challenges.[11] What they are saying is that they are making words and deeds in terms of specific frameworks, and these frameworks can help them to be logical, systematic, and coherent. Thus, in July 2001, Jiang for the first time said it is all right for the party to recruit private enterprise owners to join it, and that even if Deng were still alive, he would not oppose it.[12]

Ninth, Lee Kuan Yew, who became Minister Mentor in August 2004, once noted that: "… China has extraordinary potential power to be a superpower in the world in the next hundred years because it has all the requirements of a superpower. It might delay China's progress by putting pressure on her, but it is inevitable that China will be the superpower in the world."[13] In late 2003, he made a similar remark in Thailand. This may well be the case. Our model anticipates the day when the dialectical China become CHINA. Because there is a framework for us to see, one cannot dismiss Lee's perception as something belonging to propaganda or having an ulterior motive. Wang Gungwu also observed that by predicting a clash of civilizations in the post-Cold War era, the West was apparently retreating from its two-century-old-dominance.[14] There is a certain kernel of truth in this. Otherwise, there would be no need to talk about the clash in the first place.

10th, after reaching the CHINA stage, would it be possible for CHINA to fall again? Since two dots/points/extremes is what dialectics is all about, one should not rule out the possibility that, after the rise, there is the fall of CHINA. That is precisely why the Chinese are fond of thinking about the opposite possibility. This is why Chris M. Sciabarra describes dialectics as an art of context keeping or what I call the art of anticipating the opposite development. *Nixiangsikao* (thinking adversely) and *fanmiansikao* (thinking negatively) are familiar terms. To give one example, instead of throwing a referendum/plebiscite for Taiwan's independence, which may invite strong negative, military reaction from the mainland, pro-reunification people in Taiwan or those in the middle called for conducting a referendum for achieving the Chinese reunification. In other words, if the result of the referendum/plebiscite is below 50 per cent, Beijing leaders would get the message and they would be ashamed of themselves if they were to use force to settle the "Taiwan question." To give another extreme example on adverse thinking, CHINA could be hit by a meteorite from outer space, bringing about the destruction of CHINA, China, and china.

11th, is knowledge cumulative in this book? Yes, for the simple fact that the model has the time/space sequence component. The sequence can be stretched to a long period of time, so long as the PRC exists. Another advantage is that if this framework cannot describe and explain it, then another dialectical model can, which can accommodate new facts and phenomena arising by discovery, by serendipity, and by the flow of human history, which may be at odds with existing deeply entrenched assumptions. Thus, TAIWAN, Taiwan, and taiwan or SHANGHAI, Shanghai, and shanghai could also be set up to describe and explain other facts or phenomena. Needless to say, the dialectical Taiwan and the dialectical Shanghai are not equivalent to the dialectical China. Taiwan is a province, while Shanghai is a great municipal city. So, the Taiwan dialectical framework and, for that matter, the Shanghai framework, should be understood in the context of the PRC framework and even the dialectical China framework. By the same token, the PRC, Prc, and prc framework is not an equivalent to the CHINA, China, and china framework. The former framework is just part of the latter. It has existed since October 1949. It should disappear someday. In addition, the former one could be likened to a *Zhongguo* dynasty, whereas the latter covers a long period of time.

12th, the title of this chapter is CHINA, China, and china. But, in the subtitle, there is a question mark. Is it possible to reverse it, that is, by changing the title to china, China, and CHINA? In this connection, is it possible to make china Number 1 in reality? Yes, it is possible to change the title to china, China, and CHINA, because dialectics affords one the luxury of being flexible. Besides, we can never rule out that one day CHINA could become china. As mentioned earlier, an asteroid might hit the mainland and a great portion of the mainland became devastated as a result. Or, its nuclear weapons exploded. Or CHINA became china as a result of war between Planet Earth and other bodies in the universe. So, depending on whether one is positive or negative, that is, Positive Versus Negative, optimistic or pessimistic, that is, Optimistic Versus Pessimistic, etc., the two frameworks and others can co-exist. Of course, we do not know the answer. In other words, any one of the framework can be primary. However, there is a logical problem which needs to be solved, that is, if china is Number 1, how do we rationalize it as in the safe zone, because in the second part of this book we have said china stands for the negative aspects? If china is not good, how can it be in the safe zone? In reality, it is always possible that there is something good about being a bad china. If china is truly suffering from a natural disaster, for example, it may well be good for china to cease its existence. So, CHINA may evolve itself to be china, only to find that extinction is the best solution at a particular time/ space sequence.

13th, the KMT, the CPC, and other political parties like the DPP apply dialectics. But, the KMT and the CPC do not apply the same frameworks all of the time. One such framework is Communism Versus Socialism and its related sub-frameworks. Beijing believes in this framework. So, especially after Deng's return to power for the third time, the CPC had started to accommodate the KMT and even the ROC. In a word, the CPC is superstitious about the framework. So, can the KMT and other political parties use the framework to their advantage, disadvantage, or somewhere in between?

OBSERVATIONS

First, our dialectical model provides a holistic view of China's past, present, and the future. It is context-keeping or keeping the opposite in mind. One can look at the entire framework or just at china, China, or CHINA. One can also concentrate on the micro-level, that is, by looking at the dialectical China at each time/space sequence for each framework. In a word, due to flexibility, slotting in the data does not pose a big problem for this author.

Second, most academics like to seek truth and they want to be (more) scientific.[15] This is true of both natural scientists and social scientists. Using advanced forensic techniques and sophisticated computer graphics, a team of scientists produced what they say is the most scientifically-accurate picture of what Jesus Christ would have looked like: a highly-controversial image of a swarthy, coarse-featured man with staring eyes, dark olive skin, a prominent nose, a short beard, and wire-wool hair. In other words, these scientists claim that they have debunked the traditional image of Christ as being blue-eyed, fair-haired with flowing locks and fine features.[16] Indeed, many people want others to know the real truth. This includes some magicians who tried to debunk the magicians' tricks. The same thing is true of some American wrestlers. Kenneth Lieberthal, Joyce Kallgren, Roderick MacFarquhar, Frederic Wakeman, Jr. said all the essays in their edited volume "share a common interest in *decoding* patterns of development that help us understand why history weighs so heavily on China today (emphasis added)."[17] Wakeman, Jr., treated patterns as models.[18] Other social scientists like Mark Elvin in his 1973 book, *The Pattern of the Chinese Past*, argued that there is pattern in Chinese history.[19] June Teufel Dreyer also examined Beijing's relations with other Asian countries. On territorial disputes over islands issue, she finds a pattern of aggressive claims followed by placatory statements that do not withdraw the initial claims, followed by more aggressive claims and argues that Beijing's neighbours tend to be deeply troubled by this pattern.[20] But, in our study, we do not find any pattern. The same thing can be said of cycle. It is not possible to have a pattern, when everything is changing, even some academics and experts would rather use the term *dynamic* status quo, rather than status quo. The negation of the negation feature in our model simply shows that a pattern is not possible nor discernible. So, what it all boils down to is which approach is closer to reality, the dialectical or non-dialectical?[21]

Third, in the framework, A Dialectical Study of **CHINA** Versus A Non-dialectical Study of **CHINA**, one would have to position most publications in the West on **CHINA** at E. There are some Western publications on **CHINA**, which only mention dialectics here and there. In other words, the authors realize that the Chinese (Communist) political figures apply dialectics, but, for one reason or another, they choose to only mention it. Skinner,[22] Michel C. Oksenberg, Shambaugh, etc. are some of the names. So, those academics and experts should be positioned at 5.

Fourth, some studies resemble a dialectical arrangement. The title of Michael D. Swaine and Ashley J. Tellis' 2000 book is: *Interpreting China's Grand Strategy: Past, Present, and Future*. Arranged in terms of my version of dialectics, it would be: CHINA's Grand Strategy (Future), China's Grand Strategy (Present), and china's Grand Strategy (Past), which would evolve into **CHINA**'s Grand Strategy at the time/space sequence (n). This kind of arrangement, as one very good example, is just the opposite of Swaine and Tellis', and it is consistent with the ultimate dialectical, teleological movement from the right extreme to the left extreme.

There are other examples. The then U.S. Secretary of State, William J. Perry, in an October 30, 1995 speech, "Engagement is Neither Containment not Appeasement," mentioned the "containment-versus-enlargement" debate and referred to it as a false dichotomy. Later, he said "… China has to show that they, too, want a peaceful resolution to the [Taiwan] issue. Conducting missile tests [in July and August 1995] off Taiwan sends the opposite message."[23] Another similar example is that of the Rand Corporation's proposal of striking a balance between containment and engagement: con-gagement, which to some observers is "a blatantly hostile China policy,"[24] because the word containment is put in the first place. These resemble dialectical expressions. But, it is doubtful that Perry or the Rand think dialectically all the time.

This leads us to the discussion that some studies are non-dialectical but partly-dialectical. The problem with partly dialectical studies is that they are apt to create methodological confusion. One has to apply a model or a theory from the first chapter to the last. A dialectical framework should not be applied haphazardly in a publication. In that case, it is tantamount to saying that he or she wants to go to Taipei from Kaohsiung or from Guangzhou to Beijing. First, the person begins by driving on the provincial road, then, after a while decides to turn on to the national highway. And, finally, he or she changes his mind and continues by driving on the rail-track. This person can certainly arrive in Taipei or Beijing. But, there is a lack of methodological continuum or continuity. However, one can, after the introductory chapter, apply a dialectical model or theory in the second chapter, a non-dialectical model or theory in the third chapter, and compare and contrast the findings in the fourth chapter. Then, there would not be confusion.

Fifth, how close is one's study to the reality? This is an important question, because, as academics, we want to be as close to reality as possible. A mathematical study of Chinese (Communist) politics obviously cannot be close to reality, for the simple reason that 99.9 per cent of Chinese (Communist) political figures do not understand sophisticated mathematical formulas, such as the one for jokes: $x = (f1 + no)/p$. If they cannot understand them, would they apply them in the first place? Here, distortion and twists immediately spring to mind. What about dialectical and non-dialectical approaches? The answer is that, as mainland China becomes more open to the outside world, increasingly more and more people would regard dialectics as trammelling. So, in the years ahead, it would only be safe for us to apply dialectics to the study of Chinese (Communist) political figures at the national or macro-level. However, we still need to rationalize another related problem, that is, if one were to study the PRC from October 1949, how do we justify a dialectical approach from the day the PRC was created to the foreseeable future and a non-dialectical approach thereafter?

Sixth, in January 2001, Jiang, in his endeavour, officially advocated Rule by Virtue (*yide zhiguo*) or what I called Rule by Virtue Politics, emphasizing at the same time that the CPC has to govern the PRC by combining the Rule of Law with the Rule by Virtue. What he said in January 2001 can be traced back to the speech he made in November 1997 at Harvard University.[25] Another way of expressing Rule by Virtue is Rule Without Law Politics (*wuzhi*). Jiang is for "communitarism," not Western individualism. This thing is actually not new.[26] In ancient non-dialectical China, some emperors, influenced by Confucianism and other Chinese philosophies have advocated this. If we were to integrate this latest concept or, for that matter, another related concept by the phrase of "Rule Without Law Politics" (*wuzhi*) into the framework of Rule of Law Politics Versus Rule of Men Politics, this new concept should be positioned at the left extreme, making it Rule by Virtue Politics Versus Rule of Men Politics, with Rule by Law Politics and Rule of Dialectical Politics in between them. But, since dialectical players, to simplify reality, tend only to think of three (or up to five) concepts on a continuum, we can drop the Rule of Men Politics, and this is what the CPC exactly wants to do. In other words, Rule by Virtue Politics is 1 and Rule of Dialectical Politics is E. This means that Rule of Law Politics would be 5 and it would gradually become the main stream in Chinese (Communist) politics. Placing Rule of Dialectical Politics on the right extreme implies that those political figures who still apply dialectics should be guided to come back to the safe zone. Otherwise, punishment of one way or another may ensue. On the other hand, they could be the minority, standing in a corner. However, it can be argued that, as soon as Jiang has finished putting forward the Rule by Virtue Politics, he went back to the original framework, that is, Rule of Law Politics Versus Rule of Men Politics. This is simply because it is not possible for the Central Committee members not to practice Rule of Dialectical Politics, especially with regard to the handling of the relationship between the party and the Chinese PLA. In any case, the CPC is heading in the right direction. But, it would take a long period of time for the party to officially drop the Rule of Dialectical Politics, that is, 5 and to adopt the Rule by Virtue Politics Versus Rule of Dialectical Politics framework.

It follows that less and less political figures would emphasize ideology. Mao once observed that the PRC could just needed several hundred theoreticians who thoroughly understand Marxism.[27] But, if the PRC were to allow freedom of the press in the foreseeable future, it is doubtful whether many CPC members at the central level would be able to adhere to what is described and explained in, for example, the Communism Versus Capitalism framework. This should pose a big headache for the CPC leadership.

Seventh, Albert O. Hirschman, in an article published in the April 1970 issue of *World Politics*, said the search for paradigms could be a hindrance or barrier to understanding, because paradigms could lay down excessive constraints. Hirschman's usage of the word paradigm is not singular. It is in a plural form. This means that there are many paradigms in the human world. For example, when we say the earth is flat, it is a paradigm. Another paradigm could be that the earth is round. But, if someday, the earth's shape changed, due to one reason or another, human beings may have to change their paradigmatic thinking again. So, what Hirschman is warning should be borne in mind.

The Chinese for the last 3,100 years are obsessed with correlating almost everything in terms of *Yin* and *Yang*. Some scholars question why

Zhongguo did not move forward especially in the last 200 years or so? From the first century up to the 15th century, *Zhongguo*, on the whole, was ahead of European countries.[28] Another report said *Zhongguo* led the world in scientific and technological development before modern science appeared in the West at the end of 18th century.[29] Frescoes and other cultural objects unearthed from Mogao Grottes in Dunhuang City of Gansu Province in north-western *Zhongguo* provide such evidence. So, some scholars and experts pointed out some of the major reasons. It is the *Yin* and *Yang* which constrained the Chinese people to be creative, especially during the Ming and Qing Dynasties.[30] This is similar to the dilemma posed by Hirschman: a paradigm is both a necessity and a hindrance. Wu Dayou, a noted physicist in the ROC on Taiwan, said the Chinese have inferiority complex (*zibei*) and they are anti-foreign (*paiwai*), which eventually made them arrogant or presumptuous (*zida*).[31] Chinese people are interested in applied research, not basic science. They invent things for a specific purpose. C. G. Jung, a noted expert on psychology, also observed that the gifted and intelligent Chinese people have never developed what the people in the West called science, which "is based upon the principle of causality, and causality is considered to be an axiomatic truth."[32] In the West, researchers first study nuclear physics. Later, they would move on to manufacture atomic weapons. This means that the Chinese people are not interested in discovering the truth or pursuing knowledge for knowledge's sake and they lack the spirit of research.[33]

One should perhaps try to apply dialectics to analysis of the problem of hindrance and even resistance in academia, of both the East and the West, if he or she has not done so in the past. Or find a model or a theory, which can accommodate both dialectical and non-dialectical approaches. This requires time and other things. Perhaps one may have to bring in philosophy as well.

Eighth, continuity and change is a term often used by mainland China, Taiwan, Hongkong, and Macao academics and experts.[34] There is constant change in our model. As to continuity, it all depends on which two extremes one relies on. CHINA Versus china and CHINA Versus China are different. We do not see the China Versus china continuity in the latter framework.

Ninth, after the collapse of the Soviet Union in December 1991, the PRC became the only power which could potentially challenge th United States in the Asia-Pacific region, because it would take Russia many years to be able to economically stand on its own feet by adopting the market economy line. The argument that Beijing poses a threat, thereby de-stabilising regional security since early 1990s became vogue. However, many countries do not perceive the PRC as such. This would include Russia, Malaysia, Singapore,[35] etc. Mahathir Mohamed said: "If you look at the history of China they have never invaded neighboring countries."[36] When he took power in July 1981 as the fourth Malaysian Prime Minister, he perceived the PRC negatively. Yet, in the 1990s, he had completely changed his mind about the PRC up to his retirement in October 2003.[37] But, there are some political figures who have a different political orientation and some arms dealers who trump up the threat in order to sell more weapons. In January 2001, George W. Bush, Jr. became the U.S. President, who does not regard the PRC as a strategic partner. In the Defense Department before that, some officials did not agree with the "*Zhongguo* Threat" perception or argument.[38] They are right, because, if we were to apply our framework of thought and action, the PRC or the succeeding republic will not become a second polar bear after the Soviet Union. As China moves towards the direction of being CHINA, CHINA is cultural, a non-threat. It will not, on the whole, pose a threat to other countries and regions. CHINA is consistent with the Chinese (Communist) concept of Communism (or Utopia) or Dr. Sun Yat-sen's *shijiedatong* (Universal Harmony in the World).

10th, our study has proven that both sides of the Taiwan Strait apply dialectics in playing politics. But, each side has attempted to acquire what is good for it, dialectically and non-dialectically. Why non-dialectically? This is because many political figures in the West do not fully understand what dialectics is all about. Besides, many concepts in the West are foreign to the dialectical China context. Take the example of Taipei. The ROC political figures all know that "One China" equates to Taiwan and mainland China. ROC reflects the former and PRC, the latter. The two added together means One China. Yet, Taipei put forward the policy of One Country on each side of the Strait in August 2002. This is legally non-dialectical. But, this policy is clear to the political figures in the West, by the simple fact that the ROC has met the four basic conditions: It has a government, land, people, as well as diplomatic ties with some countries in this world. In other words, to those countries, Taipei will not touch upon the dialectical aspect. Because if it does, it will have to mean that a third party has to make a choice of either having diplomatic relations with the ROC or the PRC. So, a non-dialectical approach helps Taipei to survive.

11th, dialectics should be applied to resolve the contradiction between an enemy and oneself. It should not be used to against one's friends and allies. Yet, some dialectical players still do that, resulting in internecine war of words, battle, etc. Even though everyone knows which approach the other side is taking and given the fact that the CPC does not keep it a secret which approach it takes, still not every player can really decode and decipher every move made by the other party, resulting in misunderstanding, mistrust, etc. This is because one cannot reveal his or her own trump card to the other side. Political figures conceal their trump cards in order to to be able to score more points.

12th, there seems to be the problem of self-fulfilling prophecy in our model, given its teleological construction, with the left extreme prevailing at time/space sequence (n). Zhang Shipping, for example, said the PRC is now a small maritime country. But, it will become a big maritime power.[39] This problem should not be conceived as insurmountable; nor does it defeat rationalization, precisely because of the time/space sequence component. This is because the sequence can be stretched to 1,000 years later, if not longer, so long as the PRC still exists or, for that matter, even when it has been replaced by another regime with another national title. If the PRC were to cease to exist, it could be revived 1,000 years later by a group of political figures, who are nostalgic for the past.

13th, perception has always bothered many political figures and Bicoastal China watchers. To Taipei, for example, "One Country, Two Systems" is a threat, because it perceives that this formula may someday localize the central government in Taiwan. There are many people in the West who perceive the PRC as a threat. Andrew W. Marshall, legendary head of the Net Assessment Office (NAO) at the Pentagon, in his Under Secretary of Defence (Policy) 1999 Summer Study Final Report Asia 2025, said the PRC wants to become the ruling power in Asia.[40] Yet, Beijing does not think that its words and deeds are threatening to other countries. To the United States, its National Missile Defence (NMD) is not a threat, saying a successful missile defence system will show its allies, and Russia and the PRC, that it is in their interest as well. In a word, the NMD "threatens no one…, unless someone has an intention of doing damage to other people" as the then U.S. Secretary of State Colin L. Powell so said.[41] But, Moscow and Beijing perceive it otherwise. What if after the NMD were in force, the United States were to use its nuclear weapons to attack others first, for, to this day, Washington has not made the no-first-use pledge. With the NMD protective technology, the United States can shield itself. As a bipartisan study pointed out , in the next 25 years, the United States homeland may come under direct attack and recommends the creation of a National Homeland Security Agency (NHSA).[42]

14th, frameworks could be durable, fraying, constraining, and so on.[43] There are models in our study, which are durable, such as the Communism Versus Capitalism. It will take a long period of time for us to see which one is the ultimate winner, Communism or Capitalism. To disciples of Dr. Sun Yat-sen, there is only a degree of difference between TPP and Communism. One difference is that, as a member of the KMT, one should not advocate Communism but TPP. The Communism Versus Capitalism framework could also be fraying, because struggle exists. The same framework could be constraining, because almost everyone on this Earth and other planets can be positioned somewhere in the safe zone or the danger zone.

15th, tons of books, monographs, journal articles, occasional papers, working papers, background briefs, and opinion pieces have been written on the dialectical and non-dialectical China. In the December 2002/ March 2003 issue of *Issues and Studies*, David M. Lampton regarded the "China is China is China" belief as being narrow in Sinology.[44] We agree. Can our model describe and explain *all* the titles of those non-dialectically written publications? Certainly! Let me say something about the selected titles. Some of them are dialectical. Donald A. Jordan's *Chinese Boycotts Versus Japanese Bombs*, published by the University of Michigan Press in 1991, and *Revolution and Counter-Revolution* are good examples. In my study, the word "and" could incorporate the word "versus" but not "vice versa." In 1904, Arthur Judson Brown published a book, which is entitled *New Forces in Old China: An Unwelcome but Inevitable Awakening*. The phrase Old China is china in our study. Because within Old China there is still change, the new forces in Brown's book are trying to make moves from the right extreme in china to the left extreme in the same proper noun. Werner Klatt is concerned about model. So, his edited book stressing ideology is entitled *The Chinese Model*. He perceives that the PRC has got rid of semi-colonial status, with extraterritorial rights for foreigners and foreign-administered leased territories. The Chinese certainly are interested in viewing their place in the world. C.P. Fitzgerald's 1964 publication is entitled *The Chinese View of Their Place in the World*. A non-dialectical China does not change on the surface. Yet, non-dialectical writers such as John Gittings knows that *China Changes Face*, which is the title of his book. Joshua A. Fogel and William T. Rowe's edited 1979 book title also has the phrase, *A Changing China*. Fairbank had a book published by the Harvard University Press which is entitled *China Watch*.[45] Indeed, watching or looking at our dialectical model, we see normative changes from china to China, to CHINA, and, finally, to **CHINA**. But, such changes cannot be literally seen in non-dialectical book titles. We can only imagine there is change. Our China stage can also incorporate Yu-ming Shaw's edited book title, *Mainland China* and Ralph Clough's *Island China*, plus my own 1999 volume, *Bicoastal China*, which has integrated the island and the mainland. What one should do is to go to the time/space sequence that corresponds to China. Some books, such as Lachlan Strahan's *Australia's China*, have dialectical writings. So, on page 2, the author wrote: "Mapping out responses as a series of swings between negative and positive attitudes, the pendulum is frequently adopted by many writers as the explanatory model of Western perceptions of China." In December 1972, Canberra formally recognised Beijing. *China Returns* is a 1972 book written by a German expert on the non-dialectical China. Due to crab-like motion, China can return to china or any other letter in the danger zone. Maria Hsia Chang's book, *Return of the Dragon* (2001), suggests that China is moving back to the safe zone. China, indeed, is on the move. So, "Has China Turned Into a Frankenstein?" written by Joseph A. Bosco in the *Los Angeles Times* on March 6, 2001, will have to mean the china, which has a negative connotation. By the same token, if the stage of CHINA has been attained, it could always, as a result of decay or another factor, go back to other Numbers or Letters. Finally, in his 2001 provocative book, *The Coming Collapse of China*,[46] Gordon G. G. Chang, who is a Chinese-American lawyer and who has worked in Shanghai for almost 20 years, pointed out that the demise of Beijing is imminent within a decade.[47] If it is in that process, the PRC would be positioned in the danger zone. If it comes to pass, the PRC, Prc, and prc framework would no longer be used. In a word, our model is flexible enough to accommodate every title in the world related to the non-dialectical China.

16th, according to the latest, repeated finding by the Fudan University, the Chinese originated in Africa about 100,000 or 200,000 years ago.[48] In the West, the word "diaspora" has been popularly used. This jargon could also be applied to the Chinese. There is a Chinese joke, saying when a Chinese is alone he is a dragon and when three

Chinese are in a group they are just an insect. It will take, I think, 10,000 years, for **CHINA** to emerge. Some foreign observers argue that overseas Chinese or overseas Chinese businessmen possess 300 billion U.S. dollars.[49] This is not much, as compared to the total assets of Japanese banks—seven trillion billion American dollars. Each day, 1.3 trillion U.S. dollars are circulating. Besides, many overseas Chinese are no longer PRC or ROC citizens. Some of their relatives and family members have identified with the country in which they are residing.

With the ascendancy of mainland China, China can make crab-like moves to the left. In late 1970s, Deng designed an economic Long March in three stages.[50] Stage 1 (1980–2000) was to meet the mainland Chinese basic needs. The PRC expression for this is *fan liang fan*, meaning quadrupling the 1980 gross domestic product (GDP) by the year 2000. In March 2001, the then PRC Premier Zhu proclaimed that this target had been successfully accomplished. With a GDP of 8.9 trillion Yuan, the PRC has performed better than expected. Stage 2 is from 2001 to 2020. It is to create a solid base for the PRC's take-off into sustained growth, so that the living standard of the people can be further raised. This would be another quadrupling of the 2000 GDP by 2020, that is, in the order of US$4 trillion, using the average exchange rate in the 1990s. By 2020, the mainland Chinese economy should be the world's largest aggregate terms. Stage 3 (2021–2050) is to achieve centennial target of modernizing agriculture, industry, technology, and national defence, the Four Modernizations. When the PRC celebrates the 100th anniversary of its founding, its per capita income should be close to what the United States was in 2000. However, unless the PRC achieves three "zero growths," according to Niu Wenyuan of the Chinese Academy of Sciences (CAS), its mid-21st century dream could be frustrated: zero growth in population by 2030, zero growth in the rate of energy and natural-resource depletion by 2040 and zero growth in the rate of environmental deterioration by 2050.[51] However, in May 2001, a White Paper issued by the Japanese Ministry of Economy, Trade and Industry (METI) admitted that Japan has lost its longstanding economic leadership position in East Asia and now regards the mainland as a mighty rival, even creeping up on Japan in high-technology sectors.[52] The population factor will certainly make somewhat of a difference.

17th, there are a lot of Chinese idioms (*chengyu*), which are structured dialectically. For example, *shenglaobingsi* (birth, age, illness, and death). So, in our model, birth could be 1; age, 5; illness, A, and death E. This is the process which no one can escape from, even with the cloning technology. Of course, it is possible to reverse the arrangement. Chinese (Communist) political figures like to shackle or to enclose their (potential) opponents and enemies in a framework. Whenever they succeeded in doing so, they would feel more comfortable. This is similar to *siheyuan* (a courtyard with houses on four sides or quadrangle) of the Ming and Qing Dyanasties.[53] There is another way of saying almost the same thing: *yidiansifang* (one dot and four sides), which means that there is one centre in the Central Plains and there are the East, South, West, and North corners.[54] In a word, this structure of *Zhongguo* is like the *siheyuan*. The reason for building the Great Wall of China was to fend off *Xiongnu* (the Hun nomads) in the north. The mountains in the West form a natural barrier, so do the seas in the East as well as the South. The U-shaped line in the SCS serves precisely that function. A mainland China academic said there are two gates for the PRC to reach the Pacific Ocean: Japan and North and South Korea as a door (*yishanmen*) on the north and the Philippines and Malaysia as another door (*lingyishanmen*) on the south, with Taiwan as the bolt or latch (*shuan*). There are also two gates for the PRC to reach the Pacific Ocean and the Indian Ocean: Japan, Taiwan, and the Philippines as one door and Malaysia, Singapore, and Indonesia as another door, with the four islands groups in the SCS as the bolt or latch.[55] So, Taiwan and the four SCS island groups are very important to the PRC. If there are no external disturbances and peace can be maintained internally, the Chinese (Communist) political figures would feel more comfortable. Psychologically, they will feel superior, too. The "One China" principle is the finest example. The "One China" principle is Beijing's way of controlling Taipei. If the latter refuses to or tries to get away from this principle, the PRC will feel uneasy or even insecure. The principle is similar to the Roof/Housetop or Eaves theory as mentioned in the first section of this chapter. It could incorporate two or more political entities, which can be likened to windows or doors. Of course, when a political entity has accepted the "One China" principle framework and then jumps out of it, Beijing will hunt the political entity for betraying the principle. Similarly, in the last several years of Lee Teng-hui's presidency, Taiwan has been regarded as the subject, while the mainland, the object. If Taiwan cannot remain as a subject, many Taiwan political figures will feel insecure. So, perhaps to make both sides of the Taiwan Strait secure, a new dialectical framework has to be set up.

18th, asked about the question why most academics in the West do not like dialectics, the standard reply is dialectics is *xu*. It is difficult to translate this Chinese character into standard English. Perhaps providing some Chinese phrases, idioms, etc. could help. *Xufu*: superficial; impractical. *Xugou*: make up; fabricate. *Xuhuan*: illusory; illusive; visionary. *Xusui*: nominal age. *Xuxiang*: virtual image. *Xuxushishi*: sometimes false, sometimes true. *Xuzhangshengshi*: make an empty show of strength; bluff and bluster; be swash-buckling. My model is not Platonic, Kantian, Hegelian, Marxist, Maoist, Dengist, etc. So, there is nothing *xu* about it, due to the fact that, when making each move, the dialectical player knows precisely what he or she doing. This makes a lot of difference.

19th, would the CPC be able to move mainland China to the CHINA stage? Intuitively, it is not quite possible, mainly because the PRC, like other Chinese dynasties, has to fall one day. Jiang said at the 15th National Congress that it will take at least a few generations to finish walking the Market Economy line. But, the PRC may disappear by that time. Changing the national appellation is still a possibility. But, the CPC can always argue that the PRC may disappear for a while, it will reappear sometime in the future, even if it means 10,000 years from now, so long as the CPC exists, even as an opposition party. Such is the logic maintained by the Chinese Communists. That is how they rationalize their words and deeds. It is definitely dialectical.

20th, since Deng's *Naxun*, the market economy force has shattered ideology at the mass level. But, to this day, the CPC at the central (as opposed to provincial and local) level still maintains ideology. The problem has been worsened by the fact that more graduates of social sciences who are trained in the West are going back to the mainland. They would introduce behavioural science to their students. They may also influence the way top CPC leaders think and perceive reality. The central level of the CPC is certainly worried, even the *Jiefangjunbao* publishes articles opposing such a trend.[56] But, this should not be construed to mean that the CPC will abandon dialectics. To compromise, it could mix the two different approaches. In other words, the macro-level dialectical frameworks will be maintained. Behavioural science can complement dialectics. That is to say, so long as the things are done within such frameworks, the CPC can still accept or, at least, tolerate them.

21st, people who play games by applying dialectics show that, ironically, they lack confidence. By making what they say and do ambiguous to a second and third party which does not understand dialectics, they think that they are, at least, psychologically speaking, putting themselves in a better position.

22nd, interests of dialectical and non-dialectical practitioners may converge in the sense that the former may think that they are in the safe zone so that they can make some compromise with the latter. But, the latter may not know the exact reason, and the former may not want to reveal its inner thinking to the latter.

ENDNOTES

1   V. O. Key, Jr., "The State of the Discipline," *American Political Science Review* (hereinafter APSR), Vol. 52, (1958) pp. 961–971.

2   See Andrew C. Janos, "Paradigms Revisited," *World Politics* (hereinafter WP), Vol. 50, No.1 (October 1997), p. 119. See also Ludwik Fleck's *Genesis and Development of a Scientific Fact*, translated by F. Bradley and T. J. Trenn (Chicago: University of Chicago Press, 1979) and Thomas S. Kuhn, *The Structure of Scientific Revolutions*, second edition (Chicago: University of Chicago Press, 1970) and *id.*, "Second Thoughts on Paradigms," in Frederick Supper, ed., *The Structure of Scientific Theories* (Urbana, Illinois: University of Illinois, 1974).

3   Pye wrote: "… much of what passes as wisdom in political science is really American area studies pretending to be universal knowledge…. [R]esearchers with empirical findings about aspects of American politics can report them as scientific, and hence universal knowledge. Paradoxically, this problem has become more acute as the discipline has sought to become more scientific…. But does anyone really believe that American practices can be treated as the norm for all peoples?" See Pye (note 4, ch. 8), p. 805.

4   His email to me, dated April 19, 2001.

5   Conversation with him, dated April 25, 2001.

6   Political party in the American context is individualistic and it links with democracy, whereas it is collectivist in the Chinese (Communist) context. In the latter context, a party is a tool for unity and its power cannot be shared. Observation made by He Baogang, dated April 24, 2001 at the EAI, NUS.

7   Talk given by Wang Gungwu, dated April 24, 2001 at the EAI, NUS.

8   Wang Gungwu said, in Chinese history textbooks, the word hegemon exists. It refers to bully and it has no legitimacy. Empire is a better word for hegemon. *Ibid.* The *Chinese-English Dictionary* (Han-Ying Cidian) defines hegemony as: "to dominate; lord it over; tyrannize over." See *Han-Ying Cidian* (Beijing: Foreign Languages Press, 1978), p. 11. According to David Shambaugh, "Hegemony may be seen as good or bad, depending on how it is defined and who is the hegemon." He has also posited four possible types of hegemony that the PRC may exercise over Asia by 2015: the isolationist hegemon, the hierarchical hegemon, the cooperative hegemon, and the coercive hegemon; and he predicted that the PRC's posture in

Asia 20 years hence will likely be a composite of each type. See his research paper (note 28, ch. 7).

9   *The American Heritage Dictionary*, second college ed., p. 614.

10   Janos (note 2), p. 121.

11   See, for example, *JFJB*, March 2, 2001, p. 4.

12   Lee Kuan Yew once said if Singapore decayed he would jump out of his grave.

13   Quoted in Unryu Suganuma, *Sovereign Rights and Territorial Space in Sino-Japanese Relations* (Honolulu: Association for Asian Studies and University of Hawaii Press, 2000), p. 160.

14   Wang (note 2, ch. 6), p. 86.

15   Pye pointed out that Americanists think that their studies are scientific. See Pye (note 4, ch. 8), p. 805.

16   *ST*, March 28, 2001, p. 9. This portrait of Christ appears to be confirmed in Isaiah 53.2 *(NKJ)* "… He has no form or comeliness; And when we see Him, There is no beauty that we should desire Him."

17   See their book (note 48).

18   Wakeman, Jr. (note 42, ch. 7), p. 69. However, model and pattern are two different things. The former is fixed, whereas the latter refers to behavior on the move.

19   Skinner mentioned the possibility of historical/temporal patterns. See note 5, p. 290.

20   Edward Friedman and Barrett L. McCormick, eds., *What If China Doesn't Democratize?: Implications for War and Peace* (New York: M. E. Sharpe, 2000), p. xi. Others like Mark Burles and Abram N. Shulsky also see patterns. See their work, *Pattern in China's Use of Force: Evidence from History and Doctrinal Writings* (Santa Monica, CA: RAND Corporation, 2000).

21   Arab academics are also concerned. See, for example, Nasr M. Arif, *Western Political Science in a Non-Western Context* (Lanham, MD: University Press of America, 2000). Africanists are facing a similar problem, as one academic pointed out that "… book publishers are reluctant to print even first-rate research by Africanists for fear of commercial failure." See Hyden (note 3, ch. 7), p. 798.

22   He studied the Kaifeng cycle, the Beijing-centered cycles, the Southeast Coast cycle, and the Quanzhou cycle. See Skinner (note 6, ch. 6).

23   *American Institute in Taiwan Policy File*, BG-95–36, dated November 3, 1995, p. 4.

24   *ST*, December 7, 2000, p. 25.

25   See *The Mirror* (Jingbaoyuekan)(Hongkong), No. 286 (May 2001), pp. 36–42.

26   According to Zheng Yongnian, Jiang first talked about something related to the Rule by Virtue eight years ago. Conversation with him, dated April 17, 2001. According to another author, Ren Huiwen, the Rule by Virtue concept was first put forward by Jiang in June 2000. But, another mainland China academic said it should be November 1997 when Jiang was in the

United State and made a speech at Harvard University. Jiang mentioned *Tianrenheyi* (man is an integral part of nature or a natural harmony between heavenly and earthly forces), which is first put forward by Dong Zhongshu and which is the origin of virtue. See *HKEJ*, April 20, 2001, p. 32. See also *Jingbaoyuekan* (Hongkong), March 2001, pp. 36–37.

27   Qu Kemin *et. al.* eds., *Yu Zongshuji Tanxin* (Talking with the Secretary-General)(Hongkong: Mingpao Chubanshe, December 1996), p. 245.

28   In the 1760s, England started the technological revolution. In the 1870s, electricity was used widely, spurring capitalist development. After World War II, nuclear technology, computer science, and space technology pushed development further. See *HKEJ*, March 30, 2001, p. 28.

29   http://english.peopledaily.com.cn/200007/10/eng20000710_45087.html.

30   *ZGGFB*, May 7, 1999, p. 3 and May 21, 1999, p. 3. According to Wang Gungwu, "This conclusion is one of the most widely accepted explanations as to why Chinese science was "*luohou*" (lagging behind) in the end. But, it is an anachronistic argument when applied to periods before Ming and Qing. After the Song [dynasty], the argument is more correct." His note to me, dated August 18, 1999. Ho Peng Yoke, director of the Needham Research Institute at Cambridge University, observed that "… Science in East Asia was too general, trying to have one theory to explain everything. In the West, on the other hand, science is grounded in Greek logic and rationalism, which has become too restrictive. So now there is a need to expand beyond the barriers…. It would be best if one could achieve the golden mean—there is something to be learned from both sides." Cited in *ST*, August 27, 1999, p. 42. Yang Zhenning also agreed that the *Yin* and *Yang* plus the Five Elements affected the Chinese thinking. That is why modern *Zhongguo* is lagging behind the West. Yang also said that, in 1900, none of the people in *Zhongguo* understood calculus. In ancient China, natural sciences (as opposed to eight-legged essays) were not tested. But, the PRC launched the first *Shenchou* (Divine Ship) spacecraft in November 1999. It took the West 700 years to do that. See *TKP*, November 4, 1999, p. A13 and the February 21, 2000 issue of *Xinyashenghuo* (Chinese University of Hong Kong).

31   *CT*, May 23, 1997, p. 7.

32   See Jung's foreword in Richard Wilhelm, translator, *The I Ching or Book of Changes* (London: Routledge & Kegan Paul, 1951), p. ii.

33   It is said that Chinese relish the past and the present. As to the future, Chinese are less concerned (*guanxin*) about it and do not attach great importance (*zhongshi*) to it. People in the West stress the future. See Zheng Jizong, "*Weilaiyanjiu and Ynajiuweilai* (Future Studies and Study the Future)," *Zhongyanribao* (Central Daily News)(hereinafter ZYRB)(Taipei), May 1, 1984, p. 12.

34   See, for example, Robert E. Bedeski, "The Evolution of the Modern State in China," *World Politics* (hereinafter WP)(U.S.), Vol. XXVII, No. 4 (July 1975), pp. 541–568.

35   Shee (note 27, ch. 7), p. 350.

36   Greg Sheridan, "Mahathir Backflip on Our Asian Role," *The Australian*, May 15, 1995, p. 1.

37   Shee (note 27, ch. 7), p. 351.

38   *CT*, December 30, 2000, p. 11.

39   Zhang (note 79, ch. 7), pp. 162–163 and p. 306.

40   *CT*, February 10, 2001, p. 9. Marshall also predicted that, at that time in the worst scenario, the PRC would have succeeded in annexing Taiwan.

41   *ST*, February 13, 2001, p. 17.

42   *UDN*, February 1, 2001, p. 11.

43   Adjectives taken from Avery Goldstein's article title, "The Taiwan Relations Act: Durable Agreement or Fraying Framework," *A Catalyst for Ideas*, September 8, 1999.

44   See David M. Lampton, "Editor's Response: The Middle Way of Middle Theory," *Issues and Studies* (Taipei) Vol. 38, No. 4 and Vol. 39, No. 1 (December 2002/March 2003), p. 372.

45   See also John Bryan Starr's *Understanding China*, second edition (New York: Hill & Wang, 2001).

46   Victor E. Louis's book title is *Coming Decline of the Chinese Empire*.

47   The theory of threat surfaced in the early 1990s. The theory of unimportant China ensued. And they are followed by the theory of collapse. See the June 11, 2002 issue of *Renminribao* (People's Daily)(Beijing).

48   *LHZB*, March 26, 2001, p. 11.

49   *Ibid.*, March 22, 2001, p. 14. See also "Overseas Chinese key force in nation's revival," http//English.peopledaily.com.cn/200407/21/print20040721_150282.html, dated July 21, 2004.

50   *ST*, March 21, 2001, p. 24.

51   *Ibid.*

52   *Ibid*, May 3, 2001, p. 16.

53   One academic described the *shiheyuan* mentality in the following words: One does not depend on others and ask favors from others. The same person also does not want other people to be dependent on himself or herself and to ask favors from himself or herself. The person is agoraphobic (*zibi*) introverted, conservative, xenophobic, narrow-minded, etc. See *HKEJ*, November 25, 2000, p. 18.

54   See Yang Tingshuo, *Xinanyuzhongyuan* (Southwest China and the Middle and Lower Part of Yellow River)(Yunan: Yunanjiaoyuchubanshe, October 1992), pp. 3–6.

55   Zhang (note 79, ch. 7), p. 381.

56   *JFJB*, December 28, 2001, p. 6.

CHAPTER 12

Closing Remarks

According to the latest findings, the dialectical and non-dialectical China can be said to have a recorded history of 10,000 years. Wang Gungwu said there are many problems with Western books on *Zhongguo*.[1] Yu Ying-shih, a noted historian, also said it is not proper for us to apply theories in the West to study *Zhongguo*.[2] Tu Wei-ming wrote: "… any approach we choose to study China is inevitably theory-laden and value-laden; it is naive to believe that we can ever arrive at a totally objective analysis or strictly factual explanation of China and that our interpretation is value-free."[3] We can also mention what Shi Dongbing, who is a mainland China writer, said. By October 1999, he had written more than 20 million Chinese characters on PRC history. He, for example, interviewed more than 200 Chinese Communists including some high-ranking officials who were involved in the GPCR. But, he still acknowledged that, to seek truth from historical facts, is not easy.[4] To some extent, it is more difficult than cracking a criminal case.

Similarly, writing a theoretical book is also not easy. Editing a theoretical volume could be more difficult, because the editor must put everything within a framework, when contributors write and think differently. Failing to do that, the editor can be easily criticised. Getting it published constitutes another great hurdle. After that, how many students of Bicoastal China studies would read your book is still another problem, let alone citing and quoting it.

There are not many dialectical books on Bicoastal China in the West. There are also books or portions of them, which touched upon dialectics but not fully.[5] One example is Jorn Brommelhorster and John Frankenstein's *Mixed Motives, Uncertain Outcomes: Defense Conversion in China* published in 1997. Let me elaborate.

The subject matter of the edited book deals with defence conversion in the PRC's vast military-industrial complex (MIC). One of the editors, Frankenstein, in note 1 of Chapter 1 wrote: "… in the Chinese view, 'conversion' can swing both ways—from war production to civilian production and back again. This is consistent with the Chinese view that war and peace are—like *yin* and *yang*—two sides of the same coin, and thus, conceptually at least, the dual role of the defense industry in the larger economy and the relationships between the civilian and military sectors suggested by the '16-Character Slogan' are without contradictions...." On page 28, he also said, in the PRC, it is politics (or what I called the Rule of Dialectical Politics) in command. The question that I would like to raise is: Why didn't the two co-editors adopt a dialectical framework of analysis in their book, which can afford us at least a macro— or paradigmatic view? For this reason, I cannot agree with Herbert Wulf's argument in the foreword: "A full understanding and examination of defence conversion requires a multidisciplinary approach; no single perspective can capture the complexity of the process."

Because Frankenstein was not clear or sure, he could not understand why the two members of *China's Defense Conversion* editorial committee dissected somewhat out of order Deng Xiaoping's "16-Character Slogan"—*jun-min jiehe* (combine the military and civil), *ping-zhan jiehe* (combine peace and war), *jun-pin youxian* (give priority to military products), and *yi min yang jun* (let the civil support the military). (pp. 20–21) The reason is pure and simple: Beijing at a certain time/space sequence perceived the existing environment as peaceful and, then, decided to combine the military and civil. In other words, had the situation given rise to conflicts or war-like, conversion may end or be frozen. Throughout the volume, I have noticed that, for example, Cai Benliang wrote through the lenses of Marxism-Leninism-Mao Zedong Thought. Table 4.2 in Chapter 4 should be understood dialectically. By the way, in May and September 1997, Jiang Zemin for the first time put forward the policy of "separation of politics from enterprise." Herbert Wulf in his Foreword mentioned the dialectical phrase of "both China and non-China experts," though he may not be aware of it. In the same line of thinking, it was a mistake for Ka Po Ng to non-dialectically say that, in June 1985, the PRC had abandoned the doctrine of preparing the country for fighting an "early, all-out nuclear war," (p. 81) because even the author of Chapter 5 mentioned on page 92 "a form of dialectical process." In other words, Beijing may face that kind of situation again in the future. Likewise, Brommelhorster should not have said on page 230 that "... conversion in China was one of the results of internal political changes by the abandonment of Maoist principles ..." or for both co-editors to ever mention the phrase "a capitalist China," (p. 255) because as Min Chen rightly quoted Deng's words: "Army construction should follow the overall constructive (dialectical) plan of the country." It should also be noted that Yitzhak Shichor, who had applied the dialectical approach in the past, realized that PRC defence conversion typically reflected traditional Chinese culture. (p. 130) In any case, dialectics helps us to understand why things change *without being contradictory*. Such is the magic of dialectics, though not necessarily moving in a linear progression. (p. 256) And, of course, most books on Bicoastal China are not dialectical. Many authors choose to write non-dialectically, for one reason or another. My attempt has been vertical, because this is my third book, which applies a dialectical approach. If more academics and experts followed this author's example, perhaps a horizontal development in Bicoastal Chinese studies would come about. So, in the end, it is up to readers to choose from the following products: Do they or do they not want to read publications that have been logically presented? Do they just want to see new contributions? Do they want or not want a study which is closer to reality, if there is such a thing called reality? Do they or do they not want to have first-hand information? Do they stress or not stress cause and effect studies? Do they prefer a study, which does not apply a model or a theory, thereby risking the danger of being labelled a pseudo-scientist? The (dialectical) choice, of course, is yours.[6]

ENDNOTES

1 *LHZB*, August 13, 1998, p. 11.

2 *UDN*, May 4, 2001, p. 15.

3 Tu (note 55, ch. 7), p. 4.

4 See his book, *Huairentangzhengbian*, first volume (Coup d'etat at Huairentang)(Hong Kong: Dragon [Hongkong] Publication, Ltd., October 1999), Preface.

5 Many academics recognized ostensible polarities. Robert H. Salisbury pointed out the following: teaching versus research, technique versus substance, real world politics versus theoretically driven research. See his article, "Current Criticism of APSA is Nothing New," *PS*, Vol. XXXIV, No. 4 (December 2001), p. 767. Peter J. Katzenstein wrote that there is "… a range of dialectical processes confronting the social sciences everywhere: global versus local, basic versus applied, area versus disciplinary." See his article, "Area and Regional Studies in the United States," *PS*, Vol. XXXIV, No. 4 (December 2001), p. 791.

6 Why does this author include the word dialectical? This is because one may accept dialectics at one point in time and reject it at another time/space sequence, only to accept it again sometime in the future.

Glossary

Chinese (Hanyu Pinyin)	English
bangkongting	General Office
bangpai	faction
banxinbanyi	half-believing and half-doubting or not quite convinced
baohuguojiadajiangjun	a great general who can protect the country
baozhanghgyouli	adequate logistics
bingtuan	regular force
boudazhongyouda	a mixture of not to attack and to attack
bujinguanjunquan,	the Chinese PLA should not only control
haiyoudangquan	military power but party power as well
bukefengedetongyi	that which cannot be partitioned or carved
Changwuweiyuan	Member of Standing Committee of the Political Bureau
da	Beat
dadatantan	literally, fight, fight as well as talk and talk
dandejueduilingdao	absolute loyalty to the CPC
dangjun	party-army

dangneiminzhu	intra-party democracy
dangweizhi	party committee system
dangweizhidu	the CPC committee system in the armed forces
diaogui	paradox
diwei	position or standing
duilidetongyi	the unity of opposites, mutually complimentary, not mutually exclusive in themselves, or complimentary in opposition, like *Yin* and *Yang*
duodanghezuozhi	Multi-party Cooperation System
falunguwenchu	legal advisory panel
fan	anti-thesis
fang	defense
fangzhen	guiding principle
gaizhao	remould
gangjumuzhang	once the key link is grasped, everything falls into place
gangling	program
ganjin	vigor
geminhua	revolutionization
gemingju	revolutionary army
Geminweiyuanhui	Revolutionary Committee
gong	attack

gongzhongyoufang and fangzhongyougong	there should be defense within attack and vice versa
gongzuo	cultural work
guanxi	ties or connections
guojia	state in general and government in particular
guojiahua	making it part of the state
Guoneihepingxieding (zuihouxiuzhengan)	Domestic Peace Agreement
Hongloumeng	The Red Chamber
huanhuanxiangkou	interlinked
huiyi	conference
jiaoyu	educate
Jiefangjunbao	*Liberation Army Daily*
jiluyanming	strict discipline
jingbing	streamline of the military
jitimanyi	collective satisfaction
jituanjun	group army
jiudediren	old enemy
jizhong	centralism
jueduilingdao	absolute leadership
junduidang	literally army-party, not party-army
junhun	spirit for the Red Army and later the armed forces

junqing	military situation
junshiguoying	militarily competent
junshishiquan	actual military power
junshixuquan	nominal military power
junzhongyoudang and dangzhongyoujun	the Army is in the CPC and vice versa
lan	lazy
lian	company
liandui	company
liangdianlun	two dots/points
liangyong rencai	dual purpose personnel
lifaguize	a rule stressing legislation
lingdaobanzi	leading group
luxian	line
luxianjuedingyiqi	line determines everything
minzhu	democracy
Nanjinglushanghaobalian	the good 8th Company on the Nanjing Road
nianqinghua	making younger
paiji	discriminated against
pengtouhui	brief meeting or literally knocking head meeting
qi	business/enterprise

qiang	plunder
qiangganzichuzhengquan	all political power grows out of the barrel of a gun
qiangyingpai	hardliners
Quishou	Autumn Haravest
quxian	curve
Renmin Ribao	People's Daily
ruan	feeble
san	undisciplined
Sangedaibiao	Three Represents
santongsiliu	three links and four exchanges
santouzhuyi	mountain-stronghold mentality
Sanzhiliangjun	the task of "Three-support" and "Two-military" back up the leftist masses, industrial production, and agricultural production and support military control or supervision and military training.
shehuizhyyiminzhuzhi	Systems of Socialist Democracy
shengchan	production
tongyideduili	the opposite of the "unity of opposites"
tuanjie	unite
tuanjie-piping-tuanjie	Forging Unity-Conducting Criticism-Forging Unity
tuchuzhengzhi	putting politics in command

Tudigeminzhanzhenshizhi	The Period of Agrarian Revolutionary War
Wanshuijun	Long Live Army
weixinglun	idealism
wenjianpai	moderate
wen	civil
wu	military
wuhusihai	all corners of the country
wujuhua	five sentences
xiaotuantizhuyi	cliquism or small-group mentality
xindediren	new enemy
Xinminzhuzhuyi	New Democracy
xinshiqijunduijian-shedezongyaoqui	army-building in the new era
xiushenqijiazhiguo- pingtianxia	cultivate oneself and make oneself useful to the society, look after the family and maintain strong sense of family responsibilities, look after the country, as well as have peace and harmony under heaven
xunling	directive or instruction
yi	chivalric justice
yifazhiguo	Rule by Law Politics
yifazhijun	ruling the armed forces by law
yigejigou, liangge paizi	one organization with two signs

yinggutouliulian	the hard-boned, dauntless, or steel-willed 6th Company
yitiaobian	command like a continuous line in the safe zones of all the dialetical models
youji	organic
youjun	friendly army or forces
youjungong	has performed military meritorious service
yourenshi	has a network of personal connections
yuanze	guiding principles
za	smash
zhandou	war
zhanlue	strategic
zhanqu	*ad hoc* operational area commands
zheng	administration
zhengce	policy
zhengguihua	regularization (or standardization)
zhengyi	righteous
zhengzhihege	politically qualified
zhengzhijiguanzhidu	political organ or office system
zhengzhijuyizheng	the political commissar system, with each commissar enjoying seniority and authority over his or her military counterpart

zhenqu	win over
zhidang	governing, administrating, or managing the CPC
zhidu	system/institution
zhijun	governing, administrating or managing the armed forces
zhishihua	increasing knowledge
zhiye	professionalism
zhiyehua	professionalization
zhong	loyalty
zhongyongzhidao	middle way
zhongxinsixiang	central thought
zhualiangtou and daizhongjian	one should sustain the advanced and help the backward or those lagging behind, so as to bring the middle along
zhuanyehua	specialization or making professional
zhuti	subject
zong	general
zongfangzhen	general principle
zongpaizhuyi	sectarianism or factionalism
zuofengyouliang	good work style

Index

Other Titles on Politics and International Relations

Asia in the New Millenium: APISA First Congress Proceedings 27–30 December 2003
edited by Amitav Acharya and Lee Lai To
ISBN 981 210 395 3

Hu Jintao and the Ascendancy of China: A Dialectical Study
by Peter Yu Kien Hong
ISBN 981 210 423 2

The Changing Face of Electoral Politics in Sri Lanka (1994–2004)
by Laksiri Jayasuriya
ISBN 981 210 394 5

Parties and Politics: A Study of Opposition Parties and the PAP in Singapore (2nd edition)
by Hussin Mutalib
ISBN 981 210 408 9

Damage Control: The Chinese Communist Party in the Jiang Zemin Era
edited by Wang Gungwu and Zheng Yongnian
ISBN 981 210 251 5 (paperback)
ISBN 981 210 259 0 (hardcover)

For information on pricing and availability, please log on to
www.marshallcavendish.com/academic